No, Prime Minister!

TERESA GORMAN

No, Prime Minister!

JOHN BLAKE

Published by John Blake Publishing Ltd,
3 Bramber Court, 2 Bramber Road,
London W14 9PB, England

First published in hardback 2001

ISBN 1 904034 00 4

British Library Cataloguing-in-Publication Data:

A catalogue record for this book is
available from the British Library.

Typeset by Gdadesign
Index by Valerie Chandler

Printed in Great Britain by
Creative Print and Design (Wales),
Ebbw Vale, Gwent.

1 3 5 7 9 10 8 6 4 2

Papers used by John Blake Publishing Limited are natural,
recyclable products made from wood grown in sustainable forests.
The manufacturing processes conform to the environmental
regulations of the country of origin.

Every effort has been made to contact the relevant
copyright holders, but some were unavailable. We would be
grateful if they could contact us

*This book is dedicated to Jim, my partner for life,
who has put up with me for all these years. We worked
as a team, and he never stood in my way.*

CONTENTS

ACKNOWLEDGEMENTS

Dorothy Brain, who managed our business to perfection.

Alex Segal, who kick-started my political career.

Jill Brown, who ran my parliamentary office and did her best to keep me in order.

Karen Sheehan, my eyes and ears in the constituency.

Matthew Parris, who helped me to remember my sins.

Eithne Whaley, for her wizardry at IT and research.

Frederic Bastiat (1801–1850), who taught me that 'the state is the great fiction by which everyone seeks to live at the expense of everyone else'.

Without them, this book would never have been written.

ACKNOWLEDGEMENTS

Dorothy Brain, who managed our business to perfection.

Alex Segal, who kick-started my political career.

Jill Brown, who ran my parliamentary office and did her best to keep me in order.

Karen Sheehan, my eyes and ears in the constituency.

Matthew Parris, who helped me to remember my sins.

Eithne Whaley, for her wizardry at IT and research.

Frederic Bastiat (1801–1850), who taught me that 'the state is the great fiction by which everyone seeks to live at the expense of everyone else'.

Without them, this book would never have been written.

'Women Refresh Politics.'
MATTHEW PARRIS

PROLOGUE

'The everlasting No!'
Thomas Clyle

It was the summer of 1994. July. Parliament was in recess but Jill, my secretary, and I were still working in the office – keeping on top of the paperwork.

The telephone rang. Jill took the call.

'That was Downing Street. The Prime Minister says would you like to come over for tea with him next week?'

I thought it was a wind-up, but Jill reassured me that the call had been genuine. 'That will be me and fifty others,' I told her. These occasions are usually an opportunity to kill a lot of birds with one stone. 'Call them back and ask them.'

Jill did so, and came back into my office.

'Just you and the Prime Minister. It must be something special,' she said. 'Promotion, maybe.'

'Do you think he will have forgiven me for Maastricht?'

'That was some time ago; a week is a long time in politics.'

I had absolutely no idea what the Prime Minister could want of me – but it was worth dressing up for. At the weekend, I popped into Shelley's in Billericay High Street to buy something nice to wear.

'Sexy or sober?' asked Elizabeth, the shop owner.

'Sexy,' I replied. 'I'm going to meet the Prime Minister.'

'Is he going to promote you?'

'Some chance,' I answered. We laughed. Elizabeth sorted me out a pretty little summer suit. Floral jacket, short white skirt with small slits at the side.

'Does this look right? I don't want to overdo it.'

'You look terrific. Summery, snazzy and special.'

I walked the few hundred yards down Whitehall from my office to Downing Street. It was a lovely summer afternoon. Tourists were crowded against the iron gates that protected Downing Street from unwelcome visitors. When the policeman opens the gate, you do feel different; you feel special. Tourists stared at me, trying to guess whether I was someone whom they ought to recognise.

I waited in the lobby of Number 10, looking at the paintings on the walls, too nervous to sit down. A few minutes went by and then I saw the Prime Minister coming towards me. And he was smiling.

To my astonishment, he greeted me with two kisses, one on each cheek, continental style. This was a good beginning. I felt relaxed – even special. It's not very often that someone with my track record gets kissed by a prime minister.

He showed me into the Cabinet Room. I had never before visited, but I instantly recognised the place from television. It was a very large room. A civil servant with a note pad sat in a corner of the room, somewhat in the shadows. The PM walked down the room, sat in his usual seat, bang in the centre of the long table and tapped the seat next to him, inviting me to sit down. I wondered whose chair I was sitting in. But John Major interrupted my thoughts.

'Would you like some tea or coffee?' he asked, smiling.

'Tea, please.'

'How do you think things are going in the country, Teresa?' said the Prime Minister, opening the conversation proper. Of course, I knew John Major as a colleague. If we met in the House, we passed the time of day. But we had never before had a real conversation. Now, here I was, being asked a profound question.

I was astonished. It was barely a year ago that the Prime Minister was furious with me for refusing to vote with the party over Europe. I was head of the Tory Party's bad girl list and here was the Prime Minister himself seeking my opinion. It didn't make sense. Indeed, it crossed my mind that maybe there was some other reason for this unusual invitation.

'I think that things have settled down very well', I replied, cautiously. I was well aware that a year ago, I had been a thorn in his flesh and it was unlikely that he had decided to forgive and forget.

For a couple of minutes we talked earnestly about the political climate in the country. Out of the corner of my eye, I could see the civil servant taking notes.

Now John's eyes showed signs of glazing over. His eyelids began to droop. Whatever he was after, I was not hitting the right buttons. It was as if I had had my five pennyworth of his time and he wanted to get down to the nitty-gritty.

Suddenly, he turned to the civil servant. 'Would you mind leaving us alone? I have something confidential I wish to discuss with Mrs. Gorman.' The civil servant looked at me over his glasses, closed his note book and left the room without a word. We watched him go. The door closed silently behind him. Now we were alone together. Now I was about to learn what this charade was all about.

I felt a mixture of apprehension and excitement. Was this a ticking off or something else? Suddenly John lent across, took hold of my left hand, and placed it between his two hands. He looked me straight in the eye and said, 'There's something which I want you to do which means a very great deal to me.' He began very gently stroking the side of my hand with his thumb. My mind began to race. I didn't know what to think. 'I'm going to ask you something and I want you to think very carefully before you answer me.' I nodded. I could feel my heart beating a little faster. Feeling nervous, I crossed my legs and then realised that, with my sexy slit skirt, I was showing quite an expanse of thigh.

He was definitely caressing my hand very gently, very softly. Was he coming on to me? Suddenly I was excited and apprehensive. I knew the civil servant would not come in, but what about Norma? She might be in the flat upstairs, and then what? I drew in my breath. I might have to make a very quick decision. I admitted to myself that John Major was not unattractive. Then I told myself not to be so silly, reminding myself that he was a very tactile man. Surely, he wasn't going to proposition me? Not the Prime Minister. Not in the Cabinet Room. He began speaking again.

'In the next session of Parliament, we are going to debate an increase in the European budget and it's very important not to have another showdown over the amount. It's only £75 million.' Now it was his turn to take a deep breath. 'So, Teresa, I want your assurance that you will vote with the government this time.'

I closed my eyes briefly. For a few seconds I couldn't think what to say. In an instant the frisson of excitement had disappeared. I was the bad girl of the party once more. Whatever high hopes I arrived with were fading rapidly. Truth be told, I had secretly hoped that I was in line for a promotion. The let down was enormous. My sexy new outfit was all for nothing.

I looked at him, not knowing whether to tell the truth or let him down gently. For his sake I wanted to say 'Yes', but I just couldn't bring myself to abandon my principles, my opposition to the outrageous demands of Brussels. I had to stick to my guns.

'Only £75 million? That's a small fortune. Why do you

keep bailing them out?' was all I could think of to say.

The Prime Minister let go of my hand.

'Yes or no?' he asked, curtly. His eyes narrowed. His mouth tightened.

I took a deep breath.

'No, Prime Minister,' I said finally. 'Not even for you.'

Chapter One

EARLY YEARS

*'All of this will not be finished in the first
hundred days. Nor will it be finished in the
first thousand days ... but let us begin.'*
JOHN F. KENNEDY

I love telling everyone that I was born on the embankment
at Putney. It's not quite accurate, but very nearly.

My father, Albert Moore, a kind of Steptoe character, was
a demolition contractor. He earned his living by knocking
down old buildings and salvaging the bits and pieces of the
structure that were saleable, which he then recycled. In his
builder's yard in Ruvigny Gardens, which stretch down to

the River Thames, he would melt down the lead off roofs, and turn it into bars of solder, which he then sold to local plumbers. Tiles, timbers, doors, floorboards, pretty well everything that could be sold was sold at a profit. This was post-war London and there was a desperate shortage of every type of building material.

It was a good business to be in after the war. London was full of bombed-out, unsafe buildings that needed to be demolished. There were many other buildings that enterprising builders could patch up and put back into service again. My father was a very busy man.

Most nights he would return home exhausted, but he would usually have some little treasure with him that we would all carefully inspect as he laid it out on the kitchen table. He rarely demolished a building without uncovering something of real use to the family in those austere times.

On one occasion, he was asked to demolish the headquarters of the Swan Pen company in Curzon Street, in London's West End. He came home that night with scores of gold-plated Swan fountain pens with gold nibs, which he had found beneath the rubble in the bombed-out building. The next day, my two brothers and I took them to school and gave them to our special friends. We also gave them to other friends and neighbours, who were stunned and delighted that we had come across such a treasure trove.

Some time later, my father was asked to demolish the convent at nearby Roehampton, which had received a direct hit from a German bomber. That night he arrived home with a pile of partly singed fine linen drawers, which had presumably belonged to the nuns. My mother, Nellie, boiled them in the copper and hung them on the line to dry in the breeze. These extraordinary bloomers consisted only of two gigantic legs, which must have reached below the knee and were tied around the waist. We all thought they were hilarious. Mother was particularly perplexed by the fact that they had no crotch whatsoever. However, always a dab-hand with the sewing machine, she unpicked them and converted them into the most superb linen blouses. I was the envy of all my girl friends; in those days, school blouses were often made from old nylon parachutes.

I didn't get on too well with my brothers, because I was jealous of them. I believed that Albert, the elder, whom we all called 'Bertie', was my father's favourite child and that my younger brother, Maurice, was my mother's pet. Looking back, I think that I felt left out, being the only girl and the pig-in-the-middle.

To say that my parents didn't get on was an understatement. They would spend days and weeks, even months, not saying a word to each other. At such times, they would communicate by writing notes, which we thought was silly. At other times, the plates would fly and my brothers and I would take refuge under the kitchen table while the crockery was hurled across the room as they shouted obscenities at one another. On occasions, my mother would storm out of the house in a rage and my father would go to the trouble of changing the door locks so she couldn't get back in. I don't know where she went – presumably to one of her five sisters. When she returned home some days later, we had to let her in and, gradually, life would return to normal.

After these rows, my mother would take me to one side and talk earnestly to me, telling me that all men were brutes and that I should never become dependent on one. At that time I didn't really understand what she was telling me, but I never forgot those words of warning. It was only later that I understood that my mother had been trapped in a miserable marriage from which she felt it was impossible to escape. I grew up not dreaming of being a nurse or a teacher, like most of the other girls in my class, but of being independent – whatever that meant.

We were certainly working class, but because business was good for my father we were not hard up. In the late 1940s, we had a small family car, a hoover, an electric frying pan a radiogram, and a 10" black and white TV set. In other words, compared to the great majority of people, we were comfortably off. We also had a Singer electric sewing machine. My mother was adept at turning her sisters' cast-offs into our clothes – a skill I learned from her at an early age. By my teens, I was turning out wrap-over dresses for my maiden aunts with large bosoms at seven shillings and six pence a garment – and earning a bit of extra pocket money in the process.

On Saturday nights, my father would take us to a music hall, where we would watch comedians such as Max Miller perform. I had piano and tap-dancing lessons. I would write and recite monologues, à la Joyce Grenfell, who was a star attraction on the wireless at the time, and tap dance for the kids in the neighbourhood, charging them twopence a show.

However, my parents insisted that we children must save

half of our modest pocket money, which we were given each week by our grandparents and various aunts and uncles, and would religiously put into our Post Office Savings accounts. Whenever we wanted to buy something, such as a bicycle, we were expected to contribute half the cost. I believe this taught us the hard lesson that we had to pay for things in life that we wanted. It certainly taught me the value of money at a remarkably young age.

My mother was part of a network of women who met on doorsteps, swapped gossip and helped each other out. We would sometimes take a bowl of soup to some family less well off than ourselves, or pass on clothes we had out-grown. She also had her own way of expressing her disapproval.

'She's been putting her pudding out for treacle,' she would say of a neighbour who took in the milkman with the milk.

'She's playing Hamlet with her husband,' when a marriage was on the rocks.

Every Friday night after high tea, my mother would clear the table for my father to sort out the wages for the ten or so men he employed that week. He would count out the notes and the coins for each man and I would put them in the little brown wage packets. The following morning, we would go off with my father to visit the various sites to distribute the wages. I enjoyed that. I believe my lifelong connection and respect for small businesses was nurtured during those childhood years, so it wasn't really surprising that I ended up championing their cause.

At each site there was always a brazier burning the rubbish and on it an enamel bucket bubbling away with hot water. Around noon, one of the workmen would empty the contents of a packet of tea and a tin of condensed milk into the bucket and stir the brew with a stick that he had picked up from the ground and wiped across his grubby trousers. He would ladle the tea into chipped enamel mugs for his mates and visitors were handed a jam jar wrapped in a piece of old rag. The tea was delicious. On a cold winter's day a shovel used for mixing cement would be scraped half clean to form a frying pan on which a string of beef sausages and some rashers of bacon were placed. Ten minutes later, the sizzling sausages and bacon would be taken off, slapped between two thick slices hacked from a white loaf and handed to us to eat. These 'doorsteps', as we called them, tasted wonderful and I really looked forward to those treats.

Meanwhile, Dad's lorry was loaded with rubbish and rubble and off we would go to Mucking Flats, a rubbish tip on the Thames estuary in Essex. Forty years later, that part of Essex would be part of my Billericay constituency.

There were virtually no books in our house. Whenever I brought books home from the library, my mother insisted that they had to be immediately put away in a cupboard because she considered them dust collectors; she had little time for books. I always got the impression from our parents that books weren't welcome at home for fear they might muddle our minds or give us airs and graces above our station. Not having airs or graces was an important part of our upbringing. So, I did most of my reading under the bed clothes with a torch and kept my early scribblings, inspired by what I had read, in a box under the bed.

During school assembly when I was eleven years old, I heard to my astonishment the headmistress announce, in a monotone voice: 'Teresa Moore has passed the scholarship examination to go to a grammar school.' I turned to my friend. 'Was that my name?' I asked her.

'Yes, yes,' she replied, excitedly.

I was thrilled. No one else in the school that year had won a scholarship. The news was all the more surprising because, along with many other children, I had missed months of schooling due to the air-raids. At the beginning of the war we watched of thousands of children being evacuated from London because of the bombing. But my brothers and I were not spirited away, because my mother steadfastly refused to let us go. She argued that the family should stay together and, if it was God's will, all would be killed together. As a result, those children who remained in London missed many months of schooling. We thought the enforced holidays were great and spent hours rollerskating around the near-deserted streets, collecting pieces of shrapnel and spending nights in air-raid shelters, listening to the bomb blasts and the anti-aircraft guns.

I ran home that day and burst into the house, shouting to my mother, 'Mum, Mum, I've got a scholarship! I'm going to grammar school!' But Mum didn't share my excitement. She seemed unhappy at the idea. My heart sank when she looked up and I saw no smile on her face.

'Don't let this go to your head, my girl,' she said, speaking with her serious voice. 'Don't think we're going to waste good money on a school uniform and a tennis racquet. And who do you think is going to pay for the bus fares and the dinner money?'

I slunk out of the kitchen, went to my room and waited for my father to come home. I had a gut feeling that he would be pleased for me. But I wasn't sure. I heard him come in that evening and when I heard no shouting or yelling downstairs, I decided it would be safe to go down and tell him.

His face lit up when I told him the news. He seemed thrilled and I looked at my mother, who turned away. 'Well done, well done, what news, what great news,' he kept repeating. And I felt wonderful.

My father was the treasurer of the Putney Allotments Association and the Allotments chairman was the local bank manager, whose two daughters were already attending Putney High School, a public day school trust. My father, who harboured aspirations for me to join them, seemed very happy I had won a scholarship. He thought that Putney High might even have been a better school than a grammar school. In reality, however, my scholarship had simply become a new bone of contention between my warring parents.

My father was only too happy to pay for my uniform and the tennis racquet and I placated my mother by agreeing to cycle the three miles to school each day, come rain or shine, so that no money had to be found for travel. I didn't mind one jot riding to school, because in those days many kids cycled to school every day. I didn't even mind my mother making my gymslip rather than buying one, nor taking sandwiches to school each day if that was the price to pay for attending the school.

Alas, I didn't make it to the High School. I read fluently at the interview, but with the wrong accent. And I doubt there were many places there for the daughters of demolition workers. That said, I enjoyed my five years at the all-girl Fulham Grammar School, particularly biology and science. And I really enjoyed games. I played every game possible and felt really proud when I was selected to represent the school. During my years there, I represented Fulham Grammar at hockey, netball and tennis and became a really enthusiastic sportswoman. In my final year, I entered for the 100 yards in the National Schools Athletics at Wembley Stadium though, alas, I didn't win. Later, I would join the Selsonia Women's Athletics Club with a sports track on Tooting Common, where I continued to specialise in sprints.

My mother didn't think much of my grammar school education. Throughout my years at Fulham Grammar, she never tried to make my life enjoyable; in fact the opposite. It was the working-class ethos that a fifteen-year-old girl should be earning her keep.

As my 'O' level exams approached, my mother would talk to me of other girls in the street who were starting work, earning money, getting good jobs as shorthand typists in local firms. As a result, I felt under growing pressure to quit school, get a job and earn money for the family. It was a great relief when I finally took my exams. And I felt fantastic when I read the results – I had gained five 'O' levels – and my school certificate – my passport to the sixth form. However, I never did go into the sixth.

Fortunately for me, my father didn't want me to become a

shorthand typist. He wanted me to go into some sort of business and he suggested I became a hairdresser. His idea was that eventually he would set me up in my own shop; he would manage it, and we would have a steady little business together.

However, neither idea appealed to me. I certainly didn't want to become a shorthand typist and end up marrying some nice young man at the age of eighteen. I didn't really fancy the idea of working in a shop either, even if it was mine. I knew in my heart that I needed to further my education. But I also knew that the only way I was going to achieve my aim was to get a good job that paid enough money for me to attend night school.

I scoured the small ads searching for the best paid job and ended up working as a book-keeper in a swiss roll factory. For the next two years, I changed jobs three times, always increasing my pay packet because I was saving up for a college education. My prime concern for getting myself a better education was not to make big money, but to ensure I could look after myself and become totally independent, as my mother had urged me to be. 'Don't be a grain in a rice pudding, my girl,' she would say over and over again.

My ambition was to become a teacher, but I just wasn't earning enough money to pay towards my keep at home and save enough for college. My mother didn't want me to go to college and my father refused to fill in the forms needed to apply for a grant. I had calculated that after passing my 'O' levels, I would then need a further two years' full-time training at a teacher training college. I knew there was no way of being able to earn enough money, even working at nights and weekends, to put myself through college.

Then fate played a hand. I heard of an educational fund at Fulham Grammar School that was specifically designed to help girls like me get through college. I eventually managed to secure a loan from the school, but I had to find a way of earning enough money to pay for my accommodation and keep at Brighton Teacher Training College, where I had been offered a place in the women's college. In those days, there was no question of a girl from my background aiming for university. Barely ten per cent of their intake were women and I would need 'A' levels to even try.

But I was thrilled and excited to be going to Brighton to live and to study. I felt a wonderful sense of freedom leaving home and going out on my own. I managed to find a job, working as a shop assistant in a department store on Saturdays. I also found a good wheeze, running the college 'hop' on Saturday nights. The Saturday college hops were the place to be in Brighton during those years and the place would usually be heaving with young couples, drinking, dancing and having fun.

I loved counting the takings, buying the records, organising the refreshments, and, of course, dancing to Glenn Miller and Victor Sylvester; and jitterbugging and waltzing. I was entitled to a share of the profits and I worked hard for that money. Aged eighteen, it was the start of my business career, running a small but profitable concern.

Those two years at college were a revelation. At home, my education was always contentious – almost an aberration. But at Brighton, I found the intellectual activity not only natural but encouraged by the teachers. For the first time in my life I was independent of my parents and away from their constant, tedious squabbles.

Life back home during the holidays, however, was fraught. My mother attacked me, almost on a daily basis, for having 'airs and graces', criticising nearly everything I did. But I was not blameless. In reality, I was trying to impose my new-found middle-class attitudes on my parents. My mother considered that because I was at college I wasn't pulling my weight at home, earning money for the family. Every time I returned home, the atmosphere grew more and more intense. We would have terrible rows over the fact that I laid a table with both a spoon and a fork for pudding. I now called high tea 'dinner' and pudding became 'dessert'. My mother felt that I was being critical of the way she had lived her life and told me in no uncertain terms that I had become a middle-class snob.

However, for good or ill, college had changed me. And I knew that when my course came to an end I couldn't face returning to live once again with my parents on a permanent basis. I wanted out. I wanted to be independent.

I remember as if it was yesterday, the excitement of Fridays when I was fifteen. The dash home from school across Putney Bridge on my bicycle. The rush to get my homework done. Then off with the gymslip, the lisle stockings and the navy blue knickers. On with the flirty skirt and the beads and the jumper. No lipstick. Not, at least, until I'd escaped from my mother's beady eye.

On winter Friday nights I worked on the canteen at St. George's Physical Culture Club above the Duke's Head on Putney Embankment, where my father was secretary. It was the highlight of my week, a seething mass of weightlifters, bodybuilders, boxers and gymnasts in baggy shorts and string vests. Lycra had yet to be invented.

One Friday, in came a stranger. Jim Gorman had just been demobbed from the Royal Marine Commando. He floored everyone in unarmed combat skills honed in climbing cliffs under cover of darkness during short raids on enemy territory. It was rumoured he knew ten ways to kill a person using two fingers and a hatpin.

I usually took quite a long time to learn what these fellows coming back in the post-war period had actually done during their service. Jim was no exception. Nevertheless, I was impressed with the newcomer. In an atmosphere thick with the grunts and groans of males exercising and the clanking of the barbells as they hit the floor after a nice press and snatch or a good clean and jerk, this strong, silent stranger was beginning to register with me.

My father, who coached the weightlifters, was a middleweight champion. Our kitchen walls were covered with certificates and cups testifying to his achievements, arranged along the picture rail. My mother used to remove them to annoy him whenever they had a falling out, which was quite often.

Jim was a good listener to my endless, eclectic conversation. Soon he was invited home for my mum's bread-and-dripping suppers and to listen to our Bing Crosby collection. Dad's building yard backed onto the boatyard of Bossy Phelps, well known as a waterman who made skiffs for the school and university rowing clubs along the Thames. From Putney Bridge to Mortlake is the part of the Thames where the Oxford and Cambridge boat race is rowed. Rowing was mainly a sport for toffs, but each spring the young men from St. George's descended the iron staircase from their winter quarters to exercise their muscles in Bossy's fours and eights in the water. Jim rowed well. He'd had plenty of practice in cutters in which men were rowed onto enemy beaches for hit-and-run raids. However, actually getting this information out of him was like pulling teeth.

Jim rowed me across the river to Bishop's Park in Fulham for a picnic; our first formal date. As the summer wore on, he introduced me to his collection of motorbikes and I was really hooked. Everything from a Royal Enfield Bullet to an AJS 500. He was happiest stripping them down and tinkering with them. I was happiest with the excitement of riding pillion; arms wrapped round his middle, screaming in his ear 'squeeze it – squeeze it' as the speedometer crept up to 100 miles per hour. I loved the thrill of roaring along the roads to the Henley Regatta. Hair streaming in the wind, skirt up round my thighs, there were no crash helmets or leathers in those days. It was raw speed, it was danger, it was excitement. It was better than the Tango!

When the time came for me to leave London for college, Jim whizzed down to Sussex at weekends bearing gifts of tins of spam and baked beans; anything that was off rations. Never mind candlelit dinners – our romance blossomed over beans on toast cooked in front of the spluttering gas fire, the crumbs falling through the cracks in the lino, where they fed an army of earwigs that had colonised the space under the floorboards. Jim was the kind of man you could rely on to deal with a crisis like that without even flinching – what a find!

This being Brighton, we did a lot of marine biology. We used to dread the Low Spring, which always seemed to occur in the early hours of the morning.

'Miss Moore, it's half-past four and you should be down on the shore,' shrieked the biology lecturer as she banged on our door. With sleep in our eyes and a vasculum on our backs, we slithered over rocks collecting obscure molluscs and other invertebrates.

After college we decided to marry – Jim says I decided. Anyway, he asked my father for permission, I was still only twenty. People did things like that in those days. My mother threw a wobbly and would have nothing to do with the wedding; not after she'd spent twenty years of my upbringing warning me against the perils of men.

I took a taxi to pick Jim up. He had a nice navy blue suit for the wedding, but no tie. So we stopped on the way at Burtons in Putney High Street, where he spent his last penny on a tie – consequently, I had to loan him 11/6d for the marriage licence. We arrived at Wandsworth Registry Office so late that our witnesses, Jim's heavily pregnant sister and her husband, had left in disgust after the desperate registrar asked if they were the happy couple.

We had a fish-and-chip wedding breakfast in the garden of

Jim's mother's council house and his sister gave us a box of groceries as a wedding present. No honeymoon; all our savings had gone into a deposit on a run-down and neglected terraced house in the suburbs of south-west London. Next day we were wakened by a lad from St. George's anxious to trade his old motorbike for Jim's prized bodybuilding weights. In fact, Jim also had to sell his set of encyclopaedias and his James 250 cc motorbike to raise the deposit for the house. He figured he wouldn't have time for such frivolities anymore, and he was right.

We started working on our dilapidated new home that same day. We spent the first day of our honeymoon ripping out the old, black kitchen grate and the fireplace in the front room. It was to be the start of many such exciting and rewarding renovations that Jim and I carried out together.

Chapter Two

AMERICA AND
THE KENNEDYS

*'England and America are two countries
divided by a common language.'*
GEORGE BERNARD SHAW

The first two years of our married life was spent modernising our little home, despite the fact that we were total amateurs with no idea of plumbing, plastering, painting or decorating. We soon evolved our own division of labour; Jim knocked down the internal walls and I was his labourer, bagging up the rubble!

We both had full-time jobs. Jim was with Cable & Wireless and I was teaching at the Hurlingham Girls School, a secondary modern school, a thirty-minute bus ride from home. I taught a bit of everything. Ostensibly I was the science teacher, but in fact I also taught arts and craft, needlework and took some of the physical education classes. Because of my aptitude for various games, I was also given the job of games mistress. I had to work really hard – all the young teachers were expected to muck in and do anything they were asked. I never had a spare moment, but I enjoyed it all immensely.

Teachers were very poorly paid and I needed to pay off the money I had borrowed to attend training college. To earn extra money, I taught basket-making and a keep fit class at night school. It was called 'music and movement'; in reality, it was just PE set to music. I was enjoying every moment of a very full life but I soon realised that I would never earn enough money or be promoted unless I managed to obtain a university degree. So now I had a new ambition. I spent the next three years teaching all day and studying each evening, mostly as an external student at London University. Somehow I achieved a first-class honours degree in Zoology and Botany. Once again, I was more surprised than excited. No one had expected such a result – especially me.

I was now in my late twenties and facing the greatest decision of my young life. I was offered post-graduate scholarships to study in the United States, which would have opened the way for an academic career. The idea was tantalisingly flattering. I had always dreamt of visiting the United States and a higher degree would have guaranteed me a job there. The idea was almost inconceivable. In my wildest dreams I could have hardly imagined that a young woman with my family background would be offered such a chance.

But I had other responsibilities that I felt compelled to consider. The headmaster of Addey and Stanhope, a small co-educational grammar school in Deptford, south London, funded by the diarist John Evelyn (a contemporary of Samuel Peyps), had offered me a job teaching science throughout the school, irrespective of what class of degree I achieved. I would have let him down badly by refusing his offer and flying off to America instead. It might seem extraordinary, but I turned down an academic career in the United States to work in Deptford – at least for the time being.

I stayed at Deptford for the next five years and I loved it. Teaching biology to East End kids whose fathers were mostly market traders was a revelation. There was never a dull moment. At weekends, I took them out to the countryside pond dipping. And they all had a ripe sense of humour.

'I can't find the testicles,' the boys would cry out when dissecting.

'Maybe you don't have any,' I would retort.

Meanwhile, Jim hadn't been idle. After a few years we moved from our little terrace house in Streatham into a three-storey semi nearby. Three years later, having spent evenings and weekends repairing and modernising our second home, we moved again, this time to a lovely, four-bedroomed detached house on the edge of Streatham Common, with half an acre of garden. We were substituting elbow grease for a family fortune and going up in the world. More importantly, we were becoming independent.

And then, out of the blue, Jim was offered the chance to teach in New York. This time we seized the opportunity. America was to change my whole life. It was in 1964, just a few months after President Kennedy had been assassinated, that we set sail for New York in the QEII. Jim had a job but I needed to find one. All the New York teaching agencies that I phoned on arrival turned me down flat because I didn't have what they called a Masters Degree. My English degree was simply not accepted as good enough. I felt devastated.

We were living in a run-down hotel on the Lower East side, on 85th Street. The rooms were shabby and Jim and I would eat supper every night using newspapers as tablecloths. I began to think we must have been mad to give up our lovely detached house in south London for a life in a poverty-stricken part of New York City.

In desperation one day, I walked into the tiny employment bureau built onto the side of the famous St. Patrick's Cathedral on Fifth Avenue and asked if they had any teaching jobs. The woman who interviewed me asked, 'What subject to you teach?'

'Science', I replied, and she looked pleased.

She picked up the telephone. 'Is that the Convent of the Sacred Heart?' She then asked for the Mother Superior. 'I think I've found a science teacher for you,' she told them. After a pause, the woman said, 'Yes Mother, she's Irish, her name's Teresa O'Gorman.' After a further pause, she added,

'Oh yes, Mother, she's Catholic.'

By this time I was in a real panic. I wasn't a Catholic. I had never even set foot inside a Catholic church, let alone a convent. I waved frantically to the woman, trying to catch her eye. She put her hand over the mouthpiece and I burst out, 'But I'm not Irish and I'm not a Catholic!'

'Do you want this job or don't you?' she hissed back.

'Yes,' I replied. I needed the job.

As she put down the phone, she said, 'Well, you can go to confession when you get to the convent, they've got a nice little chapel there.' She gave me the address of the school and I took a cab up Fifth Avenue to 91st Street and the Convent of the Sacred Heart, the best Catholic school in New York. It was situated in a beautiful mansion.

It was a blisteringly hot and humid New York day and I was perspiring as I stood outside the solid wood door situated in the high wall, which protected the building from the outside world. A tiny little nun in a long black habit, her face surrounded by a nun's traditional close-fitting white bonnet, opened the door. She was obviously expecting me. 'Come in, come in my dear,' she said, smiling.

'Please wait here a moment while I fetch Mother Superior,' she added, when I had come inside, and silently disappeared. I stood in the dim, cool entrance hall, apprehensive and nervous because I was applying for a job under false pretences. That would have been bad enough if this were Bloomingdales but in a convent I suppose I was committing a sin. But I did need the job. Suddenly, I heard a rustling noise coming from at the top of the majestic spiral staircase. I looked up to see a troupe of a dozen or more nuns walking almost silently down the stairs to welcome me!

It transpired that the science teacher who had taken the job had pulled out just three days before the beginning of term and that morning the nuns had been praying in the chapel that God would find a replacement from somewhere. And here was I, standing before them, a qualified science teacher all the way from across the Atlantic. They told me later that they knew I was a gift from God.

For the next twelve months I taught science to four hundred girls who must have been amongst the most well-mannered children from the most wealthy families in New York. And they were all keen to learn. I taught them science in the English way – hands-on, practical science – so very different from the text book method they were used to. Among the pupils was nine-year-old Caroline Kennedy, the daughter of Jackie Kennedy and the late President John Kennedy. I had certainly fallen on my feet. These girls were not only delightful, they were fun to teach, and their parents were endlessly grateful that their daughters seemed to be fascinated by what went on in our science lessons. The nuns always introduced me to the parents as 'a gift from God' and told them that I had turned up in answer to their prayers. I'm not too sure if the parents believed it but the nuns certainly did.

Each day I walked to school through Central Park, which most New Yorkers believed was riddled with drug addicts, but I never encountered any problems. Maybe because the nuns prayed for me each day from 6 a.m. onwards!

It was then that I met Jackie Kennedy almost on a weekly basis, when she came to the school to collect Caroline. Of course, I had only known Jackie Kennedy from seeing her on the TV screen back home and I was frankly star struck. However, this was not the glamorous Mrs. Kennedy that I had seen on the television but just another mother who had slipped out without her make-up to collect the kids from school. Most of the time she wore a large, round knitted beret covering her hair, which emphasised her enormous cheekbones and wide-set eyes. She was as skinny as a rake. In fact, she looked like a mop on a stick with a large head and a size 6 body. Her voice was high pitched and breathy. But she was pleasant and charming, and insisted she was delighted at meeting someone from London. And, like most of the other mothers, Jackie told me how much Caroline was enjoying her science classes.

I got to know Jackie a little more when it was her turn to accompany me and the science class into Central Park for one of our natural science outings. We were chaperoned by a nun and a parent and, of course, when Caroline's class went to the Park, we were also accompanied by two armed Secret Service agents. As we strolled back to school together, the children armed with a bag full of specimens, we would chat about London and especially the theatre, in which she was very interested. In London, Jim and I had regularly attended the National Theatre and Jackie liked to talk about the plays, the actors we had seen and what I thought of the American stage. As a result, once every few weeks two tickets for Jim and me would arrive from Jackie, usually to plays at the

Lincoln Centre. We sat in the best seats surrounded by New York's elite, listening to Shakespeare played with an American accent. We had certainly fallen on our feet.

At Christmas, when the convent staged a performance of Gian Carlo Menotti's *Amahl and the Night Visitors*, not only did the composer turn up but also most of the Kennedy clan, including Jackie, Robert Kennedy and his wife as well as members of the Lawford family, whose daughters attended the school. Robert Kennedy went down the centre gangway with both arms extended, and people stretched out to shake his hand.

Before the Christmas break, the young girls clamoured to take home one of the creatures – frogs, mice, stick insects – that we had raised in the natural science laboratory.

'You'll have to bring a note,' I told them. Caroline's note duly arrived, and I still have it: '*Caroline has my permission to bring home a mouse*', signed by Jackie Kennedy.

Just before the Christmas holidays, I phoned Jackie.

'Are you sure you really want this mouse? It could escape.'

'Caroline's in love with the idea, she absolutely insists,' Jackie replied. 'Could you bring it round? We could go downtown to find a cage for it.'

I arrived at the penthouse overlooking Central Park. The drawing room was as big as Victoria station, with cream walls and cream sofas; on the walls hung American paintings, some of which I recognised as being by Andy Warhol. We went out to Bloomingdales, where Caroline picked out a cage that looked like a Chinese lantern.

'You'll need some wood chippings and something for the mouse to nibble,' I told her.

'I'm beginning to think it would have been simpler to send the children away to camp for the holiday,' Jackie confided. Everywhere we went, the detectives came too. We inevitably attracted attention. But Jackie explained that our two Secret Service chaperones were a necessary evil. 'I don't mind for myself, but I'm nerve-wracked about the safety of the children,' she told me. 'There are so many nutcases about.'

But, unfortunately, Caroline had taken home a male mouse, which was causing an unbearable smell in the vast centrally heated Fifth Avenue apartment where Jackie and the children lived. Jackie phoned the school in desperation and told me, 'You must come and take this mouse away. It's stinking the apartment out. Caroline will be heartbroken, but it's killing my social life. I would put the mouse down the john, but Caroline would never forgive me. The mouse also has a big red sore eye, so you could say that it needed some medical attention.'

When I arrived at the flat I discovered that Jackie had not been exaggerating. The smell was pervasive and strong. The mouse itself had indeed become a pathetic sight and was clearly in need of treatment, so I took it away on the pretext of letting a vet examine it. But Jackie had a guest at the flat, and introduced me to him: Andy Warhol. The Pop Artist made a quip about the dominance of the male and joked, 'I understand that you are introducing Caroline to the facts of life, including some we don't talk about in polite society.'

Jackie and the children went away on a skiing holiday the following week and by the time the children returned to school, Caroline had forgotten about her mouse. But Jackie hadn't. Soon after Christmas, I again bumped into her as she waited with the other parents to collect their children from school, wrapping them up warmly before venturing out into the freezing New York winter.

'I'm really grateful for your help with you-know-what,' she said with a conspiratorial smile. Then, as if as an afterthought, 'How do you feel about Bertolt Brecht? There is a production of *Mother Courage* at the Lincoln Centre that I am scheduled to attend. Would you and your husband like to come along?'

Mrs Kennedy turned up with Andy Warhol, who was wearing huge round glasses, and a secret service agent. The Brecht was well done, if you like that sort of thing, but the audience reaction was amazing. I can only imagine that this is what it is like being out with royalty. During the interval in the bar, every eye in the room was on Jackie.

I had my last contact with Jackie Kennedy in June 1968, not long after we returned to England, when Robert Kennedy was assassinated. I was shocked and horrified that another member of the Kennedy family had been murdered. I could imagine the terror she would be feeling, especially for the safety of her children. I imagined that she would want to get them to a place of safety – somewhere they would not be known. In retrospect it sounds crazy, but I decided to offer them the anonymity of a suburban house in South London. I knew the telephone number of Jackie's apartment from the time of the mouse incident, so I called it. The telephone rang for some time and then a man answered.

'Who is it?'

I explained my contact with Mrs Kennedy and Caroline, expressed my sympathy and asked to speak to her. I waited and then another voice came back on the line. This time it was Jackie

We chatted for a while, then I made my offer. 'Would it help if you sent the children over here – at least Caroline? I could pass her off as my niece – and she'd be safe for the time being.'

'That's real kind. There are detectives everywhere. We can hardly move out of the apartment. I just don't know how long any of us have to live in this mad country. What have American people got against me and my family?'

Caroline didn't come; Jackie wanted to keep the children close to her. Of course, it was a crazy idea, and as I look back, embarrassingly naïve. The idea that the American Secret Service would be unable to find a safe house somewhere in the vastness of the United States in which to hide the Kennedy children was absurd. I suppose that the extraordinary circumstances of a tragedy like that elicits a reaction dictated by your heart and not your head.

Jim and I finally found a two-bedroomed apartment in a run down mansion block on the corner of Broadway and 75th Street. The elderly couple who owned the apartment took the sun flight down to Florida where they stayed for the winter months. Each day on my walk across Central Park I would be followed by a New York police car because they too feared for my safety. Sometimes, a friendly cop would lean out of the car and warn me of the dangers of walking alone in such a place, something that was almost unheard of during that time. However, not once was I ever approached, possibly because I wore a ski balaclava to combat the freezing Atlantic winds that sweep across New York.

Both Jim and I were determined to see more of America than just New York. We bought a second-hand VW camper equipped with a wash basin, a little stove, a chemical loo and a table that turned into a double bed. During each school vacation we headed off across the United States and during the eighteen months we stayed there we visited New England, Boston and Chicago, and went across to Seattle and down the West Coast to San Francisco and Los Angeles. Rather than spending time at Disneyland and Hollywood, Jim and I were principally interested in America's natural history and we travelled from one National Park to another. In that way we visited the Rockies, the Arizona deserts, the Gulf Coast, the Florida swamps, the Grand Canyon and the Carlsberg caverns in New Mexico.

To our surprise, we discovered America was dotted with charming old towns with magnificent art galleries and many wonderful, hospitable people. Later, we moved on to live for a few months in Mexico, another exhilarating country with magnificent antiquities and wonderful parrots.

* * * * *

Jim and I arrived back home in October 1966 to a cold, wet London and to our house with no central heating. After America, it was a miserable let down. I found myself walking around the house wearing three layers of clothes and thick woollen stockings just to stop shivering. We had returned to England with a wealth of experience, new ideas and exciting information to pass on. But, of course, no one was interested. When we offered to show the family our slides, they accepted and then all fell asleep. And most of our other friends were convinced the Americans were so uncouth that we would surely be glad to be back. How wrong they were!

What most surprised me on my return was the attitude of intelligent people, including teachers, who genuinely seemed to believe that we could not have enjoyed the experience of living Stateside because, in their view, the Americans were so 'uncultured'. I couldn't believe it.

Jim and I had experienced a whole new way of looking at life living in the US. Raised under post-war socialism, where we took for granted the all-pervasive role of government, in America we had lived alongside people who took personal responsibility for granted. The concept of wholesale state control of industry, which we had been brought up with in Britain, was completely alien to the American way of thinking. As a result of my eighteen months in America I was now hooked on the free market and what it could deliver and I wanted to be a part of it.

Luckily for me, the same ideas were stirring amongst a group of people in the UK centred around a tiny handful of academics and the Institute of Economic Affairs. Of course, I knew nothing of that when I returned to London and our dreary, strike-ridden society.

I needed to find a job but I didn't want to stay in teaching.

I had outgrown the regimented school system in which, as a married woman of child-bearing age, I would be stuck in the classroom with little chance of promotion to a position where I could exercise my new ideas. I had to find a new outlet for my energies.

Chapter Three

SETTING UP IN BUSINESS

'Mind your own business is the only moral law.'
FREDERIC BASTIAT

America had inspired me. I found myself in a new country where people did not expect the state to be involved in every aspect of their life. We had left a Britain run by control freaks, both Tory and Labour, controlling almost every aspect of our lives. In America such an idea would seem preposterous. America opened my eyes to a totally different way of life, where virtually everything was provided not by the state but by private enterprise.

I had grown up in a country where people assumed that

only the government was capable of organising the basics of life, like health, education and housing. In America, for example, flats were easy to rent, health care was a free market, and everywhere there was a great entrepreneurial spirit. Americans took it for granted that they were responsible for their own lives. In Britain we had come to assume that the government would take care of everything from the cradle to the grave.

I didn't relish the idea of going back into teaching. I shared the Americans' 'can-do' attitude to life and found it enormously refreshing. I determined that I would try and follow the US ethic. I loved their get-up-and-go attitude. I knew that I would never make my fortune in teaching, but I did have a determination to become a real success in whatever job I tackled. I felt I had a natural flair for business because of my family background.

All I really knew about was teaching science, it was my only experience of my working life. And I had a gut feeling that I could turn some of my practical teaching ideas into a small business, supplying schools with laboratory materials. There was lots of scope for simplifying the equipment, which sometimes came between the children and learning science. Instead of microscopes and slides, we could provide transparencies of animal and plant tissues and a unique viewer for examining them. I would take the pictures and Jim would do the technical stuff in his spare time. When Jim left the Marines in 1947, he worked as an engineer in the car industry, then for Cable and Wireless, and finally transferred to teaching.

But we needed money to set up the business. My first port of call was the manager of my bank, where our two teaching salaries were paid into each month. Jim and I had never had an overdraft, so I thought my chances were pretty good. All I wanted was a £1,000 overdraft facility.

I dressed smartly and went off to see the manager of the Streatham branch of the Westminster Bank who, of course, was dressed in pinstripe trousers and black jacket. When I told him of my plan and requested an overdraft facility for my new business, he sucked in his breath as though I was asking for a million pounds. This was 1967, and women were still considered dependent on their partners. It was very unusual of them to expect the bank to give them an overdraft.

'How much were you thinking of?' he enquired, in a serious tone of voice.

I hesitated. 'One thousand pounds.'

He thought for a while, tapping the tips of his fingers together before asking, 'Does your husband know you're here?' This was not an uncommon attitude at the time. Women were unable to get any loans – or a mortgage – without a man's signature. He went on, 'At the moment, Mrs. Gorman, I don't think I could manage a thousand pennies overdraft facility let alone a thousand pounds.'

I left the bank feeling absolutely humiliated – and absolutely fuming.

As I came out, I saw Martins Bank across the road, with a picture of a small, bowler-hatted man carrying a builder's hod and climbing a ladder to success. The advertisement invited people to bring their business ideas to the bank, and guaranteed that they would receive a sympathetic hearing. So, there and then, I decided to put it to the test. I walked in and didn't even have to make an appointment.

The manager I met there was dressed in a suit, which put me at my ease. I explained my business plan, the need for the £1,000, and told him that I had a husband in work and also owned a house with a mortgage. He agreed to give me the facility on the condition that we both transferred our accounts to Martins Bank. I was only too happy to agree. I left that bank feeling cock-a-hoop.

My business – BANTA (Biological and Nursing Teaching Aids) – was born in our front room. It became an office. A girlfriend who could type came to help me and I was off and running. In a few months I was winning orders after trailing around London's schools as a saleswoman. I found that most of the teachers I met – people I had worked with professionally for years – treated me as a member of the lower orders because I was a mere salesperson. But I was determined to succeed and, because my ideas made sense, the orders began to come in.

My big breakthrough came with the Open University. They needed home teaching kits for elementary science courses for adults. Somehow I was awarded what was, relatively speaking, a fantastic order: 4,500 kits worth some £15,000, which to me was a small fortune. I drove back home from Milton Keynes that day singing 'Land of Hope and Glory' at the top of my voice. From now on I could tell the teachers who pooh-poohed my ideas that they were good enough for the Open University. The prestige of that order was a turning point. Now I had some capital to expand and produce new ideas.

Within a year or so I began to export the same products to British teachers working overseas. I began to travel, seeking new markets, mainly in Africa, the Far East and Australia. And the business began to make money.

I needed more help and so Jim quit his teaching job and came to manage the business while I concentrated on sales. Within a few years we were directly employing a dozen people and providing manufacturing work for half a dozen sub-contractors. We were out of the red and into the black.

The business grew as British teachers working abroad adopted my teaching materials, which they had first used with their classes in Britain. The aids were specifically designed to simplify science and were ideal for developing countries. For many students, this was their first encounter with science lessons. I began to design aids specifically for projects backed by the World Bank and other NGO aid agencies. I combined my globe-trotting with pleasure. Whenever my plane landed, I used the opportunity to explore. The game reserves in Africa, the unique plant life of Australia and the exotic locations in Mexico, Indonesia and Borneo were a spin-off from our growing overseas trade.

Whenever I travelled to Africa on business, I took time off to visit the local game reserve. The best safaris are where you walk through wild country, accompanied by an armed game warden, and camp at night under the stars.

One night, in Zimbabwe, we camped under the trees with orders not to venture out under any circumstances. Alone in my tent, I was awakened by the noise of something pelting the canvas. My immediate thought was that it must have been a tropical rainstorm, but as I unzipped my tiny window and peered out, the scene was bathed in the bright moonlight which only Africa offers. And there, a few feet away, was a large tree trunk. As I watched, it began to move. I was momentarily terrified. It was the leg of a gigantic elephant which was shaking the tree above me, dislodging the seed pods and scooping them up with its trunk. As it moved away, I could see we were in the midst of a herd of elephants slowly grazing in the moonlight. I, too, kept as silent as a mouse, fascinated at the scene. It was like a real-life Attenborough programme with the sound turned off.

It was treats like these, a unique culmination of work and pleasure, which made my job the best job in the world.

Then the problems began. Within a period of a matter of months we found ourselves, like every other business back in the early 1970s, in real trouble. We were faced with dock strikes, postal strikes, power cuts and even the refuse collectors went out on strike. All this industrial strife caused havoc in businesses and industry up and down the country.

Eventually, of course, we had the three-day week. The Prime Minister, Edward Heath, had ordered it to save electricity. Margaret Thatcher, Keith Joseph and Geoffrey Howe – all members of the government – supported him. When Patrick Jenkins, another minister, was caught with the lights on, using electricity to shave, it became a national scandal. And – unsurprisingly – nine months later there was a surge in the birth rate.

Sometimes, components that were vital for our business arrived in England but the dock workers refused to permit us to collect them. On one occasion, when matters were becoming really desperate, I decided I had to get hold of those components from the London docks, come what may. I made enquiries of Customs & Excise officers, who advised me there was indeed a chance I could retrieve the goods I needed. One day Jim and I hired a plain van and drove down through the East End, past a large group of dockers who were being harangued by Jack Dash, the infamous Communist leader of the dockers, who was yelling through a megaphone while standing on the back of a lorry.

Slowly we drove past the crowd of hundreds of workers into the docks. My heart was thumping. Suppose the dockers turned nasty? Some turned to stare at us. It was frightening. But we drove on to the Customs office, paid the duty and they signed the release forms for our goods.

'Can you tell us what to do, where to go?' asked Jim.

A Customs officer direct us to a particular shed where the cartons were awaiting clearance.

'You'll have to find a couple of friendly dockers to load them. You can't load them yourselves otherwise you'll be in big, big trouble.'

'Where do we find these men?' Jim asked.

'You're bound to find some of them down there who will be prepared to load them for you for £10 or so. You'll find plenty of them behind the packing cases playing cards.'

I was still nervous that something could so easily go wrong and that Jim and I might end up in the Thames. We drove the hundred yards to the shed and together we approached a group of men sitting around a packing case playing cards, exactly as we had been told.

'You stay in the van, I'll do this,' Jim ordered. 'They're less likely to give me a poke on the nose.'

He got out and approaching the men. 'Excuse me', he began, very politely, 'The Customs officers have agreed to release some packages that we urgently need for schools but I understand we need your co-operation to load them.'

We waited nervously. A couple of the men got to their feet, wandered over somewhat sullenly and Jim handed them the paperwork, which they glanced at. They were, of course, strike breaking, and I suspected that they were doing so with the collusion of Jack Dash and the union bosses, who must have been turning a blind eye. But that didn't worry us. After they loaded our boxes into the van, Jim asked the spokesman, 'How much?'

'Give us twenty quid.'

Jim didn't argue. He handed over the money, and thanked them just as if they had bought him a pint in the pub. 'I thought it was politic to do so,' he said later.

Our one aim now was to get out of the docks in one piece. Back on the road, travelling through London's East End, I felt that a great weight had been lifted off my shoulders. It was an adventure of sorts, although I didn't fancy too many more like that.

But I was also hopping mad. Why did we have to tolerate a situation where we were forced to eat humble pie by dockers who were out on strike? The country was in absolute chaos. This was just a microcosm of what was happening across the country. I knew from first-hand experience that these strikes were having a devastating effect on small businesses like ours. It was outrageous.

It was becoming impossible to run a business effectively when no one knew when or if orders could be produced and sent out to customers on time. No business knew when their machines would grind to a halt because of a sudden, totally wild power strike. Firms didn't know whether their workers could get to work because of rail and bus strikes and the month-long postal strike of 1973 meant many businesses could barely operate.

To cap it all, Edward Heath took us into the European Common Market and with it came VAT – Value Added Tax. That was bad enough but what made the imposition of VAT unbearable was the army of inspectors from Customs & Excise who were given the most draconian powers – which they seemed to relish. To the owners, directors and managers of Britain's small firms it seemed, on occasions, that the VAT men were treating them as smugglers, crooks or worse.

The papers were full of stories of VAT men breaking into firms' offices and, armed with jemmies, forcing open filing cabinets and drawers as they hunted for evidence that the firm might be hiding details of their business activities in an effort to evade paying the tax.

The government made a mistake in giving the collecting of VAT to Customs & Excise. VAT inspectors operated it the only way they knew – as if small businesses were trying to smuggle goods in and out of the country. They had *carte blanche* to do whatever they deemed fit in order to root out possible tax evaders. Most small firms were simply trying to cope with running a business and doing the government's paperwork for them.

My personal objection, as was the case with the owners of many small firms, was not only that we had to add the VAT to the cost of everything we sold, but we had to find the extra cost of paying book-keepers to set up and run this new system. It certainly distracted people from running their businesses efficiently. VAT was an elaborate, complicated tax system, the cost of which had to be born entirely by British business. For some small firms like mine, it became almost ruinous.

I think that, above any other development in Britain, it was the arrival and imposition of VAT that turned me into a political animal. Out of sheer frustration, I got together with a small group of like-minded local businessmen. We had industrial chaos, the three-day week, power cuts and never-ending strikes of one nationalised industry after another. We simply had to protest. And when Heath decided to seek a new mandate, we took the decision to put up a candidate of our own.

The first meeting took place in the front room of our house in Streatham within days of Edward Heath calling his second general election of 1974. He had come to power on a promise to reduce government interference in the business community, bring the trade unions under control and ban wild-cat strikes. Instead, we had industrial chaos and the election was Heath's attempt for a fresh mandate, to endorse his authority and increase the government's power over the trade unions.

Six of us met that night and I provided tea and biscuits. We talked into the early hours, thrashing out a platform for a new party to challenge the Conservative Party's weakness in dealing with the all-powerful trade unions. We wanted to put forward a more radical libertarian approach. We wanted less government, less taxes and more choice. We also wanted to reduce radically the power of the trade unions.

Our decision to put up a candidate to represent small business was meant to highlight the mounting problems facing all small firms. Understandably, no one wanted to be the candidate because it would mean precious time away from their business and so, finally, we decided to draw lots. I drew the short straw.

But as I drew that straw I had a mild panic attack. I suddenly realised the implications of putting my head above the parapet. I certainly wanted the free market to be applied to nationalised industries, but I wasn't political in any way. My main concern was what the neighbours and my customers would think. I had never done anything in the public arena before. I had never been directly involved in politics, I had never attended a political meeting, never belonged to a political party, although I had voted Conservative. I woke up in the middle of the night and thought, 'Oh my God, what have I let myself in for?'

One of my main concerns, of course, was the effect that this decision might have on my business. It would mean that the next five weeks of my life would be totally consumed by the election. I would have to write speeches, design and print leaflets, get our message out to the voters by running around the streets, pushing the leaflets through 37,000 letterboxes and putting up posters. All these thoughts went racing around my mind before I finally went back to sleep.

I woke up the next morning with a solution. I would stand as our candidate in Streatham if I used my maiden name, Teresa Moore. Then the neighbours and my customers wouldn't know what I was up to.

Our front room became the party headquarters. There was always a kettle brewing tea and biscuits for the small band of workers who came to help our cause, mostly personal friends and relations. Jim has a large family, eight brothers and sisters, and dozens of nieces and nephews, which came in very handy. Sometimes it seemed that we had struck a chord among the voters. We began to hear feedback from supporters in the public and enjoyed the task of getting over our message. We asked business acquaintances to design the leaflets and posters and organised teams to go canvassing and run public meetings. We were, in fact, running a kind of small business 'selling' a product and using all our commercial skills to get our message across.

That said, our public meetings were a disappointment. Only a tiny handful of people ever came to hear that message. I began to wonder whether we would do as well as we hoped. Standing up in some local hall addressing a tiny coterie of our own helpers was not inspiring. But we were not deterred and soldiered on.

We spent many hours deciding the wordings of our

leaflets, which we wanted to be bold and straightforward; in fact, they were downright witty. We were determined to get the message right so that people would understand why we were fighting both the Tories and Labour. We became even more contemptuous of all the political parties. Having connived at making people dependent on the state, they were now unable to control the unions, who were making life hell.

To our surprise, we did recruit a couple of dozen people who called us out of the blue with offers to help us in our campaign. We began to realise that there were other people around who shared our political views and aspirations. They gave us hope.

And then, we received a letter of support from the Institute of Economic Affairs, a right-wing think tank that none of us had ever heard of. It was the IEA that would later become the intellectual powerhouse behind the Thatcher free-market revolution. Somehow, they had heard about our campaign and now congratulated us on our manifesto. They promised to invite me to lunch at their headquarters on the corner of Lord North Street, Westminster, where, the following year, Jim and I were to buy another derelict, terraced house, which was to become our London home, though it meant abandoning our immaculate detached house in the suburbs.

Our leaflets pulled no punches. The message was all about freedom. We gave it straight to the voters. The politicians were ruining Britain, passing more and more legislation that had to be paid for by massive taxation. Britain needed not more but less government; Britain wanted more individual freedom. Freedom from government interference; freedom from government-induced inflation, which was destroying pensions and savings; freedom to choose good schools and freedom from massive taxation that took away our freedom of choice. And soon.

We thought up the idea of paying my electoral deposit in gold Krugerrands rather than pounds sterling, our way of showing our contempt of the constant devaluation in the British currency caused by politicians of both parties. This proved to be a stroke of genius, for we made the back page of the highly influential *Financial Times*. At last, we thought, we were making a breakthrough. In fact, this was the only piece of national press cover that we were given.

Perhaps the highlight of the entire campaign occurred in Streatham High Street on a Saturday morning when everyone was out shopping. I was standing on the back of our open truck haranguing the shoppers through a megaphone, when we came face to face with the Conservative candidate's battle bus coming towards us.

'Why are you standing against me?' shouted Bill Sheldon through a megaphone. The sitting Tory Member of Parliament seemed to think that we were really Conservatives and should have being supporting him.

I shouted back through my megaphone, 'Because the Conservative government is not doing its job of protecting the little man.'

I felt really terrific. Here we were, having our first political battle, and I felt that we had scored against the great Tory electoral machine. Everyone in the truck felt elated by the gladiatorial encounter. We laughed and cheered and felt we had the Tories on the run. Buoyed up by our enthusiasm, we became convinced that the message we were sending out was reaching the people of Streatham.

But the reality came a couple of weeks later at the count. We really did expect that we would get a few thousand people behind us. In fact, we polled precisely 298 votes. I felt deflated. I had been in the eye of the storm and I felt I had totally failed.

Heads down, we trooped out of the count at Lambeth Town Hall and made straight for the nearest pub. We needed to console ourselves and drown our sorrows. But we had learned a lesson. Independent candidates in a general election rarely make much of an impact; I would have to join a political party if I seriously wanted to influence policies.

In the pub that night, my supporters came to offer their condolences. The more they commiserated with me, the more wretched I felt. It was a bit like launching a new product only to find the customers turning it down flat. The more they tried to support me, the closer I came to tears. I felt less like celebrating and more like having a good cry.

When Jim and I eventually got home that night, the place seemed empty and desolate. We looked into the front room – our party headquarters – and saw the piles of leaflets, the half-eaten sandwiches, dirty tea cups and full ash trays, the remnants of everything we had strived for during the past weeks. We had given it our all and we had failed. We closed the door and went to bed, shattered.

Heath lost the election; Wilson took over the government,

though only with the support of the Liberals. But we took no pleasure in it. Instead, the next day we cleared the rubbish out of the house, cleaned the place and got back to the business, which I had neglected for five long weeks. I was determined never again to stand for parliament.

A political life would not have suited me anyway, I decided. I liked to get things done – under my own steam – and without having to kow-tow to other people. I was a back-me-or-sack-me kind of person – not a give-me-a-job type. The idea of hanging around waiting for someone to offer me a job in politics was anathema to me.

A few weeks after the election, when life had returned to normal, I was again surprised to receive an invitation to lunch from the Institute of Economic Affairs, inviting me to meet some other free-market supporters. Attending those lunches were economists, businessmen, academics, journalists and, of course, Tory politicians. Amongst the forty-odd guests who regularly attended the lunches were Geoffrey Howe, Nigel Lawson, Keith Joseph – rumoured to be the brains behind Thatcher – Airey Neave, Leon Brittan and, of course, Margaret Thatcher herself. The majority of these people would later become the nucleus of the Thatcher government. The day I attended the luncheon, Margaret had just defeated Heath for the leadership of the Tory Party. I had cheered with delight when I heard of her triumph. At last, a woman at the helm would surely put some common sense and stuffing into the Conservatives.

But I was amazed when Ralph Harris introduced me to my fellow guests as someone – the only person, in fact – who had fought the election on a truly free-market platform. Fellow guests congratulated me on my manifesto, part of which Ralph Harris read out to them.

Someone asked me if I belonged to the Reform Club. I looked at him blankly for a second or so, my mind racing. The Reform Club? What was the Reform Club? I had never heard of it. I had no idea of its existence, nor what it represented in our political history. The Reform Club was in fact a gentlemen's club set up by the Whigs, the predecessors to the Liberals, after the 1832 Reform Act, which extended the franchise from land owners to the middle classes, and later, in 1880, all males. Universal suffrage, including women, was only introduced in 1918. By asking me to join them, they were effectively paying me a great compliment by saying that my manifesto was as important as the recommendations in the Reform Act.

Amongst the guests who congratulated me was Alfred Sherman, an economic journalist who became one of Margaret Thatcher's main speech writers. After her leadership victory, she used the precise words, the very phrase, which had been the main plank of our manifesto – less government, less taxes, more choice. I was astounded, but also flattered. Perhaps, after all, our skirmish in Streatham had not been a complete waste of time!

Then, out of the blue, Bill Sheldon, who had retained the Streatham seat, wrote to me on House of Commons writing paper, inviting me to tea at the Commons. I couldn't have been more excited if I had been invited to 10 Downing Street. It was the first time that I had been invited to the

Commons and I dressed up accordingly. I wore a navy blue straw hat with cherries on the brim, a neat blue-and-white check suit, blue shoes and a pair of white gloves – all bought for the occasion. I know it sounds silly, but that is how women dressed for such a visit twenty-five years ago.

After some amiable chit-chat, Sheldon revealed the main reason for my invitation: 'Now we've got a woman running the show, why don't you come and join the Conservative Party?'

I told him that I would think about it, but in my heart I was thrilled that at last a woman had been given command. After all those boring bachelors and upper-class toffs, who seemed to think they were born to rule, Margaret Thatcher had broken the male stranglehold in the Tory party that had lasted for centuries.

I did not become a Conservative overnight, but I had become an instant Thatcherite. Everything she said in her early speeches appealed to me; they were the sentiments that our little upstart independent party had tried to express in standing against the Conservatives. Margaret Thatcher and her political instincts coincided entirely with my views.

Chapter Four

MY FIRST POLITICAL VENTURE

'"Helping industry" is the elephant pit of socialism, a deep hole with sharp spikes at the bottom, covered over with twigs and fresh grass.'

ENOCH POWELL

The election of Margaret Thatcher to the leadership of the Tory Party cheered me up enormously. Things could only get better. I hoped and prayed that politics in Britain would now become a fresh, more action-packed business – more like the United States. As soon as Margaret became leader of the opposition, I found her speeches and her Commons performances an ideological change of direction and a break from the former pragmatic, paternalistic Tory policies that seemed little different from Labour.

During those years the Wilson government seemed intent on piling on more and more regulations, which made life difficult, if not nigh impossible, for small firms. The Employment Protection Act seemed to be the last straw. As a direct result of the act, proprietors and directors of small firms were being hauled up before the newly established Employment Tribunals and fined large sums of money for sacking their employees, often on perfectly reasonable grounds.

I had protected myself from heavy legal bills by insuring myself against potential legal problems in my business. This insurance would cover such legal costs involving disaffected employees, but also any claims that might have been made by customers or suppliers.

Whenever I hear a chancellor telling us the wonderful things he (and it has always been a he) will do for us with our money, I see one of those small traders under the railway arches, up to their elbows in grease and driven mad by inspectors of all shapes and sizes, poking and prying into their businesses. And it makes me furious. I heard of so many cases where employers were prepared to pay off employees threatening to take them before the Tribunal simply to save themselves both the time and the aggravation. To me, many of these cases were akin to blackmail.

Having discussed these matters with a number of other like-minded business people, I decided to set up an organisation to extend these facilities to others. As a result I set up ASP – the Alliance of Self-Employed People. Membership included legal representation at an industrial tribunal when employers found themselves caught up in the web of the employment law. Consequently, employers became much more cautious when planning to take on new staff, for they feared the possible consequences if the person didn't fit in to the set-up or proved inadequate for the job. The tribunals changed patterns of employment. They bred a culture of taking on employees on short-term contracts or sacking employees within twelve months because after that time limit the employees were entitled to the full protection of the Act.

Not only small firms adopted these tactics. Middle and large companies followed suit. Even nationalised industries like the National Coal Board adopted the same tactics. As a result, the legislation had a distorting effect on job opportunities. Small firms were increasingly unwilling to take on inexperienced people and train them and large companies resorted to using outside contractors or offering short-term contracts to ensure they could not fall foul of the Act.

For me, the problems which had been building up for small employers were encapsulated in 1976 when some of the most violent picketing of the century took place over the principle of the closed shop. Grunwick, run by an Anglo-Indian entrepreneur George Ward, was a small firm that printed people's holiday snaps. It was under siege by APEX (the Association of Professional, Executive, Clerical and Computer staff), the trade union of printers, led by Jack

Droney, the husband of Harriet Harman. The might of the socialist world and the British Trade Union movement united in an effort to ruin Grunwick by refusing to handle mail for the company – the lifeblood of the business.

ASP received a call from NAFF (the National Association of Freedom), run by Ross and Norris McWhirter, asking us to join in an attempt to rescue Grunwick's mail, repackage it and post it in pillar boxes around the country. We organised it like a covert SAS operation. At dead of night, coaches smuggled out hundreds of sacks of prints and drove them to a secluded barn deep in the countryside where scores of volunteers worked all weekend repackaging the envelopes and sticking on thousands of stamps. On Sunday afternoon we dispersed small quantities of envelopes in pillar boxes across the country. The operation was a great success, and the camaraderie had been great fun and very rewarding. The operation was to play a pivotal role in undermining the strike.

Shortly afterwards, Eddie Shah – another immigrant, this time from Iran – struck another blow for freedom when he started a new tabloid newspaper, *Today*. Shortly after he launched a Sunday edition of *Today*, a youthful Alistair Campbell became the paper's news editor. The *Today* newspaper was remarkable in that it was the first computer-printed newspaper, which meant that it did not need the help of the unions. This caused many problems and picketing of the paper ensued; eventually, Rupert Murdoch rescued the ailing *Today* and, taking his cue from Eddie Shah, decided on his epic move from Fleet Street to 'Fortress' Wapping. Here,

Murdoch employed non-union printers, thereby risking the wrath of the print unions. The scenes of violence outside the tall iron railings went on for months.

In the space of a couple of years, ASP had built a membership of over 7,000 firms. We ran our own advisory and help line and many a small firm escaped the anguish and the cost of expensive legal proceedings through coming to us first. Firms that were represented by good lawyers found that they were winning far more cases and as a consequence, instead of simply capitulating to troublesome employees, they were prepared to fight them in court.

My experiences with ASP led me into writing articles for newspapers about the cases thrown up by the legislation that seemed to have been intent on making life difficult for small firms. I eventually found myself writing articles in the national press every month. As a result, think tanks approached me either to join their committees on employment or to give talks on the many problems the Employment Protection Act had created. These think tanks included the influential Adam Smith Institute and the Centre for Policy Studies, set up by Keith Joseph and Margaret Thatcher and headed by her favourite guru, Alfred Sherman.

I felt that my campaign had achieved real success when I received my first invitation to appear on the BBC's *Any Questions*, with Jonathan Dimbleby. But it was the mail bags that I received following such programmes that opened my eyes to people's concerns about the welfare state and the fact that the government was taking over every aspect of our lives. The hundreds of letters showed me that people across the political spectrum and from all walks of life were finding the state was taking over, and they resented it. By this time I was appearing on numerous political chat shows, the sort that were usually aired on Sunday mornings or late at night.

As ASP began to take off, we realised that we would need research staff and a base to work from. Daphne Macara, who ran her own small publishing house, joined me and wrote the newsletters that helped keep the organisation alive. But the Alliance of Self-Employed People really came into its own with the introduction of the hated tax – VAT.

Undeniably, VAT hit small businesses like a sledgehammer. It diverted them from business activity. They fought to keep their turnover under the level for registration. They felt angry with the time it took to fill in the forms that some believed would ruin their businesses and drive them to the wall, destroying what which they had spent a lifetime steadfastly building up. Of course, ASP took their cause to its heart and lent all possible support in doing battle with the government. All small firms rely on the amount of time you can put into them and government demands were stealing their time.

Then the newspapers reported that an old man who had run his own business for forty years had been raided by VAT officers. The officers smashed their way into his offices and were forcing open filing cabinets with jemmies when he remonstrated with them, asking them to wait while he collected the keys from his home. But the Customs & Excise officers refused. They sent an officer to his home to collect the keys from his daughters, but the VAT men still at his office refused to wait and broke into all the drawers and cabinets. After they had removed all his books and files from his office and left, the old man hanged himself. This outraged us. It was time for action.

We decided to organise our own demonstration against the VAT bully boys. We spent the weekend in the garden designing banners that spelled out our message succinctly: 'VAT KILLS. KILL VAT'.

At the appointed time, about twenty like-minded people, mainly members of ASP, assembled outside the VAT headquarters in London's Haymarket, holding up our banners. We drove round and round the Haymarket, and through Chinatown with our loudspeaker van demanding an end to VAT – the tax that killed.

As we drove around, the windows of the VAT headquarters overlooking the Haymarket filled up with staff wanting to see what was going on. Some of them were gesticulating, giving us the 'V' sign. There had never before been any such demonstration against Customs & Excise; we were totally inexperienced in such an area and, to be frank, weren't sure what we should do next.

Fortunately, a police officer guarding the entrance to the VAT offices came over to us and said, 'The Chief Executive of Customs & Excise will receive a delegation if you would care to come and see him.' We were flabbergasted. We hadn't asked to see him; indeed, we had no idea that he would agree to see us especially as we were, more or less, calling him and his officers killers.

Together with two other ASP members, Jim and I were ushered into the offices and escorted in a lift to the Chief Executive's office. We had not planned this and we weren't at all sure what we should say. He welcomed us nervously and asked why we were demonstrating and what we wanted.

I piped up, 'The first thing you can do is to get your staff away from the windows, where they have been standing, giving rude gestures to us.'

He was clearly taken off-guard by this piece of news. Recovering himself, he immediately left his office and returned saying, 'I've dealt with that. What else do you want.'

I continued. 'We have with us the two daughters of the poor man who hanged himself after his business had been raided by VAT inspectors.' We described the bully-boy tactics that were being used on a daily basis on our members and on hundreds of other small firms. We complained at the tactics being used by Customs & Excise. We also asked that there should be a review of the methods being employed by VAT officers who should stop treating businessmen as smugglers.

The Chief Executive agreed to examine the case of the suicide and thanked us for coming. I think we did have some success because, to judge from the number of complaints that we were receiving from small firms, Customs & Excise did modify their behaviour towards small businessmen and, to a certain extent, dropped their bully-boy tactics.

From the Haymarket we marched down Whitehall to lobby our Members of Parliament – minus our banners, of course, which the police made us leave at the other side of Parliament Square. This was my first-ever experience of lobbying. I quite enjoyed it.

Nicholas Ridley, then in opposition, came out to speak to us and promised to organise an adjournment debate if we would write out the substance of our complaint. We thought this was marvellous news, little realising at the time that an adjournment debate is very small beer.

When the day arrived, some twenty ASP members filed into the strangers gallery late at night to hear the debate. We were taken aback to find the Commons all but empty. Only Nicholas Ridley and the Minister who had to answer his question were present. Ridley read largely from the briefing notes we had supplied. It was all over in thirty minutes. Little did I then realise that, in fact, no one takes a blind bit of notice of adjournment debates. It would be some years before I understood that they are a perfect example of gesture politics.

However, on a personal basis, I had to get on with my own life, concentrating on running my own business. BANTA, fortunately, was going from strength to strength. It was hard work, but I loved being in charge. In fact, Jim did what I referred to as the boring bit: supervising the manufacturing side, making sure the orders went out on time and the like. I had a marvellous manager, Dorothy Brain, who kept the books in order and supervised our growing staff of a dozen or more.

Meanwhile, I was travelling overseas three and four times a year setting up science teaching projects in developing countries as well as supplying the UK market with my teaching aids. I continued to work with major aid organisations such as the World Bank designing science teaching programmes in parts of the world where science teaching had never before been introduced. Some schools even lacked gas, electricity and, unbelievably, running water. The classes were often of fifty or more pupils. It seemed those obstacles were impossible to overcome but somehow we managed it, mainly because the children were so keen to learn.

Chapter Five

LORD NORTH STREET

'A man's house is his castle.'
EDWARD COKE

When Jim and I began our business venture, which we hoped we would build into a successful and profitable concern, finding that vital 'start-up' finance proved difficult for there was no one, including the local bank manager, who would supply the amount of capital we needed to expand. In the end we had raised an additional mortgage on our small, not very valuable home – which, thankfully, had gone up in value considerably as a result of Jim's handiwork. Owning your own property and borrowing against it is the classic way for small firms to get started.

The business consumed our interest. You get a great thrill out of seeing your ideas come to fruition. Even better, they produced a healthy profit. But, as every small entrepreneur understands only too well, it took hard work, long hours and absolute commitment. We were building our capital by restoring old houses. Moving to a larger, more expensive house became part of our life. It enabled us to raise more money from the bank. Children hadn't come along and so we were both able to spend most of our waking hours building the business, or rebuilding the house!

Jim proved to be a great DIY man. As a young man during the war he trained as an engineer and served with the Royal Marine Commandos. He was a practical man, good with his hands. He became expert at turning a shambolic wreck of a house into a lovely home. In the space of forty years or so we moved house half a dozen times and each time we would select a run-down, dilapidated, ramshackle shell of a house in a good area that we both felt had real potential. We took great care to select the right area of London. At times, some of our friends thought we must be crazy for buying one dilapidated house after another, working on it every spare moment making the place not just habitable but lovingly restoring it, only to sell up and move on. But we enjoyed the whole process.

Thank goodness we were both young and healthy. We had a surplus of energy and were prepared to work all day and then spend all our free time – evenings and weekends – painting and decorating. The partnership worked brilliantly.

The houses we tackled and renovated shot up in value and, as a result, whenever we needed more money to fund the business we could prove to the banks that the value of our homes far outweighed the loans we required.

It was ironic that we first spotted the next house that we would move into on one of our visits to the Institute of Economic Affairs, the organization founded to spread the gospel of free enterprise in the aftermath of the war. The 'For Sale' board was barely readable. It had obviously been there for some time. The moment I saw the place, I knew I wanted to buy it. It was in a part of London that I had dreamed of during those weekend walks.

The house was part of a beautiful Georgian terrace in Lord North Street, a tiny area that had somehow survived the war-time saturation bombing of that part of London north of the Thames near the Houses of Parliament. The Luftwaffe targeted the heart of government, and reduced the area to little more than rubble. Fortunately, the Houses of Parliament suffered relatively little damage.

Lord North Street was built in the early 1700s on land reclaimed from the River Thames and later named after Lord North, the prime minister tarnished with the reputation of being responsible for the measures that brought about the loss of America. The location of the house was brilliant for anyone involved in national politics, as it was situated within a two-minute walk to the Houses of Parliament, a five-minute walk to Downing Street and only a ten-minute stroll across St. James's Park to Buckingham Palace. It is one of four streets radiating off a beautiful square in the centre of which is St. John's Church, built in 1706 for Queen Anne and known locally as Queen Anne's Footstool. The church was later restored and converted into a concert hall by the family who would become our neighbours, the Sainsbury family. By one of the coincidences that seem to haunt my life, long ago Jim and I had attended the opening night there, when Joan Sutherland sang and her husband played the piano – I remembered it vividly.

Thirty years after the war the condition of those houses, and particularly the one we wished to buy, was truly horrendous. The small terrace was originally built for government servants. In Victorian times, they became lodging houses and sometimes seven or eight families lived in one three-bedroomed house. If this had still been a working-class district, they would surely have been condemned as unfit for human habitation and pulled down.

As we walked past the house on Sunday afternoons, gazing into the grimy windows and peering through the letterbox at the piles of mail inside, I fell more and more in love with the house. I was sure we were meant to buy it. Time and again, we would return to Lord North Street, walk up and down, take a look at the other properties and plan what we should do. Even before we had taken a look inside the house, we both recognised that one hell of a lot of work would be needed to simply get the place habitable, let alone to try and restore to its former glory.

We did notice, however, that some of the houses were smart and that the cars parked outside them were expensive, which suggested that there must be some snag to this property otherwise it would have been snapped up before. On further investigation, we discovered why the house was empty and had been for years: it only had a thirteen-year lease. We also learned that as soon as anyone bought the house, the local Westminster Council – which owned the freehold – would have the authority to order a full repair and renovation of the place, which could amount to tens of thousands of pounds.

With a lot of pleading on my part, Jim agreed to buy it. During the 1970s there was talk of leaseholders being granted the right to buy their freehold, or at least an extended lease on the property. There were many such dilapidated houses around the country, but particularly in big cities, that were lying empty because of the law permitting the freeholders to force leaseholders to repair short lease properties in which they lived. As a result, any property with a short lease was a bad investment. The houses were left to rot.

Jim had his doubts, but I was determined. It was a gamble, but how else could we have afforded to live in the centre of London? So we sold our bijou, four-bedroomed detached house in the leafy suburb of Streatham, with its lovely manicured garden, and spent all the money on buying a thirteen-year lease on Number 14 Lord North Street.

The house had belonged to the once-famous theatrical producer Hugh 'Binkie' Beaumont, the Lloyd Webber of his era, whose influence on the West End theatre world stretched from the 1930s to the 1960s. 'Binkie' Beaumont was the impresario who presented most of the Ivor Novello musicals and Noel Coward plays in the West End – indeed, he was good friends with both gentlemen.

And 'Binkie' was also famous for throwing some of the great parties of that time. After West End shows, he would invite not only the stars of the show but also the most influential theatre people and backers to his home in Lord North Street. His housekeeper, Anna, who by now was working for the Sainsburys, our new next-door neighbours, told us that 'everyone who was anyone' in London's theatre world had slept in the principal bedroom on the first floor, including Marilyn Monroe and her playwright husband Arthur Miller, and Marlon Brando.

The house certainly had a history. It had in its years also been home to a blacking manufacturer, a mason, a tailor, a printer, a bricklayer's labourer, a butcher, a needle-woman, a coach joiner, a plumber and a gas fitter. It wasn't until 1916 that the great and the good started to move into Lord North Street, when Gladys, Marchioness Ripon, combined our house with the one next door into one residence, developing Lord North Street into a truly fashionable address. Later, the house was to become the home of Lothar Henry George de Bunsen, whose son, Bernard de Bunsen was the inventor of the bunsen burner.

We got the keys and went inside. The house was in a terrible state. And after we had climbed the five storeys to the top of the house from the basement I seriously wondered if we hadn't bitten off more than we could chew. It was a gamble. We had no spare money in the bank for the necessary major repairs – it was all tied up in the business. We faced the prospect of years of hard work.

The lace curtains that had been left at the windows disintegrated when I touched them, ending in little piles of black dust on the dark green carpet, which didn't look as though it had been swept or cleaned for decades. The house was full of nooks and crannies. There were thousands of cobwebs and scurrying spiders, millions of dust mites and the dried up remains of dead mice. The basement kitchen looked Dickensian, the only bathroom was stained and filthy, and an additional lavatory built at the back of the building at first-floor level was about to fall off the wall. Even the stairs, with their beautiful sweeping banister, seemed dodgy and some of the ceilings looked as though they were on the verge of collapsing. Where to start?

First, we had to make just a few rooms habitable so that we could at least live in the place. We planned to work our way slowly up the house until perhaps, one day in the far-off future, we hoped to have a wonderful, fabulous home. But it looked as if it might take us all of the remaining thirteen years of the lease to complete the necessary restoration.

So we called up our friends and invited them round for a working lunch. They duly arrived with buckets and scrubbing brushes, paintbrushes and rollers, brooms and dusters and every other type of cleaning appliance they could lay their hands on. We provided the necessary cleaning materials and gallons of tea and coffee as well as something stronger for the end of the day when everyone would collapse, exhausted. Weather permitting, we sat in the back yard under an enormous plane tree, the roots of which were undermining the foundations. Incredibly, some of our friends returned for another hard day's work the following weekend, for which we were eternally grateful.

We called in Westminster Council and the Heritage Department because this house was a listed building. It was wood panelled from the ground to the second floor. They approved of our plans to restore the house and agreed that we should remove the later additions to the original structure. But planning permission was not needed unless we intended to make major alterations.

It was not long after we arrived in Lord North Street before we took in a lodger. The cleaning lady must have let her in. She was sitting on the landing at the top of the stairs leading down to the drawing room when I came home one night.

'Who the hell are you?'

No answer.

'How did you get in here?'

The same cool stare.

'Where do you come from?'

She turned her head sideways, sizing up her surroundings.

'Don't think you can stay here. I've got enough to do.'

She stood up, stretched out and walked slowly down the stairs and out onto the doorstep. She looked up and down the street and strolled off. The next day, she was back. This time waiting outside the door.

'You're back. Haven't you got a home to go to?'

Again, the look. But this time it was more pleading.

'Oh alright, you can come in. But I'm not saying you can stay.'

And so began our love affair with the cat – a tortoiseshell tabby – big eyes, house trained and almost silent but for some guttural noises whenever I came home from Sainsburys with the shopping.

'Name?' said the vet when I took her in for a medical.

'Pussy.'

'I know it's a pussy, but what is its name?'

'OK. Pussy Pussy.'

The vet wrote regularly to remind us when she was due for a check-up. The card was addressed to Pussy Pussy Gorman.

She wasn't my cat and I didn't want to get too attached to her. She had a fondness for walkabouts. She often stayed away for days and turned up in the queue of patients waiting outside Dr. Muir's Surgery round the corner. Mrs. Muir would often phone me to say, 'Your cat is in our surgery. I don't know why she keeps coming. There is nothing wrong with her.'

'Are you treating her on the NHS?'

'Well, no, our patient list is full.'

Mrs. Muir had been sniffed out as a cat lover. I suspect we were both on probation. For whatever reason, Pussy Pussy decided to live with us. Ten years later, when I became an MP, she was still with us and was always there when I came home tired and weary in the small hours of the morning.

We soon discovered that our neighbours were a wonderful cross-section of society and a most interesting bunch. One earl, one prime minister, one Member of Parliament, one multi-millionaire, one publisher, a high court judge, a banker and a used car salesman.

Soon after we arrived, Jim called at the local newsagent in nearby Horseferry Road to order the newspapers.

'Address, sir?' asked the man behind the counter.

'Fourteen Lord North Street.'

'Name, sir?'

'Gorman, James Gorman.'

'Title, sir?'

'Just Mister, Mister James Daniel Francis Gorman. I'd like the *Mail*, the *Telegraph* and the *Spectator*.

'*Times*, sir?'

'No *Times*, thank you.'

Lord North Street had its fair share of titled people. It was that sort of neighbourhood. Not long after we bought the house, Jim was carrying out the unenviable task of cleaning out the grimy, filthy basement, lamenting the fact that much of the eighteenth-century plaster ceiling was in pieces on the floor, when the doorbell rang.

Covered with black dust and looking like a chimney sweep, he opened the door to an elegant, white-haired lady with a cut-glass voice and a slight foreign accent.

'Is your mistress in?' she enquired, looking Jim up and down.

'No, but I'm expecting her,' he replied.

'Well,' she went on, 'will you tell her that if she has any parcels delivered before she moves in, my maid will be pleased to take them in for her.'

'That's very kind of you, mam,' Jim replied, 'I'll let her know.'

This was our first encounter with our next-door neighbour, Lady Lisa Sainsbury, wife of Sir Robert, one of the four founding brothers of the supermarket empire.

Lady Sainsbury, who was a member of the famous Van den Bergh family, would often stop and enquire how the building work was progressing. I frequently reflected on what tolerant neighbours they were because they never once complained at all the banging and noise throughout the months of repairing and restoring the building. Much later, when I had become a Member of Parliament, Lady Sainsbury would stop me in the street and ask, 'How is my niece Harriet getting on?' She was referring to Harriet Harman, the Labour Member for Camberwell and Peckham. 'Harriet,' I would reply, 'is doing awfully well.' But I never did discover what the actual blood line relationship was between the two women.

Each weekend, Sir Robert's chauffeur-driven limousine would arrive and the maid would pack the boot with their suitcases before Sir Robert and Lisa were driven off to their country estate, where Sir Robert cultivated his prize orchids.

But even more interesting to us was Anna, the Sainsburys' maid-cum-housekeeper, who had previously worked in our house for 'Binkie' Beaumont. She told us all about Binkie's friends and of his odd little habits. She even offered to show us around the Sainsburys' house while they were away. I was keen to see how their house, more or less identical to ours, compared. I guessed that it might contain original pieces of eighteenth-century furniture.

As the world now knows, Robert Sainsbury and his French wife, a former ballet dancer, were great collectors of modern art. And as soon as we walked into the hall I could see why it was necessary for them always to employ live-in servants and why the house was equipped with a highly sophisticated security system. There, on the wall was a magnificent Modigliani, an original, which by itself must have been worth a fortune. In the first-floor dining room staring down at the dining table was a positively hideous self-portrait by the English painter Francis Bacon, whose art sets out to highlight the repulsive in the human shape. One eye was missing and the mouth was twisted round to the ear. 'That's enough to put anyone off their grub,' quipped Jim as we stood, transfixed by the large painting.

But the oddest thing in the entire house was Sir Robert's bedroom. A single bed had been placed in the centre of the room. Surrounding it on three sides was a shelf some two feet above the bed. It was a bit like a bunk onboard ship. On the three wide shelves were displayed a collection of life-size models of human skulls, all of which had snakes and lizards twisting in and out of their mouths, their eye sockets and nostrils. The skulls sent a shiver down my spine and seemed utterly bizarre. As Jim put it, 'Well, you wouldn't need to go to sleep to have nightmares; fancy waking up in the dead of night to this lot.'

It seemed perfectly natural when a Sainsburys van stopped outside their house and a delivery of groceries was taken in by the maid. However, on occasions, it wasn't a Sainsburys van but one from the upmarket grocer, Fortnum and Mason.

Opposite us, at Number 8, lived Lord Drogheda, then chairman of the *Financial Times* and Chair of the Governors of the Royal Opera House, who would throw parties and hold concerts and musical events in the private theatre at the back of the house. During the Queen's Silver Jubilee in 1977, Jim and I stood, night after night, peeping through the holes in the rotted net curtains like the Bisto kids watching the comings and goings in the Drogheda household.

After ten o'clock, when Covent Garden performances had ended, a procession of chauffeur-driven Rolls, Bentleys, Jaguars and Mercedes purred into our street and a procession of posh totty, accompanied by their men in dinner jackets and black bow ties would walk into Number 8 for the main event of the evening. Everyone who was anyone in London society that summer of '77 seemed to attend, including Princess Margaret. Ambassadors and their wives, people from the world of politics, the law, the City and the Church were all regular visitors. At Number 8, they would be entertained by principal soloists from Covent Garden. It seemed we were watching a bygone generation in a world long-since forgotten.

It was Jonathan Aitken, then a promising young Conservative MP, who bought Number 8 when Lord Drogheda retired from the *Financial Times*. It was, of course, the perfect home for an ambitious MP, not only architecturally beautiful but a wonderful place for entertaining his political friends, a mere stone's throw from Parliament. And Jonathan and his glamorous Yugoslavian wife Lolicia seemed to love to entertain. They would hold frequent parties, both in the winter and summer evenings but now the purring limousines were from various government ministries, as the top brass of the Conservative Party came to dine.

The Conservative Philosophical Society, which Jonathan ran, met regularly at his house, where star speakers from the world of politics would entertain an array of star-studded guests. Former US President Richard Nixon was one visitor. Some years earlier, Jonathan had written a study of Nixon's presidency and the two men subsequently became firm friends.

Between the IEA lunches at Number 2 and Jonathan's meetings at Number 8, Lord North Street hosted a multitude of stars from the world of politics and the Establishment. Frederich Hayek, the celebrated German economist and a favourite of Margaret Thatcher's who won a Nobel prize in Economic Science in 1974, was one guest speaker. Half the Cabinet, including Norman Tebbit and Norman Lamont, regularly attended. In his lecture, Lamont dared to suggest that the United Kingdom could leave the European Union if this provided the best alternative, a view with which I couldn't have agreed more. Sometimes I was invited to hear them. It was the place to be seen and heard and a great compliment amongst senior Tory Party members to be invited to those evenings.

From our side of the street, it seemed as though Jonathan, tall and handsome, talented and rich, with powerful friends in politics and the City, was living a golden life. Margaret Thatcher did not promote him but John Major did shortly after Jonathan made a very supportive speech when John returned from the conference on Maastricht. In addition to his stunning wife, Jonathan had three lovely children and a safe seat.

Not many people knew that when Diane Abbot, the maverick hard left Labour MP was elected, Jonathan managed to snap her up as his pair. Securing a pair is vital for MPs, because it means that by agreement, you can both miss a vote and cancel each other out. It helps you to live a more relaxed, sociable life outside politics without the need to race back to the House late at night to cast your vote. For most MPs, life without a pair can be tedious as well as ruining your social life. At that time, pairs were at a premium and wealthy Tories were rumoured to be offering up to £5,000 to anyone who would pair with them. Diane chose Jonathan for his charm and their shared interest in economics. In Westminster, politicians from the opposite ends of the political spectrum often become good friends and when Diane had her baby Jonathan threw the christening party at Number 8.

When I finally became an MP, my Labour pair was George Galloway from Glasgow, who had a reputation as a bit of a ladies man. We too hit it off, although George did have some questions to answer to his constituency party when the news of his relationship with a rabid right-winger like me appeared in the gossip columns of the press.

I was never a close friend of Jonathan, but we shared the

same views on Europe. And after his sad fall from grace, I felt dreadfully sorry for him. One minute he seemed to have the world at his feet, the next he had lost everything, including his liberty. After he was released from jail he returned quietly to Lord North Street. The photographers, TV crews and press pack who had haunted the street during the trial, no longer laid siege to his house, a place that had once been brimming with activity. I thought of him sitting alone in his great drawing room feeling down-hearted and miserable, so I decided to try and cheer him up. I picked up the phone and invited myself over for coffee, telling him that I needed to have a chat.

I arrived with a bag of doughnuts from my favourite restaurant in our office block at Number 7 Millbank, and took along a bottle of champagne. I found Jonathan subdued but still dignified and, as always, impeccably polite. We chatted about the Commons, various politicians and the current political climate. He told me he was planning to write a book about his life inside, but that first he had to teach himself how to use a computer.

At another house in the street, life was very different and very bizarre. There, too, there were lots of parties, but with a different kind of guest list. The house belonged to the debauched offspring of the old aristocracy – a man in his forties whose summer drinks parties spilled out into the street and managed to keep us awake with their revelry, high jinks and prodigious drinking. The dresses of some of the women seemed very risqué, several yards short of a complete garment, while some of the men seemed to have difficulty standing upright. On party nights, we would wait until the noise level died down to an acceptable level before going to bed to try to get some much-needed sleep. But quite often we would be woken an hour or two later with the noise of a stereo pounding out music at full blast. Our neighbour was in the habit of falling into a drunken stupor only to wake in the small hours. The street wasn't very wide and the power of the music would rattle our windows. On one such night, Jim dragged himself out of bed and went to the window hoping he would be able to see the man and ask him to turn down the volume.

'Look at this,' Jim said, a note of wonder in his voice, 'you must come and have a look.'

I tumbled out of bed and went over to the window. There was our neighbour, standing stark naked in front of his long Georgian window, showing the world his God-given attributes. Everything was revealed by the light of the gas lamps that lit the street. In his hand he appeared to be holding a baton with which he was vigorously conducting an imaginary orchestra. It was an awesome sight.

Sometimes, Jim would telephone and politely ask the ageing party animal to turn down the volume. But after a while our calls went unanswered and the music continued. We had to resort to putting pillows over our heads in an effort to block out the din. One night, Jim could stand it no longer and decided to take some action. With his dressing gown thrown over his pyjamas and wearing only carpet slippers, he walked down the road and rang the doorbell. Seconds later the long window above Jim's head flew open and our neighbour, naked as usual, leant over the windowsill, and, shouted at the top of his voice, 'Why don't you piss off back to the suburbs,' before slamming the window shut again.

'Well,' said Jim on his return, 'he's certainly researched our pedigree. I wonder if we're in Debrett's?'

The following morning I met our other next-door neighbour, the wife of a judge, and asked whether she too had been disturbed by the antics opposite. 'My dear, it's been going on for ages,' she said with a smile, 'I have often seen him with his bollocks on the window sill. I can tell you, it's not a pretty sight.'

She told me that the former owner of her house, Number 15, another effete member of our ruling classes, had been even worse. Apparently he had spent nearly all his money on drugs and eventually set fire to the upper storeys and had to be rescued by the fire brigade.

Number 19, the end house in Lord North Street, belonged to a Mr. Wiggins, who had made his own fortune running the famous Wiggins Car Auctions. We had something in common – we were both in trade. I could only guess what our posh neighbours thought about that. He certainly seemed to have friends among senior politicians. However, it seemed that some of our well-bred neighbours had their misgivings and rather shunned him. The gossip was that he was the epitome of the *nouveau riche*, someone who had made a lot of money but had no taste whatsoever. This patronising remark was based on the fact that the original, wooden Georgian front door to his house had been replaced with one made in Indonesia. The trouble was that the rest of the street had to live with it. Poor Mr. Wiggins was a bit like us; up from the sticks and self-made.

Number 5 Lord North Street appeared to us to be more of a bordello than the London home of a highly respected Member of Parliament and barrister. William Rees-Davies, or Billy as he was known, was well into his fifties when we moved into the street and appeared to be single and living on his own. We learned later that his marriage had broken up and was finally dissolved in 1981. Rees-Davies was educated at Eton and Trinity College Cambridge and was renowned as a great all-round athlete. He was commissioned into the Welsh Guards during the Second World War but discharged after losing an arm. He represented Thanet as a Conservative MP from 1953 to 1983.

But it was the comings and goings at Number 5 that caught our attention. Poor Rees-Davies was a sorry sight. He looked to us more like Quasimodo with his tousled hair, his hunched back and what seemed like his other arm always held behind his back. It was later that we learned that he had lost the arm in the war. At around 11 p.m. two or three times a week, a taxi would arrive outside his home and a young woman would pay off the driver and run to the front door of Number 5. A couple of hours later it would return, and stand with its engine running until the young woman would leave around 1 a.m. Sometimes, two young women would visit him at the same time.

Some time later, I was having a chat to the woman who lived with her family next door at Number 4. She complained that whenever Rees-Davies entertained his young ladies the amount of noise, shrieking and screaming and bumping against the walls was so loud that eventually she had to move her children's bedroom to another part of her house because they couldn't sleep.

The distinguished people who lived in Lord North Street generally kept themselves to themselves in a very English way, not wishing to pry or appear nosy or interfering. Most of the news on the street was passed from house to house by 'the staff' – the maids, chauffeurs and cleaners who worked there. If there was any hot gossip it didn't take long before anyone in the street who was interested knew all the facts.

By this time, we too had a 'maid' – well, a daily help. She was Swedish and a good worker, but very melancholy. Although we didn't know it when we engaged her, she had a penchant for alcohol. One day, Jim poured a gin and tonic for a friend who, after tasting the drink, said 'Can I have some gin in this, unless you are running out of money, old chap?'

Jim sniffed the bottle, then another, and another. All the white spirits had been replaced with water. I didn't begrudge her those weird bottles of Schnapps and other foreign drinks that people bring you when the come to visit. But I hated to think of all the people we had served with gin or vodka who went home convinced we were unbelievably mean.

Then one day, I received a call from Lolicia Aitken, who lived opposite.

'Could you come and collect your maid,' she said, 'she's flat out on our basement floor and blind drunk!'

The brother of the famous novelist Graham Greene, himself a publisher, lived at Number 11. He would wave and say a cheery 'good morning' when leaving for the office in his gleaming, chauffeur-driven Mercedes. Soon we learned that he travelled to Europe quite frequently and after we met he offered me a lift to the City airport any time.

'If you should ever be going there my chauffeur would be happy to give you a lift. Just ask,' he said, airily. As a matter of fact, I had never been to the airport and was unlikely to. Most of our trips abroad were by charter flights – except when I travelled on business – but it was a kind thought. From time to time we read about Mr. Greene's matrimonial affairs in the national press. And rumours certainly circulated about him amongst the servants.

But at the time we moved into Lord North Street, our most prestigious neighbour was without doubt the resident of Number 6: the Prime Minister, Harold Wilson, and his quiet and unpretentious wife, Mary. It was, of course, the only occasion in modern times that Lord North Street could boast of having a current prime minister actually living in the street. When Harold Wilson was returned to power in the general election of October 1974, Mary refused to move back into Number 10 Downing Street because she had so hated living above the 'shop' during Harold's first stint as prime minister, from 1964 to 1970. She felt that her husband could never relax when they lived at Number 10 and would spend too much time popping into the 'office' when he should have been having a break from the job.

As a result, Lord North Street had its own permanent police guard outside the Wilsons' front door and a policeman at each end of the street. Needless to say, Lord North Street also boasted the lowest crime rate in the entire country. They were very helpful when our cat went walkabout.

'I'm looking for Pussy,' I would say to one of them, anxiously. 'Have you seen it?'

'No mam, I don't think so. What does it look like?'

'Its sort of light brown, a tabby, tortoiseshell coloured.'

'What do you call it?'

'Pussy. Well, Pussy-Pussy to be exact.'

'I see mam, I will do my very best to find it.'

It's not very often in London that you find two uniformed policemen combing the streets for a cat!

Early each morning, the milkman would arrive and outside the Wilsons' home he would leave two pints. Without fail, a few minutes later, Mary would make her first appearance of the day, wearing her long dressing gown and fluffy pink slippers, her hair tousled from sleep. We saw very little of Harold, for he hardly ever seemed to step outside the house except to take the few short steps from his front door into the waiting black official car. On a few occasions I caught a glimpse of Marcia Faulkender, Harold Wilson's personal secretary and the most important member of what became known as Wilson's 'Kitchen Cabinet'! Marcia was always smartly dressed and always carried a handbag in which, we later learned, she kept her personal recommendations for the celebrated Honours List written on lavender-coloured notepaper. That contentious list would later bring Harold unwelcome criticism from all corners of the House including his Labour supporters.

Mary was a vicar's daughter who would on occasion

confide that she wasn't sure what she preferred her husband Harold to smoke. In reality he far preferred good-quality cigars to a pipe but smoked the pipe primarily for the benefit of the Labour voters, who wouldn't want to see their champion of the working class smoking a bloody cigar! Harold also believed his pipe was a useful signature, in the same way that Winston Churchill used his cigar. Whenever Churchill was seen in public during the last months of his life a cigar would be lit and put in his mouth before he stepped outside. Once in the car an aide would take it from his mouth and keep it alight until popping it back again between the great man's lips for the photographers at the end of his journey. It's extraordinary how tobacco became a symbol of masculinity. Can you imagine the reaction to a woman MP – let alone a prime minister – who appeared in public with a cigarette in her mouth?

Two doors from us at Number 16 lived Lady Davidson, part of a genuine Conservative dynasty, whose family connections with the Party went back decades. Her husband, Lord Davidson, had been Private Secretary to Prime Minister Stanley Baldwin. Later he had become a Member of Parliament and Chairman of the Party. Lady Davidson succeeded him. Now she was in her eighties, a dear old lady with an encyclopaedic knowledge of the politics of fifty years ago, but no memory of whom she'd met the day before.

Whenever I met her in the street, whether shortly after we arrived or some years later, she would stop and say terribly politely, 'How do you do? You're new here aren't you?' Before I could tell her that we had actually lived in the street for some years, she would continue as though I hadn't said a word: 'I live at number sixteen. I've lived in this street for more years than I would care to remember. I was an MP, you know, and so was my husband before me.'

Then she would launch into her entire family lineage, explaining who was who, how long they had lived there and how they were related to people whose names I had never before heard. She would always end the rather one-sided conversation with the words, 'Do come in for a cup of tea, it would be lovely to chat.' Each time I met her in the street she would relate exactly the same lines time after time. It was a sort of monologue that never got past the opening lines.

I already knew something of the family. Her granddaughter, Ann Strutt, worked with me building up the Amarant Trust, when I campaigned for awareness of HRT (more of which later). Ann was a dynamo; without her organising talent, we would never have raised the money for our first clinic. She once stood for parliament and would make a splendid MP – but she settled for marrying Bernard Jenkins, now MP for Essex North, the son of Patrick Jenkins, notorious for shaving during the three-day week.

The most remarkable servants in our street, were, to my mind, Lady Davidson's two faithful maids; two tiny, elderly women barely four feet tall, both pale and grey-haired, Mrs. Boyland and Betty. They had spend most of their lives below stairs, and only emerged to polish the brass doorknobs on the front door and to take the King Charles Spaniels for a walk. There were all sorts of suggestions as to the ancestry of these two dear old ladies. But the gossip was that they had lived in the basement for as long as anyone could remember.

At the back of us, in Gayefere Street, lived the Hattersleys, whose bathroom faced towards our kitchen window. But for the steam, I could have had a bird's-eye view of Roy emerging from his tub. As it was, all I saw was a rather large pink blob – with no discernible features. Perhaps that was just as well. Roy was in Wilson's Cabinet and each morning the chauffeur-driven government car would stand outside his door waiting to whisk him and his red boxes away to Whitehall.

I remember vividly the day after Margaret Thatcher became Prime Minister. The car purred along the street as Roy emerged, briefcase in hand. But it failed to stop. Instead, it glided into Smith Square to pick up a new minister in Margaret's Cabinet while Roy followed, hand in the air, trying to hail a taxi. There is no sadder sight than a former minister in a failed government rejoining the rest of mankind.

We enjoyed life in Lord North Street, and I took a secret delight in living in such an historic neigbourhood. The neighbours were quite entertaining too. We loved the peaceful weekends when the government offices were closed and many of our neighbours left London for their weekend retreats. Sometimes it seemed as if we were the only people on the planet, but for the occasional crocodile of tourists, complete with guide, on walking tours of London. They would peer into our windows, trying to see how the rich lived. We would spend Saturday and Sunday walking around St. James's Park, feeding the ducks. We sometimes took a quiet stroll along the Thames from Westminster to Chelsea bridge for a pub lunch. It was a few miles down the river from the embankment where I played as a child and Jim and my brothers rowed in the summer.

We were also very fortunate. Shortly after taking the greatest gamble of our life – putting all our savings into buying a house with a thirteen-year lease – the law was changed and we were able to secure our future there by buying the freehold. It was just as well, for both my business life and my political career were to centre around that house.

Chapter Six

TOILETS, CEMETERIES AND SHIRLEY PORTER

'A councillor is like a mushroom. You're kept in the dark and now and again, manure is thrown over you.'
ALEX MAGOWAN

Most people do not realise that much of Westminster is in fact low-cost housing, with huge estates either run by the local authority or two major charities, the Peabody and Guinness Trusts. The ward where we now lived covered the area behind the Tate Gallery and stretched out to Pimlico and Victoria Station. Soon I was cajoled by Alex Segal, the local chairman, into canvassing and knocking on doors for new recruits. I had long since honed my skills as a natural saleswoman and I somehow managed to recruit new members from areas we had never before penetrated or gained a foothold in. On one occasion, I recruited twenty-six people from the Peabody Estate, an unheard of success. And I rather enjoyed the fun of canvassing, chatting to strangers on their doorsteps. I found a number of Peabody tenants were very genteel people, retired nannies and civil servants surviving on meagre pensions. Council tenants often preferred the Peabodys, despite their grim appearance, and would ask to be moved into them.

Life became more hectic. The business was going really well but it needed constant attention and my role was to keep it going, bringing in the business, promoting and selling. But I found time to become involved in the campaign for Sunday trading as well as PULSE – the Public and Local Services Efficiency campaign – to force local councils to put their work out to tender. Some years later, the Conservative government adopted both policies and when I see the massive B & Q stores heaving with happy shoppers on a Sunday, I often think that I played a role in liberating them from the Lord's Day Observance Society.

In 1982 I was asked by Alex Segal, if I would stand for Westminster and become the Tory candidate for Millbank Ward, an area composed almost entirely of low-cost public housing. Labour had held the seat for twenty-six years. I didn't, in fact, have the time let alone the inclination to become a councillor, but Alex assured me that there was no chance of winning so there was no need to worry about having to find time to carry out council work. He was honest enough to tell me that he was asking me to stand mainly because of my canvassing skills but also because there was a dearth of Tory candidates.

'You will have to canvas the ward but you'll enjoy it,' he said, 'and don't worry – there's not a cat in hell's chance of winning.'

As I went from door-to-door in the council blocks behind the Tate Gallery wearing my large blue rosette, it soon became obvious that there were many Irish people living there. It seemed that every third person spoke with an Irish accent and they were all hostile, some fiercely hostile, to the Tories. They would tell me straight out, 'We'll not be voting Tory in this house; the Tories have never done anything for us.' They would make these comments despite the fact that Westminster Council had been Tory for as long as anyone could remember and the council flats were well looked after.

I am a natural mimic and as they spoke I soon found myself replying in an Irish accent.

'Are you Irish too?' they would ask.

And I would reply, 'Do you know what my name is? My name's Teresa O'Gorman.'

'Jesus,' they would reply enthusiastically, 'and where are you from?'

That was the tricky bit because, of course, I was born and bred in Putney, south-west London.

'Er, Cork', I replied, 'I'm married to a man from Cork.' I didn't know exactly where Cork was in Ireland, but Jim's family had originated from there.

The woman at the door shouted to the rest of the family, 'There's a Tory here from Cork, would you believe?'

'You've got our votes.'

'All of them?'

'Surely,' she replied, 'we'll all be votin' for you.'

I had to be very careful not to step inside the front door, although I was asked to on several occasions. I knew very little about Ireland or Irish politics. That would come later.

When the results were announced, I had won a seat, and I was both horrified and elated. Elated to be elected to something for the first time in my life; horrified at the prospect of attending endless council meetings. I'd like to claim the credit for the victory, but thousands of people turned to the Tories at that election as a result of Margaret Thatcher's victory in the Falklands War. Patriotism is a powerful political force for the Tory Party and Margaret Thatcher embodied it in spades.

I had no idea of how local councils worked, and, partly because I knew no better, I landed on the General Purposes Committee, always described as the 'Odds and Sods' committee. The Chairman of that committee was Shirley Porter, the millionaire daughter of the famous Jack Cohen who founded the Tesco supermarkets.

Shirley was a human dynamo. She had all the time in the world for her work and magnificent self-confidence. She was fond of telling the people of London, 'The only reason I came into politics was to clean up the rubbish in the streets. Litter is dreadful and I hate it. I am determined to do something about it.' Ironically, Shirley earned her spurs when she was photographed standing on piles of rubbish that had accumulated in Trafalgar Square as a result of the wave of local authority strikes during the three-day week.

Like me, Shirley had been inspired by Margaret Thatcher's message of free enterprise and deregulation and was keen to put council work out to tender. Her beady eye fell on Westminster's cemeteries, which were owned by the council. At that time they were costing a million pounds a year to maintain. Shirley was determined to be rid of them and offered them for sale. But no one was interested. In the end, of course, she sold them as a job lot for a nominal £1 to some enterprising entrepreneur who realised the potential of redevelopment at some later date. When the story leaked out to the press, there was outrage. Pages of print were devoted to Shirley's disregard for the dead and the bereaved. There were stories of bodies being dug up to make way for new housing. In the end, the council bought them back for 15 pence when the buyer realised there was no chance of redevelopment.

In the Soho ward, a group of elderly ladies of refined taste constantly petitioned the council to clean up the sex trade of the area, which had become intolerable to them. For decades, Soho had been recognised as London's red-light district with its massage parlours, seedy night clubs, strip joints and hundreds of prostitutes. Soho was of course also famous for some wonderful restaurants and a traditional hotchpotch of nationalities from across the world.

Shirley recognised there were votes to be won and went on the attack. She decided that one way to curtail the trade of the massage parlours was to withdraw the licence to use the shop for that purpose. I protested mildly against the policy because, I argued, if we drove sex out of Soho it was bound to surface elsewhere, maybe in some nice suburban area, which is exactly what did happen.

Some of the men on the committee urged me to go to Soho

with them one night and see for myself how degraded the area had become. 'Dress down,' I was advised, 'We don't want to look like inspectors. We must try to look like punters.' Thus, when the night came, the men were in polo-necked sweaters and I was dressed quietly like a suburban housewife. We went firstly to a small cinema in Windmill Street and watched a blue movie for a few minutes. It was pathetic, more like some 8mm silent movie with nubile girls flashing their bits and pieces at the camera. I almost felt sorry for the handful of pathetic-looking men dotted sparsely around the cinema.

We next popped into Raymond's famous Revue Bar, where the more classy, but in a way, more degrading, performances were on show. The cabaret seemed more comical than sexy but I did marvel at some of the girls' athletic antics and wondered how they got themselves into such bizarre positions.

Our next port of call was one of the Ann Summers sex shops. The shop window displayed lacy, sexy underwear in bright red and black. But inside was a real disappointment. It looked more like Woolworth's, its counters divided into compartments filled with curious-looking objects, many of them made of rubber. There were trays and trays of condoms in an amazing variety of colours, some of which looked more like bizarre invertebrates. I knew all about those from my biology lectures. My constant enquiries to my colleagues was, 'What are you meant to do with this?' Even if they knew, my colleagues were too embarrassed to tell me. It was left to my imagination. The visit to the Ann Summers shop seemed to dampen their enthusiasm for the expedition and I had seen enough. We called it a night.

Those few hours in the red-light district did not, in fact, change my mind. I held the view that people should be allowed to go to hell in their own way, so long as they didn't break the law. Better to have a market for sex in one district – Soho – than to spread it all over London. In a free society, people should have freedom of choice.

But despite my liberal attitudes and my opposition, Westminster Council revoked many of the licences. Some of the shops closed down, others went to the suburbs, some went underground. Politicians like to think they can alter people's behaviour but all they do is drive it underground.

Then came the brouhaha over Westminster's public lavatories, some of which were almost landmarks. Most were kept spotlessly clean, the brass polished every day by hard-working men and women attendants who took great pride in maintaining them. Some attendants put fresh flowers in the establishments every day, even tasteful pictures on the walls. They were very important to taxi drivers and tradesmen, who earned their living moving around the city. I had always judged a city by the quality of its public lavatories.

However, Shirley's eagle eye had fallen on the amount of money being spent maintaining them and she demanded action. The options were to sell them off or close them down. Many were underground, and she believed these could be sold off and become some new form of enterprise, like kiosks or wine bars, which would then earn the council extra funds from increased rates. Once more I found myself at odds with Shirley in committee. I asked her one day, 'Where is a tourist visiting London to go when they need a lavatory?'

Shirley expressed astonishment at this argument. 'There are dozens of hotels in Park Lane which all have excellent lavatories,' she replied, scornfully. I had visions of thousands of tourists who visited the area crowding into the Dorchester or Grosvenor House to be greeted by a friendly doorman showing them the way to the toilets. We were obviously poles apart. Shirley saw the problem from a millionaire's viewpoint. I was thinking of weary backpackers being turned away from five-star London hotels because they were improperly dressed. In the end, however, we voted to get rid of the lavatories and only I and a London taxi driver voted against. It was not a very promising start to my political career. Voting against your own party does not win you friends or mark you down for promotion. But sometimes it has to be done.

We replaced those discreet, traditional, well-maintained London lavatories with a French product, little better than the urinals you find all over France, where people had to queue up in public and pay to get in. These loos restricted people to only a couple of minutes' duration before the lavatory automatically flushed and the door flew open. In the interests of research, I forced myself to sample one and once inside, I not only had an attack of claustrophobia, but was terrified that the door would fly open and catch me in the act. But Shirley was pleased when the responsibility was contracted out to a French company, who would pay for a lease on the site, thereby increasing Westminster's spending power for more worthy projects.

Within a year, Shirley Porter was voted leader of our ruling group on Westminster Council and made me vice-chairman of the housing committee. More and more of the council's work was put out to tender, which I thoroughly approved of. But that did not mean that there was no scope for uncovering waste or mismanagement.

Towards the end of those four years on Westminster Council I came to realise that my presence on the council had achieved little, if anything. I wouldn't agree to toe the party line if I felt strongly about something, no matter what the pressure. I felt it just wasn't a very productive use of my time. I had a business to look after, a pressure group – ASP – to keep an eye on, and I was writing occasional articles for the national press that I vainly hoped would change the climate for small businesses. At the next election I lost my council seat and was much relieved to be able to resume a more normal life.

More importantly, I had been co-opted by Margaret Thatcher's think tank, the Centre for Policy Studies, which set out to produce new ideas and circumvent the research department at Conservative Central Office. We met perhaps once a month and my primary interest was to work into government legislation the relaxation of red tape that was still accumulating even under a Conservative administration, despite the lip service paid to reducing this burden.

I had started to write political pamphlets. I nursed the illusion that putting my ideas down on paper would have some effect. I hoped that politicians of different persuasions would read them and that we would be pushing back the frontiers of regulation. It wasn't until I became an MP that I realised how slim were the chances of any government – even a Tory one – dismantling the web of regulations that the mandarins in

Whitehall really believed were necessary to protect the public.

My idea was not, in fact, revolutionary. I had read about Italy's progressive, free-enterprise culture. In Italy, small firms that employed under twenty people, or five in agriculture, were exempt from government regulations on employment that larger firms had to obey. These small firms, called *artisanos* – of which there were vast numbers – contributed enormously to the Italian economy. Many large Italian firms, including Fiat and Benetton, also outsourced many of their smaller tasks to the *artisanos*, helping to keep their costs down by up to thirty per cent. These cottage industries worked brilliantly throughout Italy, which now boasts the largest numbers of cars per head of population, drinks more of our whisky and has more second homes than any other country in Europe.

Indeed, even today, most Italian production of textiles, clothing, shoes, furniture, tiles, small electrical items and office machinery takes place in firms employing fifteen people or less. In Naples, for example, a vast clothing and shoes industry has developed; it exports five million pairs of gloves a year but does not have a single glove factory! Sophisticated machinery for the production of clothes and small leather goods can be found today in poverty-stricken districts around Naples where friendly, family, cottage industries carry out sub-contract work for many of Italy's leading fashion houses. And they make good money. Even today these cottage industries are not burdened by heavy bureaucratic regulations as the small firms of Britain are. I believed strongly that the Italian experience could and should be adopted in Britain's depressed industrial areas.

Some apparently depressed regions of Italy have become mini silicon valleys over the past twenty years as they trained local people and specialised in high-technology industries. These products have been highly successful, sometimes even capturing monopolies in world markets.

The Roman Catholic Church plays a key role in all this, with the local priest acting as co-ordinator, creating new wealth locally and preventing the traditional migration of people from the poorer south to the richer north of Italy.

I believed that if Britain adopted such a scheme, involving deregulation and giving individuals a chance to flourish without government demands, then Britain's depressed areas might prosper, creating more jobs and more wealth for the nation. Instead, we chase our small entrepreneurs from pillar to post, always breathing down their necks, labelling them 'tax dodgers'.

One of my first political pamphlets – 'Worried To Death' – eventually landed on the desk of John Redwood, then working in Margaret Thatcher's policy unit in Number 10 Downing Street. Out of the blue, he telephoned me and invited me to Downing Street for tea. It was the first time I had ever visited Number 10.

At last, I thought, I had made a breakthrough. Surely someone so close to the Prime Minister could have a word in her ear. I lay out my arguments in what I hoped was an easy, forthright and convincing way, firstly examining the damage that excessive legislation was doing to the British economy and then proposing a plan of action for the Tories to reverse the trend.

In my pamphlet, I attacked the rapid invasion of state power into the private sector and warned of the new source of regulation stemming from the European Community in Brussels. I showed how businesses were being harassed through government regulation and how small firms, in particular, had to shoulder the greatest burden. I also showed that the imposition of new regulations on the business community hit not only the firms but also the consumer. As small firms failed, jobs were lost where they were most needed, in the poorer communities where people lacked professional skills.

One example I gave was that nearly all one- and two-man fishing boats around Britain's coastal waters had to cease operating because health and safety regulations had required all fishing boats to install £10,000 worth of safety equipment.

I suggested ways in which the growing burden of regulations could be lifted; out of date regulations thrown out altogether and new proposals where the cost/benefit position is unclear should be re-examined. And I had a practical solution. I proposed government legislation to deregulate small firms, by simply raising the starting point of VAT, cutting local rates for small firms and releasing them from the provisions of the Employment Protection Act. In other words, I wanted government regulations off the backs of British business.

John Redwood told me that he was impressed with the pamphlet and would bring it to the attention of the Prime Minister. I left feeling cock-a-hoop. But I was quickly brought down to earth. As I left Number 10, I paused on the doorstep to have my photograph taken for our ASP magazine. At that time members of the public were permitted into Downing Street and would stand opposite the entrance to Number 10, watching all the comings and goings.

'Who's that? Who's that?' I could hear people calling to each other wondering who I was.

'Is that that Shirley Williams woman?' someone shouted. 'Yeah, it's Shirley Williams.'

She was hardly likely to be a visitor to Number 10. Shirley Williams, a minister in Harold Wilson's government, had a brilliant mind and a very sexy voice, but had little time for her appearance. The papers said she always looked as though she had been pulled through a hedge backwards. I had spent a long time and not a little money on looking my very best for my first visit to Number 10.

My visit to Downing Street brought unexpected results. I was flattered to be invited by a second think tank – the respected Adam Smith Institute – to write a new, wide-ranging pamphlet named 'The Enterprise Culture – An A–Z Guide Through the Regulatory Maze'. This was a golden opportunity to put forward ideas that had been fermenting in my mind ever since my time in America. Now, I felt, I had a real opportunity to make my mark in an area I desperately wanted to be involved in.

I wrote, 'The free enterprise system is dynamic and innovative but our politicians are parochial and obsessed with protecting the existing pattern of jobs. Nowadays, it is not industry that creates jobs but Government; its rag-bag of regulations stifle change.

'To develop an enterprise culture will take more than

rhetoric. We need a political vision and radical changes. Zero interference with enterprise is the ideal with zero business rates and taxes. This may not be possible now but it represents a goal we should strive for, where money is left with the people who know how best to use and invest it. The more we reach towards those targets the more we will stimulate the wealth-creating talents in society and choice for all of us.'

In the pamphlet I stressed that Britain's open society was being seriously threatened by the growing mania for regulation. Vested interests in the government, education, trade unions, trade associations and the EEC were pressing for more regulation and control. Standard qualifications were being envisaged for every type of job and new businesses were being forced to apply for a licence to trade. I warned that controls and penalties introduced by government-appointed bodies were suffocating enterprise.

Finally, I urged that the way to keep open the traditional avenues to new enterprises was for the government to rigorously reject schemes, however plausible, to raise standards by regulation and wage war on the statutes that threatened the enterprise culture.

Of course, I wasn't the only one writing pamphlets for the Tory think tanks. There were others writing on many subjects. Government advisers, and some government ministers, paid lip service. But I did find myself wondering whether anyone was really listening to our words of wisdom.

The closer I came to the source of political power the more I found myself seduced by life in the political arena. When asked to write a pamphlet I would sometimes consult Alan

Walters, an academic and a regular visitor to the Institute of Economic Affairs, whom I sometimes felt had become my political and economic guru. He acted as the Prime Minister's private economic advisor. During these exciting years, Alan's liberal economic ideas became increasingly important. He explained why the nation's long-term decline had gone hand in hand with the rise of trade union power and the decline of a free-market economy. Margaret Thatcher found his ideas and his plans for the economy matched her own.

Within a short time, Alan was installed in a small office in Number 10. Nigel Lawson, then Chancellor of the Exchequer, certainly did not appreciate this. He didn't like the fact that Margaret turned more and more to Alan Walters, preferring his advice on Britain's economy. Nigel came to resent Alan's intrusion in his territory. Frustrated and infuriated that his authority was being undermined, he delivered an ultimatum to Thatcher: 'Either Walters must go or I will'. In the end, of course, Lawson resigned and Alan Walters became even more influential.

I respected Alan Walters enormously. I enjoyed his dry manner and his droll sense of humour. He hardly ever raised his voice above a whisper, which meant that you had to concentrate if you wanted to hear what he said. Like me he was a keen free-marketeer and, intellectually, someone to be admired. There was an exclusive group of young free-market MPs and think-tank intellectuals, who called themselves the 'No Turning Back' group, who were keen on reducing the size and power of the state. When I arrived in Parliament, I rather hoped to join them. I had plenty of ideas. But it was not to be.

I was blackballed by members for being 'too frivolous'.

By 1986, as I found my interest in local politics waning, I was becoming more involved in national politics. I enjoyed getting things off my chest by writing political pamphlets and articles for national newspapers expressing my views and my concerns of those men and women like me who were running small firms and suffering from escalating government regulations. I felt I was part of Mrs. Thatcher's revolution and began to believe my own rhetoric, that soon we would begin to roll back the tide of state controls on enterprise. Alas, how wrong I was.

For some time, Alex Segal, my Tory Party branch chairman, had been urging me to think seriously about entering national politics. I thought long and hard about whether I really wanted a future in national politics. I was certain that a career in the House of Commons would take up a vast amount of time and I feared my business, to which I had devoted much of my adult life, might take a turn for the worse.

Our prosperity relied on bringing in new orders, which was my main job and that meant constant travel to keep in touch with my customers around the globe. Most small firms shaped around the founder, who is the driving force, have the same problem. They often decline if they are not nurtured. On the other hand, I had been in business for more than a decade – long enough in any job – and a change might revitalise me.

And I was lucky. I had a wonderful band of people helping, advising and working really hard to make BANTA successful. I knew I could rely on them to keep the business going. And after all – I told myself – you only live once!

Chapter Seven

INTO PARLIAMENT

'The beginning is the most important part of the work.'
PLATO

Still regulations continued to pour out of the government. And now they were added to by Brussels. I began to think that if I entered into national politics, I could stop the rot. I could do something about it for small firms whose problems had been created by government. Like many before me, I deluded myself that, in Parliament, I would be able to make a real difference. I was convinced that only by throwing overboard the red tape would more people be encouraged to set up their own enterprises. By now, I was well known as a champion of self-employed people, but I was under no illusion that I would have an easy job jumping the all-important first hurdle, becoming an approved Tory candidate.

Since moving to Lord North Street, I had been actively canvassing for Tory Party candidates at parliamentary elections. I pounded the streets of Westminster for Peter Brooke and John Wheeler. I climbed the stairs of dozens of tower blocks in Paddington and Maida Vale during those elections and would end each day exhausted but happy. I was after all, an old hand at canvassing from my days in Streatham – and on Westminster City Council.

Firstly, I had to apply for the official Candidates List. I needed sponsors. Fortunately, Alex Segal, my local chairman, constantly encouraged me to apply. My other two sponsors were Rhodes Boyson MP, an ex-headmaster and a robust supporter of Thatcherite policies, and Ralph Harris, one of the founders of the Institute of Economic Affairs.

Before applying for seats, you have to get the 'seal of approval' from Central Office, and getting on to the approved list is a lengthy and difficult process. There is always stiff competition, whether at election time or between elections. You have to write to Central Office and fill in a long and detailed questionnaire about your age, marital status, children, religion, education, jobs, interests both political and non-political, experience, work done for the party, and explain why you think you would make a good MP. It is here that you include the names of your referees, which, if possible, should include at least one MP and a constituency chairman. They are then asked to fill out another lengthy questionnaire about your character, party loyalty, knowledge and awareness of politics and Westminster, speaking ability and your experience of politics. It is only if you pass this selection process that weeds out the 'hopeless' that you will be invited to an interview with a parliamentary selection board, which lasts for a weekend and is the last hurdle to getting on the list.

Sara Keays nursed the ambition of having her own political career for many years, while working as personal assistant to first Cecil Parkinson and then Roy Jenkins, when he headed the European Union in Brussels. She was an active member of the Bermondsey Conservative Association, and decided to apply for selection for the 1983 general election. Although she was not on the list of approved candidates, as an active member she was able to apply directly to the branch chairman, and made it through to the final shortlist. Although she was not selected, she was the second choice of the selection committee. However, when local MP Bob Mellish announced his early retirement, making way for a by-election, their first-choice candidate withdrew, announcing that it was too close to get time off work.

Sara would have been the natural choice for a replacement, and could have been automatically selected. But Cecil intervened. He wrote to the committee advising them to discuss the matter with Central Office before announcing that Sara should take over the candidature. The excuse was that she was not on the approved candidates list. Central Office proposed a complete re-selection process, inviting new and existing candidates to apply. The chairman insisted she reapply and told her on the phone that she would get through to the final shortlist.

However, Cecil stepped in once again and Sara never got that promised interview. Instead, Central Office had decided that it would be better for a man to stand in such a tough Labour safe seat. The by-election was attracting a lot of media attention. The Labour candidate, Peter Tatchell, was using the election as a platform for the homosexual debate, and the Liberal Democrats were expecting a large swing from Labour.

Sara later confided that before the first ballot, Cecil had rung her, not to wish her luck, but to express doubt about her standing for fear of their long-standing affair becoming public. There is always much more media attention focused on candidates at by-elections, as there are so few candidates when compared to the number at a general election. Cecil was concerned that the media would dig into their private lives and discover their romance. He assured Sara that he was acting for her own good, promising a safer seat, where she would have more chance of winning. And she believed him.

A few weeks later, I met Sara Keays on the selection weekend for the approved candidates list, a step towards getting the seat she had been promised. It was attended by about thirty men and a handful of women. I dressed soberly, as I supposed a woman MP should do, choosing a dark blue suit. My heels were not too high, lipstick not too bright, and I wore contact lenses to facilitate eye contact. I looked more like a blue-stocking than my real self but I wanted them to think that I was suitable to represent the party. Sara was much more obviously a typical Tory woman: middle-class accent, quietly self confident and with impeccable manners. She also seemed to have natural leadership qualities. I marked her down as an obvious winner.

Cecil spent that weekend at Oxford for the selection weekend, but no one noticed anything between him and Sara, even though the affair had been going on for some time. He sat in on a number of sessions in which our talents were tested in mock-up situations. There was a mock debate in which we took opposing arguments; a mock constituency meeting as though we were the MP addressing the local members; a mock political article of one thousand words for a mock national newspaper. We were broken up into groups of eight, each of which had to first choose a leader and then build up a case for a particular piece of legislation in which the group leader, acting the role of a government minister, presented the piece of legislation to the House of Commons.

We were under scrutiny throughout the entire weekend by senior officials and members of Conservative associations. They watched and made notes. During meals, particularly dinner, I wondered if they were checking our table manners, our accents and how we might handle ourselves on the 'rubber chicken' circuit, a routine part of the life of an MP. We were led to understand that the average pass rate was under fifty per cent. I remembered what Marcus Fox, the bluff Yorkshire MP, who was in charge of the candidates list, had told me: 'People who have succeeded in their chosen career fancy themselves as Members of Parliament. Star turns are a ten a penny; what we are looking for are team players.'

Later, he would become chairman of the prestigious 1922 committee, the Tory back-benchers' trade union, and one of the most influential wheeler-dealers throughout the Thatcher years, responsible for all the Tory appointments to the all-important select committees. Or in my case, the non-appointments!

Both Sara Keays and I were selected to join the approved candidates list, which meant that we would be able to apply for any available Conservative seats from the list sent out by Central Office each month. If you are interested, you write to the local association and ask for information. If it is a safe seat, there are many potential candidates eager to enter the selection contest. The local paper can also be very helpful, because they tell you about the constituency and what interests the voters.

But the seat promised to Sara in the 1983 election never materialised, and she was extremely angry. She had her revenge at the party conference, four months later when she made her relationship with Cecil public and announced that she was having his baby. The conference was in uproar and Cecil was forced to resign. Later still, when the media attention surrounding the incident had died down, Sara again tried to get publicity, this time about the illness from which her baby daughter was suffering. The Official Solicitors Office imposed gagging orders on her and all but threatened to take the child away from her if she continued to embarrass the party through media attention to the case. When *Private Eye* devised an article about the child, it was banned from publishing it.

In 1997, Cecil again took up the daunting challenge of Party Chairman. We had just suffered a landslide defeat and it was a mark of his enduring popularity that he was persuaded – reluctantly – to take on the job. I met with him when I went on a visit to the company that built the Queen Elizabeth Bridge on the Thames at Dartford, which connects part of my constituency and the North side of the Thames, as well as the North and South of London's ring road, the M25. Cecil is the director of the company, and insisted on welcoming me. The company is desperate to build more bridges over the Thames, at their own expense, and I support them. London desperately needs better links between the North and the South banks of the river, as there are not enough bridges within London itself and none between the Queen Elizabeth and Tower Bridge. With me on the Transport Committee and Cecil in the Lords, perhaps between us, we could have drummed up some enthusiasm for the project. I would have loved to work with him to achieve this objective – but alas, I ran out of time. Perhaps one day, we will have a government that trusts the free market to solve our transport systems. No one loves the railway system, but at least it is doing a better job now than when it was nationalised. The trouble is, people in Britain always look back to a golden age that never was.

I remember applying for a constituency in Crewe and visited the railway centre there. I applied to constituencies all over the country including Sheffield, Tyneside, Thurrock, Derby and Maidstone, which achieved notoriety in the Tory Party for once, famously, turning down Margaret Thatcher.

They interviewed four women on their short list including me. That was remarkable, if not unique, but the Maidstone Conservative Association was determined to have a woman candidate to wipe out their remorse. Anne Widdecombe won – and she has more than fulfilled their expectations.

But there was no denying the fact that women were, usually, at a considerable disadvantage. Most constituency associations prefer their MP to live in the immediate area or, at least, have a house or flat in the constituency. That often makes it very difficult for women. There are few women who are able or willing to drop everything and move house. If they are single they probably can't afford it, and if they're married they have husbands with jobs to consider. Men, on the other hand, find it easier to achieve a sort of balancing act, with the backing of a supportive wife.

At selection meetings, candidates are always asked to bring their spouse along to meet the association members so that they can give the spouse the 'once over'. In the Tory Party, it is very important that their MP should have the right calibre of spouse. Those men who don't have a wife – and have no intention of getting one – often parachute in a 'phantom fiancée' for the evening, a woman who is happy to play the role for the occasion. Bachelors such as Edward Heath and my predecessor at Billericay, Harvey Procter, were once quite acceptable. Some never married. Even today there are not many prospective candidates prepared to state openly that they are gay and therefore have no girlfriend, fiancée or wife. They believe that would spoil their chances of being selected. Some even marry just for show.

The image of a conventional marriage is so important in the Conservative Party, that long after his premiership was over, our perennial bachelor, Ted Heath, felt the need to tell the *Sunday Times* of an early 'romance'. The story goes that he met Kay Raven, the daughter of the local doctor, after he was knocked off his bike by a car, and the two became childhood sweethearts. However, the war separated them and when Ted returned, Kay had moved to another part of the country and later married.

The article said that there was pressure from the party for Ted to marry. It was unusual for a prime minister, or even a member at that time, not to have married, but he remained single and, in the words of Alan Watkins of the *Independent*, exhibited all the enthusiasm of those giant pandas at London Zoo, when questioned about marriage.

Even today, most constituency associations seem to want a middle-class, fortyish male with a pretty, demure wife and two polite children and, in the case of a young couple, one on the way. Selection committees are completely atypical of the population as a whole, tending to be late-middle-aged, middle-class and, politically middle-of-the-road characters, though usually extremely patriotic. Many of the questions asked at these meetings seem to have been devised by some central organisation. There are nearly always questions on capital punishment, the state of the armed forces and whether you think the country is going to the dogs!

I was once turned down for a seat because, whenever they asked me the inevitable question on defence, I turned to look at my husband. This was interpreted as a lack of confidence in my own opinion. The real reason was that on the drive down we had rehearsed many possible questions, including the one they asked. Our exchange of glances was in reality simply a private joke, by which we acknowledged to each other that we had guessed correctly.

On another occasion, I reached the final selection at Chelmsford. I drove down on a lovely summer's day wearing a yellow dress with pretty yellow shoes to match. Someone remarked that the shoes were inappropriate for canvassing and, indeed, later, I was informed that my yellow shoes had been my downfall. It seemed unbelievable that an association, whose duty it was to select a parliamentary candidate for their constituency, had turned down an application solely because of the colour of the individual's shoes. Men, of course, don't have such problems. Always dressed in a boring two-piece suit, white shirt and sober tie, they are all carbon copies of myriads of politicians during the past hundred years. And when I see rows of politicians lined up for some official photograph, it's nearly always male politicians that are featured. I just pray that their intellects are more imaginative than their dress sense.

These days most Conservative associations have a woman in the final shortlist because of pressure from Tory Central Office not to look sexist. They are sensitive to criticism in the press that the party doesn't have enough women candidates. But, despite the fact there is usually a token woman in the finals, overwhelmingly, they still don't end up being selected.

One of the more outrageous questions put to a woman

candidate was, 'What will your husband do for sex when you get to Westminster?' Apart from questions of this nature, much of what is asked at interviews does not relate to a woman's experience and interests. She must become a surrogate man for the purpose of being selected. Questions will, more often than not, concentrate on finance, law and order and defence. Commons debates on these issues are well attended, even packed, but when social issues, which interest women more, are debated in the House the number of MPs who attend plummets dramatically – and most of them are women. Yet, three-quarters of our national spending goes on health, education and social services, areas in which women have first-hand experience.

Men cultivate influential people who can pull strings; women are not good at that. Women are more reticent at pushing themselves forward, the idea of cold-calling people out of the blue to stress their attributes makes them uncomfortable. Men are better at acquiring a mentor – a sitting MP prepared to make phone calls on their behalf to the association chairman when a safe seat becomes available. With the inevitable large number of applications, this influence can at least ensure an interview. It accounts for the fact that so many recent entrants come from the ranks of the 'team players' preferred by Marcus Fox. They are parachuted to safe seats without the necessity of fighting a hopeless one and they end up on the front bench deciding policy.

The women I have known within the Tory women's organisation have always been enormously supportive to me. On several occasions it was women that brought vacant seats to my attention and who offered to help get me the vital first interview.

Even today there are far more men than women wanting to stand for Parliament, particularly in the Tory Party, despite the fact that we had the first woman prime minister. But one swallow doesn't make a summer. I believe numbers do matter; there should be more women Tory MPs. And more women would apply to become candidates if they saw the Tories selecting more women.

Government needs markets. Markets don't need government. Yet businessmen are conspicuously thin on the ground in Parliament. In 1987, with a Commons featuring its largest-ever Tory majority, a number of successful entrepreneurs with a wealth of experience did manage to win seats on the back benches, and there they remained. They would be more than a match for the Sir Humphreys who drive policy and frequently control their minister, and whose agenda inevitably is to expand the influence of Whitehall to acquire more power – and introduce more controls. The Sir Humphreys' idea of reducing the size of government is to create first-hand agencies such as the Highways Agency, Food Agency or a Health and Safety Agency, the Campaign for Racial Equality and Equal Opportunities Commission. Worse still are the quangos. They justify their existence by identifying a 'crisis' and then we are off on another cycle of regulations, controls and court cases – the whole government merry-go-round.

There is only one way to stop the growth in the public

sector. It is the way used by Margaret Thatcher to restore industry when it was in the grip of the trade union movement. Slash and burn. But it requires a government led by a personality, fired up by conviction and big enough to overcome the storm of protest from vested interests.

The great majority of today's candidates offered safe Tory seats have come through the party apparatus, have usually worked at Central Office, and have often been appointed personal assistants to a minister. The Conservative benches in the House of Commons are peppered with young men who went straight from university to work as research assistants for Members of Parliament. These young men are voraciously ambitious and will frequently work free of charge simply for the opportunity of learning the ropes. They are prepared to work night and day if necessary because they see politics as their one and only career. Many of them are gay and enjoy the social camaraderie and networking. The young women seen around the Commons are mainly secretaries, most of whom haven't had the privilege of a university education. They spend their hours glued to their computers or coping with the mountains of mail that arrive every day. They are the unseen, unsung heroines of parliamentary life.

Fate took a hand in my own rise to political prominence. I believe it was my connection with the small business movement that finally came up trumps for me in Billericay, a small town, close to the Thames Estuary and not a million miles downstream from where I grew up. The day that Harvey Procter resigned I was giving a lecture at the RAC in

Pall Mall on the benefits of the free market. During the lunch break, the buzz went round that Harvey Procter had been arrested and charged with indecent acts with underage boys and, of course, had been forced to resign.

That evening I received a phone call from a friend in the Billericay constituency who ran a small business and who asked me to apply for the seat. In my view, Tory Central Office would have arranged for Procter's successor because it wasn't as though his resignation had come as a surprise. The 1987 General Election had already begun and I felt sure they would have had a candidate standing by – as indeed they did.

I decided it would be a waste of time to put myself forward. However, at five the next morning, I woke determined to have a go. I jumped out of bed and read through my CV, checking that everything I had written was relevant to the Billericay constituency. There was one problem: my age.

At fifty-six I knew some people on the committee would believe I was over the hill. At forty-six I believed I would be a more attractive candidate. So I took a chance. I became forty-six.

Two hours later I was on the A13 in my little Ford Fiesta with thirty copies of my CV as requested by my deep-throat contact. The Billericay Tory Association's selection panel met at 11 a.m. and a list of suitable candidates had already been supplied to them by Central Office. My name was not on it.

According to my contact, who wanted to remain anonymous because of the in-fighting within the constituency, the place was a melée of people arriving from all over the country. Billericay was an ultra-safe Tory seat and consequently, overnight, had become the target for every desperate, ambitious person who had so far failed to be selected to fight the imminent general election. After all, Procter's majority had been some 15,000. My contact said that the CVs from Central Office were arranged around the table for the selection panel and so he went round discreetly putting my CVs amongst them.

At nine that evening I received a phone call from the chairman of the association, Ron Turner, telling me that I was now on a short list of twelve candidates and the only woman! At this point I began to think I might have a chance. I knew there was no chance that the association would run the risk of selecting another bachelor after the embarrassment they had just suffered.

But I didn't rest on my laurels. There was work to be done. I had just forty-eight hours to swat up on Billericay. I abandoned my plans for the day and headed for the local public library to scan the local newspapers. I phoned the editor of the *Billericay and Wickford Gazette* for a chat. My contact arranged for someone to drive me around the constituency and point out the landmarks such as the local hospital, St. Andrews, the major employers like Ford and Shell Haven and the famous Tilbury Docks. I soon learned that Billericay provided the victuals for the *Mayflower* which set sail for America in the seventeenth century from Tilbury. I was now more confident that I could talk to members of the panel about Billericay and its problems and interests.

By Wednesday I was on the shortlist of just three, one of

whom – Ian Sproat – would have been the obvious Central Office favourite, because he was a 'retread' – someone who had been a Member of Parliament but had lost his seat. A former junior Tory minister, Sproat would have been perceived as a safe pair of hands. However, I figured that on this occasion a married, middle-aged woman might have the edge on either of the male candidates.

Thirty minutes after the selection committee began to make their final selection the chairman walked into the room where we were all waiting and turned to me, saying simply, 'Mrs. Gorman, you have been selected.' It was probably the fastest selection procedure in the history of the Conservative Party. I was astonished, flabbergasted. I had become used to being rejected time after time. Now I was thrilled. I had finally made it.

Two days later I was presented to the whole of the Billericay Conservative Association, who had been invited to meet their new candidate. I addressed the meeting, attended by some three or four hundred people, in Billericay High School. I stressed my background in teaching and small business and sprinkled my talk with local references. Above all I spoke of my wholehearted support for Margaret Thatcher and my love for Britain and its traditions, both of which are very important to Tory voters. The audience seemed to love it and gave me a rousing ovation. Then the meeting was thrown open for questions.

From the back of the hall a tall, well-built man rose to his feet. He was Councillor Vic York, and he had been barred from applying for the seat. This was as a result of the constituency association being driven by two factions – the pro- and anti-Harvey Procter groups, and in an attempt to ensure that the association did not split, all local candidates were excluded from standing.

'Could the lady please explain the report in a national newspaper today that shows her date of birth to be ten years earlier than she now claims it to be?'

The audience turned their heads to see who had asked the question, but I froze. I felt the blood draining from my face and I felt sick and icy cold. I rose to my feet slowly, my mind in a turmoil, as I searched for the words I should use to explain this predicament. I feared this might mean the end of my political ambitions. Suddenly, a middle-aged woman in the front row leapt to her feet and turned to address the man.

'Who the hell cares how old she is,' she shouted, 'it's time we had a woman in Billericay. At least we know she won't give us the same trouble as our last Member of Parliament.' The woman was Daphne Hart, the Chairman of the Women's Branch, who was to prove a good friend and staunch supporter. The audience roared and applauded her. She had saved the day. Now I knew I was on my way to Westminster. That said, Harvey Procter was to haunt me for my entire parliamentary career – I was once introduced as 'a female MP who pinched Harvey Procter's seat, and there's not many women who can say that'.

Once selected, I cleared the decks of my other activities. I could no longer travel the globe selling teaching aids. The business was sold. The membership of ASP was transferred to another organisation. And I relinquished my involvement in the day to day running of Amarant – a trust that I'd started up to promote HRT (Hormone Replacement Therapy) – which now had its first clinic up and running. (HRT is an area that interests me greatly, and one that I will deal with more thoroughly in Chapter 17.) I would still work for all my goals, but this time, in the Mother of Parliaments. Now I could concentrate all my energies on my main aim in life, repealing the regulations destroying small businesses. Looking back, I had set myself a Herculean task, but with Margaret at the helm, I thought it could be done. It would require a change in the whole culture of Parliament and Whitehall – that government knows best – a change that, for the first time in my life, would be within my power to influence.

The driving force behind the increase in rules and regulations was now Europe. The European Common Market is not a free market. Products from countries outside Europe are strictly controlled by quotas. And where their prices undercut production costs in Europe, they are artificially raised by tariffs to prevent what is euphemistically called unfair competition. I'm not phobic or even sceptic about Europe, I simply loathe the protectionist economic system that the EU seeks to impose.

I had spent the whole of my life living and working under socialism with its dead hand on private initiatives. I saw our increasing integration with Europe as an intractable conflict between those who want to centralise society and those who want to liberate it. This was the lesson I had learned from America and it was the journey that Margaret Thatcher had begun.

Chapter Eight

BILLERICAY

'There is a mob of their constituents ready to hang them if
they should deviate into moderation.'

EDMUND BURKE

The constituency of Billericay, near to the Thames Estuary,
is not so much a single town, as a fascinating collection of
small towns and villages that grew up around the railway
lines connecting the City of London to the Essex coast. As
well as its historical connection with the pilgrims of the
Mayflower, the area has a royal connection: Queen
Elizabeth I travelled to Tilbury to knight Sir Francis Drake
for his maritime exploits. It was here that she was reputed to

have said, 'I know I have the body of a weak and feeble woman, but I have the heart and stomach of a king.' That was just the qualification you needed for a seat in Parliament.

During the Depression, between the two world wars, much of the farmland in the area was divided into plot-lands, from a small field to a few acres. The railways ran special trains to bring Eastenders out of London to buy these patches of land as a weekend retreat where they could grow vegetables and enjoy a breath of fresh air. Today, most of their original two-roomed bungalows have been replaced with grander private houses owned by young City commuters.

These people are the original, and much-maligned, Essex men and Essex women, and I would rather trust them than the men from Whitehall any day. I admire their initiative and their vibrancy. They have pulled themselves up by their bootstraps, founded successful businesses, bought smart cars and even private aeroplanes. And they all voted Tory when Margaret Thatcher led the party. Strongly patriotic, they prefer their independence to state handouts – and they hate the regulated society we live under today.

Before the Second World War, MPs were elected to represent an area in Parliament and some never set foot in their constituency from one election to the next. Today, an MP is a combination of a local celebrity and an extended social worker. When a constituent has tried every other way to sort out a problem, they make an appointment to see their MP. You are their route to sheltered housing for their parents, their passport to a better school for their children, their fast track to a hospital bed and to the director of their disability benefits. All roads lead back to legislation. Surgery cases are a reflection of the degree to which the state now controls our lives. As an MP you can speed up somebody's cataract operation, hip replacement or the statementing of a child (the modern substitute for old-fashioned special school system).

But in the midst of the stories of the city's street riots and child cruelty, it is good to remember that away from the city, people still live quiet, decent lives. When I come to my constituency, just thirty miles outside London, I am in a world with nice ordered schools and aspiring people, who put something back into the community. Parents take their small children to the library on Saturday mornings and help them to choose a book. The Billericay Arts Society fills every classroom of an old Victorian primary school every evening with people exercising their artistic talents.

Essex people may go to boot sales on a Sunday, but they still go to church. The churches in Billericay are full on Sundays. Members of the local Methodist Church give up their Sunday afternoons so that the small children of broken families can meet and play with their 'absent' parent, usually their father, while the mothers watch television in an upstairs room. Every exit from the building has to be discreetly watched lest the parent should try to make off with the child. And it takes a dozen or more volunteers just to offer this service.

The local hospitals at Orsett and Basildon have almost 200 voluntary workers, mostly older women, who help at the reception desk, run the hospital shop, ferry patients to and fro for routine treatments and raise money for the general funds. Even more surprising is the sheer number of voluntary organisations flourishing in the constituency – over 150 in Billericay alone.

The degree to which people are prepared to help themselves and their neighbours gives the lie to our political beliefs that the government must provide everything from the cradle to the grave. But you cannot set them free to make their own arrangements while government takes so much of their income in taxation.

In the aftermath of the ERM disaster, 'Black Wednesday', people arrived at my surgery who had never asked for a handout in their lives. They had lost their homes and businesses when interest rates soared and the banks called in the loans. Unlike similar situations involving farmers or large industries, there were no subsidies or government grants to see these people over the crisis created in their lives by bungling politicians. Instead they were reduced to the – for them – humiliating position of having to seek council accommodation for themselves and their families. And they were not impressed when Chancellor Lamont, who was responsible for the crisis, told them, 'Je ne regrette rien'.

These are decent people leading decent lives – a million miles away from the caricature of Essex man, and Essex woman, being common, blonde and brainless and wearing white stilettos. They would much prefer lower taxes, less interference, more freedom and more control over their own lives. Their votes carried Margaret Thatcher to three spectacular victories, but we lost them over Black Wednesday. The Conservative Party will not win power back unless we regain their trust and support.

The early morning trains from Billericay station to Liverpool Street, in the heart of the City of London and the financial centre, are packed with their sons and daughters – City whizz kids – who earn annual bonuses calculated in telephone numbers. And most of them have no higher education.

I have a favourite story, which I like to tell when I am invited to present the prizes at our local schools, to cheer up the ones who will not collect a prize. It concerns Alexander's baker's shop in Billericay High Street, which, as the local MP, I formally opened soon after I was elected. The proprietor was a local man, hardly out of his twenties. I was surprised when he told me that this was his fourth baker's shop. He left the local comprehensive without a single academic certificate to his name. The only job he could find was sweeping up in a bakery. There he learned to bake delicious bread and even more delicious Belgian buns, my favourite.

'Just think how much more you might have achieved if you had paid more attention to your schooling,' I said to him, naïvely.

'I expect I would have become a pen-pusher – a civil servant,' he replied. Touché. That's Essex man for you.

Most people know that businesses are started by individuals. What is less well known is that, with the exception of the professions, most of these individuals have, to quote Samuel Smiles, 'come up from the ranks'. They are predominantly from the skilled working class with little formal education beyond the statutory school leaving age and no formal qualifications for their work. Some may not have had the opportunity to stay on at school, but for the majority, formal schooling has little interest. They belong to that small but vital group of people whose school reports, like those of Winston Churchill and Albert Einstein, predict disaster for them in adult life.

Others start their businesses some time after leaving school, and in a field where they have little or no previous experience, they learn what they need from books, as did Bernard and Laura Ashley, whose company, Laura Ashley, now enjoys worldwide success. A recent study showed that seventy-five per cent of businesswomen do not have A levels and that eighty-one per cent did not go to university.

One thing is certain. If these people were required by law to obtain formal qualifications for their jobs, many of them would not be in business at all. The open society where such talent flourishes is now seriously threatened by the growing mania for credentials. Vested interests in the government, education, trade unions, trade associations and now the EU are pressing for regulation and control. Not since the trade and merchant guilds of the Middle Ages has the government exercised such a suffocating grip on enterprise

A study of the early lives of people who start up their own firms shows a number of common elements. They frequently work for small firms or in a family business where they get the chance to see the complete pattern of enterprise. And there is often an element of hardship, such as the loss of a job or some other form of rejection, in their history.

This background is shared both by local tradesmen, who service our daily needs, and by those who become the giants of industrial development. Henry Ford, Bill Gates, Marks & Spencer, Unilever and Taylor-Woodrow all began in a similar way. If these men were at school today, everything would be done to steer them through formal education channels into the ranks of the white-collared middle class.

The middle classes place a high priority on security and see higher education as the route to it, so it is not surprising that they are poor source of new firms. Empirical evidence suggests that higher education actually deters people from starting a business of their own. Academic qualifications are the passport to a secure job in an established organisation where an important element in promotion is the length of service. To break out of this hierarchical structure, risking seniority and pension rights for a chance of being your own boss, takes a strong nerve or a strong stimulus, like losing your job.

On the other hand, people with only a basic education are more likely to work in small firms where the boss is self-taught and much less interested in academic qualifications. He may even be suspicious of them. But work here is less secure and the opportunities for promotion fewer. For employees, starting a business of their own may represent not only independence, but a kind of security as well. There should be plenty of room for these contrasting patterns to coexist, but unfortunately, the people with credentials dominate politically influential institutions, not least Parliament itself, and they continually seek to impose their formal standards on the informal, small firms sector.

Henry Ford, of the Ford Motor Company, which is the biggest employer in this part of Essex, once said that he never read books because they 'messed up his mind'. It is arguable that for many youngsters, the best education they could get is not in the formal atmosphere of school, but in the world of work. Perhaps riding as a driver's mate in a delivery van, learning not only geography but road sense and customer relations. But it's a safe bet that education authorities, who frown on activities such as those of part-time paperboys or girls, would stamp on the idea. They want to regulate everything and everybody to protect them from their own instinctive desire to earn money and get on in the world. They impress their inappropriate attitudes and values on the rest of society, particularly schools.

Essex man also has an undeserved reputation for ignorance and bigotry, as well as a lack of generosity to immigrants. Nothing could be further from the truth. People in Essex are no different to the rest of the population – and they have a legitimate right to be concerned about who is and is not allowed to settle in their country. Increasing numbers make a point of retaining links to their country of origin. This is not what happens in other parts of the world.

Britain has a proud record of hospitality to people in genuine need. But people can be given the right to settle here permanently, without any commitment, on their part, to our country.

People regularly promise to uphold the way of life in Australia, America and Canada. In America, swearing allegiance to the flag is a regular occurrence. It is seen as a cohesive force and to ensure that people appreciate their country. And if not the first, then the second generations are fully integrated. They may continue to call themselves Japanese-Americans, Afro-Americans, even Anglo-Americans – but they are all Americans. That is how it should be in our country.

In Germany, an application for citizenship can only be made after you have lived there for ten years. To qualify, the applicant must be of good character, able to support him- or herself and able to speak, write and read German. They must also renounce any other nationality they hold. Even then, they are only granted citizenship if it is in the interest of the German state. This is not the case in Britain, where the residence requirement is five years, three for the spouse of a British citizen, and there is no requirement for the applicant to demonstrate suitability.

If we insisted on a similar commitment in our own country, there would be fewer objections to new arrivals. In Britain, many of the people who apply for naturalisation have poor English. In many cases, this is due to customs brought with them from their home country. Women particularly are restrained from spending time outside the home on matters which are not set down in their beliefs.

In 1992, I introduced a Ten-Minute Rule Bill to establish an oath of allegiance in Britain. People were expressing concern that our distinctive national character was being ignored. That demands made by immigrants for access to the benefits of a British life included none of the responsibilities that go with it. As politicians, we have a duty to represent their concerns, whether the politically correct presenters on the BBC *Today* programme like it or not. British people, from all sections of society and all political parties, feel that their concerns are being neglected in a bid to accommodate the needs of a multi-racial, cosmopolitan Britain.

Many members of our society do have to take an oath of allegiance. MPs have to when they take their seats in Parliament. Judges have to before they are elevated to the bench. Britain is not a bed and breakfast hotel. When people come here with the expectation of starting a new life, and for many a better life, they should be proud to uphold the interests of their new country.

Ann Cryer, Labour MP for Keighley, has recently called for immigrants in her constituency, particularly women, to be required to learn our language for their own benefit. And David Blunkett seems to agree.

Civil servants are known to keep a pile of 'spare' bills – or 'crap' bills as they are known in Whitehall – for newly-appointed ministers without ideas of their own to pilot through the Commons. Perhaps, one day, my Ten-Minute Rule bill will turn up on the statute book.

Chapter Nine

MR. MUDD

'Mud sticks.'

Anon

I had barely been officially introduced to the Commons and taken the oath of allegiance there, when I clashed head on with another male chauvinist, Mr. Tony Mudd. He described himself as the chairman of the Billericay Conservative Businessmen's Association and he informed me that he was also the chief fund raiser of the Billericay Association.

He told me that Harvey Procter, my predecessor, had readily agreed each year to reserve three dinner dates at the Commons to which members of his Businessmen's

Association were invited. He told me that there was competition for those bookings and that therefore he wanted me to be there in person at the beginning of September to secure the bookings on the dates he had given.

Of course, at that time I knew nothing of such procedures so I checked with the Commons catering management. I learned that each member was limited to three bookings a year so, before making the reservations, I thought it would be prudent to consult with the association chairman. He informed me that Mr. Mudd raised just £500 a year for the association, which, he emphasised, was not a large contribution, so I decided to reserve just one dinner. I wanted to keep my options open in case other groups within the constituency wanted to use this opportunity.

Mr. Mudd ran what he claimed was the largest accountancy practice in Essex but he was not a qualified accountant. I also discovered that Mr. Mudd ran an agency entertaining American visitors at his 'stately home' – the Clock House at Little Burstead, known as 'Muddy Towers'. His sales brochure included 'highlights of the English social scene', including 'dinner with an English aristocrat, a real, live Lord, at the House of Commons'. Commercial advertising of these events is a breach of House of Commons rules, although Mr. Mudd had been organising these highlights for some years.

He was also well known around the constituency, and owned two brown Rolls-Royces – with the licence plates MUD 1 and MUD 2. One of them was usually parked prominently outside his block of offices at the top of

Billericay High Street. He had lots of local businessmen as his clients.

Within weeks of my becoming the local MP, Mr. Mudd phoned me, all but ordering me to attend his annual masked ball, which he held in a marquee at his stately home. He told me it was the biggest social event of the year in Billericay and would be attended by five hundred people; he also told me that I must wear a ball gown. It was at this event, where all the men wore black ties and the women expensive dresses, that I learned that the only money the Association would receive from the event was the proceeds of the evening's raffle. All the proceeds from the entrance sales, at £40 a head, and from the bar went straight to Mr. Mudd for his overheads. The top table appeared to be filled with Americans who, to my surprise, told me that they were staying as paying guests at Mr. Mudd's home and that the highlight of the visit was a Commons dinner.

Some weeks later I learned from the Association chairman that the raffle proceeds of some £1,200 had not been handed over. Mr. Mudd complained that as a result of my lack of cooperation over the Commons dinners, he had had second thoughts about handing over the money. And he went further. He agreed to hand over the money on condition that he had a guarantee that I would be more cooperative in the future.

I decided to seek advice and turned to the Tory Party hierarchy. The chairman at that time, Kenneth Baker, had always told me to go and see him if I had any problems and I decided the time had come to take up the offer. We met in the Members' lobby and I outlined the problem to him about the difficulties I was having with a prominent local businessman, who, I had reason to believe, was short-changing the party while trading on his Conservative Party connections. Ken listened carefully, paused for a moment, and then, in an unctuous tone of voice, said, 'Oh Teresa, I'm sure someone like you will be able to cope admirably with this problem.'

And with that my audience was at an end. I walked away feeling let down. I was sure that a brief word from the Party Chairman would have brought Mr. Mudd to heal. Now I knew the Mudd problem had to be resolved by me and I was determined to see it through. I would just have to tackle the matter on my own.

I agreed to go with the local chairman, Ron Turner, to Mr. Mudd's office to discuss the problem. We needed to come to an amicable settlement and collect the £1,200 cheque. To my surprise, Mr. Mudd's entire committee of businessmen arrived in their smart, shiny suits while we waited patiently for Mr. Mudd's appearance.

Mudd arrived, took his seat at the head of the table and began haranguing me. He addressed me as if I was a junior member of his staff, the office girl. After several minutes he suggested that I apologise for my conduct in refusing to book him three Commons dinners. He also demanded that, in return for the cheque, I must give him my full cooperation in the future.

I had heard enough. I banged the table with my fist and, speaking softly but icily, told him, 'We have not come here to be reprimanded by you. We are here to collect the proceeds of the raffle which were raised by Association members at the summer ball. Now can we please have the cheque?'

Mudd was not used to people answering him back, especially women. He prevaricated and said that he could see no good reason why he should give us the cheque.

'Well, I must inform you that we will not be leaving here tonight until we get that cheque,' I replied.

I was gambling, but I knew I had to win this battle. I wasn't about to apologise to him. If anything, he should apologise to us for failing to pay up. He left the room and I held my breath hoping that he would return with the cheque. We waited. No one spoke.

Mudd reappeared looking like thunder,

'Sign this receipt,' he demanded, pushing a piece of paper under the nose of our chairman.

'May we check the amount?' I said. Mr. Mudd had threatened to deduct £500 to pay for the raffle prizes. Reluctantly, he handed the cheque over. We both scrutinised it while Mudd waited. Satisfied, Ron Turner signed the receipt. We left, relieved in the knowledge that we finally had our money. Unfortunately this would not be the end of the matter. Mr. Mudd had other plans.

Within a couple of weeks I began receiving notes from dozens of other MPs telling me that they were receiving requests from Mr. Mudd asking them to book Commons dinners for the Billericay Businessmen's Club. I explained the situation and they left the matter with me.

Mr. Mudd decided to bring the matter into the public arena. He asked Lady Olga Maitland, then writing the *Sunday Express* diary column, if she would arrange bookings for him in the Lords dining room because I was unwilling to organise the dinners for him in the Commons.

I knew Olga. We had met occasionally at briefing meetings for potential party candidates. Olga was on the candidates list. She phoned, telling me she had spoken to Mr. Mudd who complained that he was having 'difficulties' with me. I told her that I would only be too happy to explain the situation to her but it would be a conversation which I assumed to be on lobby terms. (When MPs speak on lobby terms to journalists, they are speaking in confidence – they cannot be directly quoted.) To my horror, Olga wrote a piece in the *Sunday Express* after our meeting, quoting my remarks:

'The fact is that Mrs. Gorman took umbrage when Mr. Mudd, a mere man, gave her strict instructions on how long she might speak at a fund-raising dinner in the House of Commons (three minutes) and insisted on chairing the evening himself ... things went from bad to worse and Mr. Mudd responded with a spoof press release making fun of his Member of Parliament ... Mrs. Gorman is full of fight ... she tells me that Mr. Mudd monopolises the fundraising, that he only ever raised £4,000 in all when we should get more.'

I phoned Olga to demand an explanation, saying that I thought what I had told her had been in confidence. I pointed out that she was interfering in my constituency and breaking the rule that candidates never involve themselves in someone else's constituency.

'Well, I'm not an MP yet so I don't have to obey your rules,' she replied.

The following week, Olga returned to the story in her column. Once again she repeated elements of my conversation with her. I decided to write to the *Express*'s editor and didn't pull my punches.

Mudd now had his tail up. I advised the Association to set up their own Businessmen's Association, which should raise upwards of £10,000 a year. We found a local businessman, Tony Page, a complete contrast to Mr. Mudd, who was willing to take on the job. Over the years he raised substantial amounts of money – more than enough to pay the costs of the next general election and fulfil our quota to Central Office.

Mudd was determined on revenge. He began to leak stories to the local Essex papers that showed me in a poor light. The stories suggested that I was out to damage the local business community. My life became plagued by calls from newspapers asking me to comment about various petty accusations. I had to respond. I could not ignore these stories. If I refused, people would say 'there's no smoke without fire'. A bitter feud broke out that was to end in the highest court in the land, in what Mr. Mudd referred to as an expensive game of Russian Roulette.

I heard on the grapevine that Mudd was arranging meetings with local businessmen in an effort to win support to get me de-selected. As the next date for the association's annual general meeting approached, it emerged that a moribund ward of the constituency had recently sprung to life and had enrolled more than one hundred new members. At the AGM, held in the Billericay Community Hall, we noticed the car park was filling up with really expensive cars: Porsches, Mercedes, Aston Martins and even Rolls-Royces. Into the meeting strode sharp-suited businessmen, none of whom were recognised by the chairman, Ron Turner, who was sitting at the entrance checking membership cards.

Ron, a policeman with a meticulous attention to detail, had taken the precaution of checking the validity of the ward in which they were registered. The branch had not been properly constituted. Their membership was invalid. One by one, these Flash Harrys presented their cards to Ron, who scrutinised each one and then informed them that they were unable to take part in the meeting. It later transpired that Mudd himself had paid for their membership fees, at the minimum subscription of £5 per head. Five hundred pounds to get rid of me would be cheap at the price.

But Mr. Mudd did not give up that easily. His next ploy was to circulate a scurrilous mock press release, that reeked of malice, to every Association official and leading businessmen in the local community. It questioned my background, my ability and my work as an MP.

This time he had gone too far.

I was now spending most of my time attending to these nefarious accusations, constantly answering phone calls from the local press asking for comment. 'What the devil's going on at Billericay?' they asked. If you give an explanation, the story keeps and it will run and run. But 'No

Comment' gives a minor boost to your adversary. I was stuck between a rock and a hard place.

I had reached the end of my tether. I decided the time had come to see a solicitor. I wanted to bring this farrago to a conclusion, but Mr. Mudd would not be satisfied until he had my head on a plate. The solicitor wrote on my behalf to Mr. Mudd, requesting him to stop these petty accusations and give an undertaking not to repeat them. He warned Mudd that if he refused the matter would wind up in court. Not surprisingly, Mudd refused to comply with the request. Things now looked grim. I had two options. I either had to forget the whole matter and put up with his attempts to undermine me or I had to sue him for libel.

A year later, I walked into the Law Courts in the Strand still wondering if I had made the right decision. I quickly cast my eye over the jury. There were seven women. I also wondered what the judge, Mr. Justice Drake, would make of the whole affair. Many people would see it as a storm in a tea-cup. To me it was matter of principle. I faced the possibility of being driven out of Parliament – by malice.

The action dragged on for thirteen days while Mr. Mudd's barrister tried to undermine my reputation and blacken my name. I had to endure three days of cross-examination in the witness box while Mr. Mudd's barrister tore my character to pieces. He tried to convince the jury of a serious flaw in my character because I had once knocked ten years off my age. He said I had misrepresented my assertions about the money Mr. Mudd raised and his motives. He brought in Councillor York and Harvey Procter as witnesses against me.

At one stage his questions became so personal that my counsel asked the judge to intervene.

My barrister called Mr. Cliff Allick, an official at Conservative Central Office and an authority on these businessmen's associations. He confirmed that a well-run organisation in a safe seat could be expected to raise £10,000 a year and more. So far so good.

Then, in cross-examination, Mudd's barrister made a cardinal error. He asked Mr. Allick a question to which he, the barrister, did not know the answer.

'What do you think of a candidate who was found to have lied on an application form?'

'That could be a serious matter.'

'And what do you think about Mrs. Gorman lying about her age on her application form?'

Mr. Allick paused.

'But all women over forty lie about their age, don't they?'

The court erupted with laughter. The jury were convulsed. Even the hint of a smile crossed the judge's face.

In his summing up, Mr. Justice Drake returned to the key accusation that I was not fit to be an MP. He reminded the jury that I had misinterpreted my age.

'But is that such an important issue for a woman?' he asked

It took the jury just over three hours to return a verdict. They awarded me £150,000 in damages, plus all my costs. Mr. Mudd, who was sitting at the front of the court, with his entire family, appeared to fold in half.

The case had attracted so much media attention that when

we left the court room we had to fight our way along the corridor through a phalanx of reporters. When we emerged into the sunlight outside the Law Court, the TV crews and the mass of photographers fought to get pictures. I was more relieved than happy. Mr. Mudd would have to leave me in peace.

'What will you do with the money?'

'Will you give it to charity?'

Alas, Mr. Mudd had not finished with me. He appealed against the level of damages and the Appeal Court reduced the damages to £50,000. And although I was awarded costs, these did not cover the full amount that Peter Carter-Ruck, our solicitor, charged. He was one of the best and didn't come cheap.

Some people will undoubtedly say why bother? A libel action turned a storm in a tea-cup into national news. Only the lawyers win libel actions. In court it is a beauty contest – the winner is the one whom the jury dislikes least. But court action is the only way to recover your reputation, which is a most precious commodity for an MP. The public and the press will soon forget, but not your party. It will be several years before the memory fades and any other merits you may have are outweighed by your time in the spotlight.

Chapter Ten

SETTLING IN

'Politics is the only profession for which no preparation is
thought necessary.'

ROBERT LEWIS STEVENSON

I arrived in Westminster in June 1987 bright eyed and bushy
tailed and raring to go. After fifteen years of actively
campaigning on behalf of small firms, I had arrived at the
centre of power; now I would begin to sort out the mess. Or
so I thought.

It seems extraordinary that, save for the policemen on
duty, officers usually at the end of their careers, no one takes
a blind bit of notice of new members, except to check your

identity. The police officers are always pleasant, always prepared to assist newcomers find their way around the building. And, because of the majesty of the centuries-old building, a new MP doesn't want to appear so stupid as not to know where the loos, the bars, or the tea room, the library or the 'ladies room' are located. So, many new MPs spend hours sitting alone in the Commons library, looking all forlorn and feeling stupid. It is a bit like arriving in a hotel to find that you have no reservations and no room.

The party Whips, who should be responsible for assisting newcomers, are too important and much too busy to act as nannies to the new MPs. The organisation of the Conservative Party is a cross between the Public School system and the hunting field. The Whips (whippers in) are the school prefects whose job it is to discipline the back-benchers and see that they turn up to vote. Each Friday, members are sent a timetable (known as the Whip), which indicates the following week's legislation. The degree of importance is indicated by a one-line Whip (please yourself), a two-line Whip (turn up unless you have agreed with your pair both to stay away) or a three-line Whip (come in even if you are on your deathbed). If you fail to answer to a three-line Whip, you will be in real trouble – the ultimate punishment is banishment from the parliamentary party. Because of this system, you can never be sure if you can turn up in the constituency for a meeting until a few days before, and even then, there is no guarantee that something will not come up, or the Whip will be changed and you will have to stay in the House for another vote.

I had a number of contacts within Margaret Thatcher's circle. I had served on Westminster City Council with Mike Forsythe and Frances Maude, both now ministers in the Thatcher government. I had worked with Nicholas Ridley on legislation to reduce red tape. I had met a number of government ministers and advisers, including John Redwood, when he was in charge of the Number 10 Policy Unit, and Michael Portillo at functions at the Centre for Policy Studies and the Adam Smith Institute. But not a single one of them offered so much as a greeting, or even a cup of tea on my arrival at the Commons. I am no shrinking violet, but looking back, I think that this had more to do with the fact that, as ministers, they hardly ever appeared in the tea-rooms or bars around the House. In the Commons, you are thrown in a the deep end, sink or swim.

As a new member, I was unlikely to invite myself round for a friendly visit, even if I could track them down. So I sat in the library, day after day, ploughing through my post-bag and mugging up on how Parliament worked. The library staff are wonderful, very professional and discreet, but I could have done with someone to talk to.

One day, however, as I crouched over my papers, I felt a hand on my shoulder.

'How are you, Teresa? How are you settling in?'

It was John Major, then Chancellor of the Exchequer, smiling down at me.

'Slowly,' I said, 'still groping around in the dark but there is light at the end of the tunnel.'

'Don't worry, it will all fall into place soon enough.'

He squeezed my shoulder in a friendly gesture. And with those few words he was gone. But I treasured those words because he was the first person to take the time to acknowledge that I was there at all!

I was to learn that the Commons is a strange world for those without connections to some specific grouping. The public school. University. The military. The law. Even some sporting activity – hunting, shooting – will give you an entrée. But few women fit in to these fraternities. I received terrific support from the CWNC (Conservative Women's National Committee), when I was seeking a parliamentary seat. But sadly, the Conservative women in the Commons never act as a group. There was no welcoming mat from them.

Election to the House is not a beauty contest or an obstacle race. It is a procedure to select a jury for the whole nation whose role is to keep an eye on what the government is up to and women have a right to equal representation. But in 1987, they were noticeable by their absence.

Then, one day, I bumped into Marion Roe, the Conservative member for Broxbourne, a long-standing member. She eventually took pity on me and another newly elected woman MP, Maureen Hicks, who had captured a Labour seat in Wolverhampton. She tipped us off that she had vacated an office somewhere off an upper corridor inside the Palace of Westminster. There we squatted for several months, undisturbed, while the Whips took their time sorting out what should have been a simple matter of allocating rooms.

Above: Early days. My first dance with Jim when I was sixteen.

Below left: Jim and I leaving Wandsworth Registry Office on our wedding day. He bought the tie and I bought the marriage licence!

Below right: A happy moment together, as Jim and I cut our wedding cake.

One of my teaching jobs was in New York, at the Convent of the Sacred Heart. Here I am, pictured with two of the nuns (*top*). One of our pupils there was Caroline Kennedy, daughter of John and Jackie – she is the pupil examining something under the microscope.

While I was still in the teaching profession, the Duchess of Kent visited my stand at a teaching aids exhibition.

Inset: My first visit to No 10, to protest against the introduction of VAT.

An exciting day in Lord North Street: Anthony Hopkins and the camera crews came to do some filming right outside our house.

Above: Margaret Thatcher joins me hot on the campaign trail in 1987.

Below: Our tireless campaigning bears fruit as the 1987 election night results are announced.

"Nicholas Winterton yelled a bit but Teresa Gorman quite enjoyed it!"

JAK's Christmas Annual is now on sale at leading bookshops, price £3.9

WHIPS' OFFICE

EU vote

'Teresa Gorman has started a girl gang!'

© Peter Brookes

Left and above: A selection of cartoons from the press depicting events in my political career. The press had a field day over our position on the Maastricht Treaty and also frequently portrayed me as the Conservative feminist.
Below: On safari with Michael Grylls MP, sadly now deceased.

Above: With Jonathan Dimbleby, with his glasses, before *that* operation.

Below: Visiting a North Sea oil rig with a group of MPs. The good thing about being 5ft 3in is that you always get in at the front of the picture! Notice a younger William Hague at the left.

I learned later that it isn't that simple. There is a fiercely contested pecking order in the parties. Ministers fight to get the rooms they want, followed by old hands. New members get what is left over. It is time that these technical matters were handed over to the Sergeant at Arms Office who administer what is called the Westminster Estate. There are hundreds of offices scattered over Westminster. All that new members need is somewhere to settle down and get to grips with the strange new life in the House of Commons.

I had come into Parliament with high expectations and brimful of enthusiasm. I believed I had reached the powerhouse of British politics where things happened, ideas prospered, enthusiasm encouraged. This was the era of Margaret Thatcher's enterprise culture initiative, to which I had directly contributed before arriving in the House. I had written numbers of pamphlets for Tory think tanks and many articles in both the *Daily Mail* and the *Daily Telegraph* on the plight of small business. I would write human interest stories, highlighting cases such as that of the West Indian baker closed down because his traditional techniques upset the Health and Safety officer, or the builder who could no longer find casual labour for love nor money since the new tax exemption rules were introduced.

I had an encyclopaedic knowledge of the legislation surrounding small business activities in Britain. For fifteen years I had been campaigning through the ASP. I was already an acknowledged spokesman on the subject, appearing regularly on radio and TV and writing many articles. I was also a member of the Conservative Party's own Small Business Bureau.

Newcomers are always told that everyone who sits in the House of Commons is equal. We are not employees, but the people's representatives. Our duty is to our constituents, not our party of the government. But it wasn't long before I realised that, of course, this was not the case. Life in the Chamber has an unwritten code of its own. You can sit there for hours attending debates and hope to catch the Speaker's eye, but I soon realised that priority was always, but always, given to more senior colleagues.

On one celebrated occasion, I actually sat through four days of debate at the budget, a total of eighteen hours of parliamentary time, waiting to be called. I was becoming more frustrated as people wandered into the Chamber, made their views known in a ten- or twenty-minute speech and then walked out again. I sat and waited and tried to catch the Speaker's eye, all to no avail. I decided on action. I walked down to the side of the Speaker's chair and asked the Speaker, Bernard Weatherall, 'Why are all these people allowed to come into the Chamber and be given priority to speak? I've sat here through four days of debate and I have never been called. What do I have to do to be called?'

He tipped his wig towards me, one eye still on the Chamber.

'These people are privy councillors or the chairmen of back-bench committees and therefore must be given preference in any debate,' he explained.

'Even if the House has heard their views dozens of times?' I asked incredulously.

'I'm afraid so. It's tradition. You're time will come.'

From that moment on, I knew that MPs were not all equal. I realised that I would have to fight hard to make my views known.

People often ask whether MPs have a special seat in the Chamber. Only the front-bench seats are reserved, for government ministers on one side and opposition on the other. The rest is a free for all – except that some members are more equal than others. Since 1974, ex-prime minister Edward Heath has sat sulking in his corner seat below the gangway, glowering at the woman who took his place. Opposite him, on the Labour benches, sat Dennis Skinner, labelled the Beast of Bolsover by Norman Tebbit; he is fearless and has made the Chamber his permanent place of residence. From there, he regularly heckles the front benches opposite and, occasionally, his own side. You can bag a seat for a day, by placing a green prayer card into the slot on the seat where you want to sit, provided you turn up at 2.30 p.m., when Parliament officially opens for the day.

If you think small children are petty, you should try a day or two in the Chamber. People vie for the best vantage places. Since the cameras arrived, the prize seats are immediately behind the leader – where you can be seen on camera – and hopefully be recognised by your constituents watching the Parliamentary Channel. You might even appear behind the leader in a ten-second slot on the news bulletins.

As I watched the parliamentary proceedings on television, the cameras soon revealed our dark secret, that there were precious few women on our benches. I reported it to the Whips, but they weren't much interested. So I phoned Downing Street to alert the leader, but she was not available.

I had more or less forgotten the idea and was preparing something for Sunday lunch when the telephone rang.

'I have a call for you from Chequers,' said the operator. 'Is Mrs. Gorman free to speak to the Prime Minister?'

I gulped and almost dropped the receiver.

'Ah, Teresa. You telephoned me yesterday. I'm sorry I was unable to take your call.' It was Margaret Thatcher.

I was astonished and flustered.

'Its not all that important. But whenever PMQs is on the television, you are surrounded by men in grey suits. It's important that women should be in the backdrop. The men, frankly, don't see the problem. A word from you would do the trick.'

I see your point. I'll have a word with them. And thank you.'

I had in mind some of the younger women, but Dame Jill Knight and Dame Elaine Kellett-Bowman, the two most senior members, were delegated by the Whips to do the job. They took their responsibilities very seriously. It was the first time in their long parliamentary careers that the fickle finger of fate had touched either woman. Not for them the tedium of an early morning start to put in their prayer cards.

They were there by the command of the leader, and woe betide any male colleague who dared to sneak in.

* * * * *

When a secretary of state is sacked, or as we say, is relieved of office, it is a big shock to the system. He also loses the chauffeur-driven car, the prestige red boxes, the deference of his officials – and his place on the front bench and half his salary. Too grand to join us in the tea-room, let alone in the scrum to find a seat at 2.30 p.m., he will, when he has overcome his humiliation, seek to join us on the back benches. He enters the Chamber and pauses, standing at the bar of the House. Like a hawk, he surveys the back benches in search of prey. We, who inhabit them, watch anxiously, wondering whose seat he will target.

A departing secretary of state may be granted the right to make a farewell statement (a sort of self-composed valedictory speech). Back-benchers may wish to sit within camera-shot, because his speech will undoubtedly attack the leader, which will guarantee him an appearance on the ten o'clock news. But on great parliamentary occasions, when the benches are crammed full, his search for a seat can deteriorate into a great piece of theatre.

It was the first Budget speech after Norman Lamont had resigned. Sitting in a prime seat from which he could challenge his successor was Angela Knight, a junior Treasury minister. Norman mounted the stairs and stood at the end of the row indicating for her to move up. No one moved. So without a word, he sat on her lap. I watched transfixed as all of a sudden, Angela popped up like a pip squeezed out of an orange and retired, beaten, to sit on the steps in the gangway.

* * * * *

Soon after my election, I was approached by a reporter from Northern Ireland, I suspect because of my name.

'What do you think about the election results in Northern Ireland?' he asked.

In truth, I knew little about the results, but I was convinced that Ulster is a part of the United Kingdom and like everyone else, I despaired of the civil war between British subjects and the unofficial Irish Republican Army, backed mainly with funds from the Irish Community in the US.

'I look forward to the time when the people of Northern Ireland vote Red or Blue – not Orange or Green,' I replied.

I have always been a strong supporter of the union, and deplore the situation tolerated by both Labour and Conservative governments, where a foreign power is allowed to wage civil war against British subjects. It is hard to imagine any other country, let alone the USA, whose citizens largely fund the IRA, tolerating something similar on its own territory. Can you imagine a situation where a Mexican guerilla force was allowed to commit bombings, torture and cold-blooded murder in Texas and New Mexico?

Neither Conservative nor Labour Parties field candidates

in Northern Ireland. Both parties prefer to keep on the right side of the MPs representing local factions. The effect of my brief remarks – reported on local news bulletins in Ulster – surprised me. But I resisted requests for more interviews. I was intrigued when I received an invitation from a group calling themselves the North Down Conservatives, inviting me to meet them. The meeting took place on the outskirts of Belfast, in the garden of a lovely house belonging to Lawrence Kennedy, a consultant at the Queen's Hospital. Here I met about thirty people who looked like Tories, behaved like Tories, but were apparently not allowed to be Tories officially.

They desperately wanted to form an official branch of the Conservative Party and to introduce the full range of mainstream politics into Northern Ireland. I immediately offered to help them. On my return, I arranged a meeting with the Party Chairman, Kenneth Baker.

'We don't want to upset the Unionists, They always support us in the House. Don't interfere,' he advised me.

'But the Unionists are a one-issue party,' I argued, 'we need to broaden our approach, get them talking about a range of policies, take the focus off their internecine warfare.'

But Conservative Central Office was not about to budge.

To support the group, I became vice-chairman of the unofficial Northern Ireland Conservative Association – and campaigned for their candidate, Lawrence Kennedy, in the European Elections. He won a respectable number of votes, though not sufficient to get him elected.

I managed to wangle some passes for these frustrated

Tories to attend the Conservative Party Conference. With the help of a large number of delegates, we won a place in the ballot to raise the issue of admitting Northern Ireland Conservatives to full membership of the Party. The motion was overwhelmingly supported by the grass-roots members of the Party from all over the country. But still Central Office resisted.

By this time, Lawrence Kennedy had become a well-known figure in the politics of Northern Ireland. One evening, while he was working at the hospital, three thugs broke into their house. They bound and gagged his terrified children with sticky tape, locked them in the bathroom and tied up his wife. Then they settled down to wait for Lawrence to arrive home. As the evening wore on, somehow his wife managed to manoeuvre herself close enough to the panic button – which had been installed in their house by the authorities – and set off the alarm.

The police arrived in force and arrested the suspects – leaving the family to await the return of their father. The incident had a devastating effect on the family. Lawrence, who was now a target for the terrorists, was unable to continue his work in a mainstream hospital because the police could not guarantee his safety. He was forced to leave his job at and develop private practice. Eventually, the family decided to move to Scotland to regain a normal life, leaving behind their relatives, friends and their beautiful home in what is a lovely part of Northern Ireland. The suspects were eventually charged with burglary and given suspended sentences.

This tragic episode, the first involving Northern Ireland with which I had a personal connection, illustrated for me the failure of all parties to bring Northern Ireland into the mainstream of UK politics. Kate Hoey, Labour MP for Vauxhall, who hails from Northern Ireland, held similar views to mine. She too tried to persuade Labour to establish a base in Ulster. We often exchanged views about the tragic situation when we bumped into each other in the Ladies Room.

'Wouldn't life be different if women ruled the world?' she once said and I agreed. We had a woman Prime Minister, but there was so much more to do. Our policy in Northern Ireland was weak and cowardly. You can never appease a bully.

'There would be more law and order and less blood and guts in politics if we had our way,' I agreed. Kate was one of a handful of MPs who would have been equally at home in the Conservative party

* * * * *

Soon after my arrival at Westminster, I approached Marcus Fox, who was then chairman of Select Committees, to ask if I could join the Select Committee on Trade and Industry because, of course, that is where my interest in small business lay.

'There's a waiting list. You have to wait until someone decides to drop out.'

'How long could that be?'

'I don't know, you'll have to be patient. I'll keep an eye out for an opportunity where you might fit in. You've plenty of time.'

There are two views on how to hold the government to account, which is more important than ever since the rapid expansion of legislation that has taken place since the war. One of these is by debate in the Chamber. The other is through select committees, which monitor each government department, such as the Treasury or Social Services.

It was originally thought that these committees would make for better government. But government diffuses the more sensitive scandals, like BSE, by shuffling them off into judicial enquiries, which can be dragged out for ages until the public, and even the media, have forgotten about them.

Prime ministers, as a rule, do not like the committee system. Committees as a means of curbing the power of Government are a delusion. Their power comes from the government, which is not about to relinquish any of it.

Under Labour, much of government legislation is now announced directly to the media, through press conferences by-passing Parliament altogether. Once people have been told what to expect, there is not much that Parliament can do about it.

Select committees only serve to distract attention, and members' time, from the proper parliamentary forum, the Chamber. Members have a great workload, and committee work adds to this and is a further and possibly intolerable strain. The demands of the committee meetings hold up the genuine business of the House. While members are sitting bored in a committee room, they cannot debate on issues that may be important to them or their constituents, and means that they find it increasingly difficult to fulfil their constituency role.

Enoch Powell once said that 'Everything which diminishes true debate on the Floor of the House of Commons strengthens the Executive and weakens Parliament. We must, in order to do our business, be uninvolved. We are not participating in government, we are not experts, we are even less the puppets of experts. We have our own expertise, and our expertise is as politicians and would-be Ministers facing other politicians and actual ministers. We can only do that through debate, we can only do that on the floor of the Chamber.'

After my experience of serving on a select committee, I totally agree with him. Select committees are a waste of MPs' time. In addition, the composition is based on the size of the parties, and the chairman is usually a member of the governing party. They tie up twenty back-bench members across the parties for days at a time. And they give a new lease of life to the older members – whom I call Klingons – and the has-beens, might-have-beens and never-would-have-beens who serve as chairmen, which makes them feel important. When the BBC cannot persuade ministers to give their views, the chairman of a select committee will usually oblige, although they have no real power. If a chairman is doing the job of criticising policy, the government will find ways to dump them.

Select committees love to order celebrities to attend their meetings. If you are into celebrity spotting and you wait long enough on the committee corridor, all the great and the good of our land can be found, sitting outside the committee rooms waiting for a grilling. They can also order ministers to attend. The only select committee of any importance is the Public Accounts Committee, which sifts through government spending and is, by tradition, chaired by a member of the opposition, who at least has the incentive to hold the government to account.

In my fourteen years in Parliament, I managed to avoid serving on a select committee until, in my last parliament, I was more or less ordered to join the Select Committee on the Environment, which included Transport chaired by the formidable Gwyneth Dunwoody, who looks as if she was carved from the base of a very large tree trunk without the curves. To her great credit, she is a thorn in the flesh of Tony Blair's government, which may account for the fact that she failed in her bid to succeed Betty Boothroyd as Speaker. Gwyneth, who always has a brilliant grasp of her brief, towers over the committee and is capable of turning to jelly the great and the good that she summons to appear before us.

After Hatfield, Railtrack was a favourite target. And more times than I can recall, Mr Corbett, the chairman, was hauled in to be given a rollicking bringing with him enough of his senior staff to make you wonder who was running the railways in their absence. It was like watching a cat with a mouse. Superficially the enquiry was about the safety record of Railtrack. In fact, it was a continuation of the political battle between old Labour and the Conservatives over privatisation.

Before each inquisition began, we were handed a list of

questions prepared in advance by a phalanx of select committee clerks. We were not encouraged to ask our own questions. But occasionally I broke ranks. And I chose to do so with Mr. Corbett.

'Isn't it true that, in the four years since privatisation, two years have been almost accident free and but for the tragic circumstances of Hatfield, the safety record is far better than under nationalisation?' I suggested to Railtrack's much-beleaguered chairman.

Gwenyth frowned – this question was not scripted. Instead of rising to the opportunity to bring some balance into the proceedings, Railtrack panicked. They had come prepared to take their medicine, not to be complimented. Once more, I demonstrated my incapacity as a team player. No one actually scolds you. But a lot of tut-tutting goes on after the meeting.

In my experience, the whole pointless exercise is entirely destructive, and, again, there is no scope for members of the committee to contribute ideas of their own. Everything is decided between the chairman and the clerks.

* * * * *

MPs spend a lot of their time examining government proposals for new laws in standing committees. This would be easier and more effective if they were written in plain English. Drafting a government bill is an antique cult, practised by teams of civil servants specially trained in the art of gobbledegook. Because the language is incomprehensible, we spend hours, days, weeks and months scrutinising every word and every phrase to try to discover the loopholes.

There is a method in this madness. The civil service tries to cover all angles so there are no comebacks for them. But the average citizen would need an interpreter to discover its meaning and avoid the pitfalls of failing to comply. And this is why hapless businessmen engage an army of highly paid advisors and accountants, partly to protect themselves from falling foul of the law and partly to find loopholes of their own that they can exploit.

The Citizens Advice Bureau provides the same service for ordinary people, and an MP's advice bureau should see the casualties of the system, those who have fallen through the net.

Government back-benchers on the committee are not encouraged to hold up the bill by asking awkward questions. But it is a field day for aspiring opposition members, who are encouraged to do anything they can to delay the proceedings. It is a good place to sharpen up your political skills.

Outside organisations with an interest scan the bill for possible opportunities to add their demands and look out for a sympathetic committee member to put their point of view across. Sometimes it works, as it did when I sat on the Children's Act with David Mellor. Mellor had a sharp tongue and a short fuse. We were discussing the protection of children in care. There were, and are, some awful cases of abuse within care homes – where children have no one to turn to outside the system.

I proposed a new clause to ensure that each care home

prominently displayed a telephone number and name of a person which a child could call – an extension of the Childline concept. David did not agree that we needed to add the clause to the bill. He became irritated by my persistence and spun around to face me.

'Why doesn't the honourable lady from Billericay get off my back?'

'I thought that was what I was here for, Minister, to offer my opinion. Please correct me if I'm wrong,' I replied, sweetly.

'Order, order, the minister must not be so fierce with committee members,' cried the chairman.

The altercation could not have lasted more than a few seconds. But the next day, I received a two-page handwritten and rambling letter of apology from David, which, I suspect, was prompted by the Whips.

But my clause was added to the bill. And when David presented the finished product to the House, he paid me an ostentatious complement on my achievement.

As a back-bencher, you have no say on the content of a bill, or its presentation. But you can draw some small comfort from amending a bill. It is from these small crumbs that we draw our sense of achievement. And it gives us something to boast about in the tea-room.

* * * * *

In the Commons, there are unofficial committees on just about every subject under the sun. Committees to promote friendship with other countries. Committees to promote awareness of health problems. Committees to keep an eye on the world of entertainment and our heritage. Committees of friendship with every other country on earth. These are well patronised because they frequently offer the chance of a fact-finding mission to a country you have always wanted to visit. There is hardly an issue that does not have a committee of its own. Anyone with a bee in their bonnet can persuade a Member of Parliament to set up a committee to air their grievance and give them publicity. I am also guilty, as I once set up a committee to highlight the health needs of older women in the days when it was taboo to mention the menopause.

The more prestigious of these committees, which have some wonderful outings and wonderful trips abroad, are hogged by members who have all the time in the world to organise their election and re-election. And here lies the problem. Like elderly proprietors of the family firm, they smother new blood and fresh ideas. And so we present a geriatric image to the world.

Their influence can remain long after they have been sent off to that resting place for geriatric Klingons – the House of Lords. The supreme example is Michael Joplin, now Lord Joplin, who had a distinguished career as a minister, but who for donkey's years held the chairmanship of the prestigious Anglo-American Committee. It decides who does and does not take part in official visits to Washington, but in some committees where the trips are so much in demand, they are a wonderful way of settling old scores. In my view, chairmanships should be limited to two terms.

If only Margaret Thatcher had had the good sense to quit after two terms, she would have been spared the wrath of those frustrated males who saw no other way of getting their hands on the job but to get rid of her. But of course, the people in whose hands the power lies to make these changes are the very Klingons who have most to lose.

* * * * *

I'm a great fan of Desmond Morris. His book, *The Naked Ape*, inspired my early interest in animal behaviour. But my favourite work is *Manwatching*. It has had a seminal effect on my relationship with men ever since. Desmond taught me how to break down the barriers between men and women, without actually being hauled off to bed by one of them. And I have applied it ruthlessly and without shame throughout my parliamentary career.

A remarkably high number of male colleagues behave as if they haven't spoken to a woman, much less been touched by one, since they parted company with their nannies. Indeed, they can only cope with women as nannies, grannies – or fannies!

Whenever an uptight, grey-suited MP talked down to me, I would reach out and squeeze his arm, tap the side of his nose or even link arms with him if we were side by side at a road crossing. The reaction was instantaneous; you could feel the frisson of excitement surging through him. From that moment on, he would be putty in my hands. The scowl would be replaced by a lovely smile, and invariably we would become friends.

Sir Peter Tapsell was one of my great conquests. Tall, elegant and a touch superior, as befits a man who entered politics as PPS to Anthony Eden, he would sit in a corner seat in the Chamber, legs crossed, arms crossed, barely acknowledging me as I squeezed past him to take my seat.

'Why do feel threatened by me, Peter?' I asked, teasingly.

'What do you mean? That's absurd,' said he.

'But your body language is very defensive. You are protecting all your vital organs.' Peter was shocked. I imagine that, in his circles, women are seen and not heard, and certainly don't mention such things as organs.

'How should I sit, then?' he asked.

'Uncross your legs and set them just a little apart. Stretch one arm along the back of the leather benches towards me and rest the other hand on your lap. There, doesn't that feel better?' I could positively see the icicles between us melting.

'What nonsense! It's all those hormones you are taking.' But I could tell that he rather enjoyed the attention.

Peter could never quite bring himself to use my first name; that would be a tad too intimate. But these little flirtations helped to oil the wheels in a workplace full of hostile, elderly gentlemen who still believed in their heart of hearts that Parliament was no place for a woman, and that we had invaded the best men's club in the country.

Chapter Eleven

TICKET
TOUTS AND
TATTOOISTS

*'If freedom were not so economically efficient, it certainly
wouldn't stand a chance.'*
MILTON FRIEDMAN

The longer I remained an MP, the more frustrated I became
at the difficulty of making a constructive contribution to
political debate in the House, much less introduce new
thinking. In desperation, I joined the army of MPs tabling
questions to the relevant minister. The newspapers' lobby
correspondents offered another opportunity of getting your
views across to the general public. Anything an MP says to
a lobby correspondent is meant to be confidential. You can

sometimes fly a kite – or get a hare up and running – through them.

MPs who speak to a lobby correspondent must make it known before raising a subject that 'lobby terms apply' – in other words, they are free to use the information in their reports but never to reveal the MP's identity. However, if you forgets or fail to insist on 'lobby terms' then you could be quoted and find themselves in big trouble.

Only one month after entering Parliament I came a cropper over the lobby system. It was just as Wimbledon's annual tennis tournament was about to begin. In the chamber, Menzies Campbell, Liberal Democrat spokesman on law and order was rabbiting on about ticket touts, a suitable old chestnut for Wimbledon week. To listen to him, you'd have thought they were guilty of spreading rabies. He was calling for £10,000 fines and prison sentences to banish touts from our great national tournaments. I wandered out of the chamber into the Members' Lobby and bumped into Chris Moncrieff, the Press Association's famous lobby correspondent.

'What's going on in the Chamber?' he asked, casually.

'Ming Campbell is on about the Wimbledon ticket touts. He wants to lock them all up,' I replied.

'Do you agree with him, Teresa?' Moncrieff asked.

'No, I certainly do not,' I replied. 'Ticket touts are simply stockbrokers in cloth caps. They buy cheap and sell dear to make a profit. What is the difference between touts and some of our own colleagues who earn a living as stockbrokers in the City?'

Chris, a wise old bird with donkey's years of experience in the art of extracting a good quote from a novice MP, got out his notebook and began scribbling in his impeccable shorthand.

'Have you ever bought a ticket from a tout?'

'Yes I have.'

He licked his pencil.

'Do you think the Wimbledon authorities ought to do something about the touts?'

'The All England Club? They are the cause of the problem. People with spare tickets can only recycle them through the touts. They're nothing but a bunch of Edwardians pickled in aspic.'

I was rather pleased with my first attempt to defend the underdog.

The next day I was hugely embarrassed to find myself all over the front page of the *Evening Standard* under the banner headline, 'Gorman Supports Ticket Touts'. I had forgotten the cardinal rule – only talk to lobby correspondents on lobby terms. In the tea-room the next day, older and wiser colleagues looked at me and shook their heads in sorrow.

A few days later, I visited Wimbledon as a guest of David Evans, the Tory member for Welwyn Garden City. I went down by train and walked up the hill hoping to avoid recognition. But as I neared the gates a reporter spotted me and within seconds I was mobbed by cheering ticket touts. Some tried to grab me, egged on by the press, wanting to pick me up and carry me shoulder-high through the famous gates. It would have made a terrific picture.

At tea-time, David and Janice, his wife, who were debenture holders, took me off to the Members' Tent. An official stopped us and stared at me. He took David on one side, and suggested that I might not be welcome. David brushed him aside. He would hear none of it and in we went. I looked around furtively to see if anyone else had noticed, but no one paid us any attention.

It is easy for an MP to come to the defence of three-legged dogs and small babies, but defending the rights of ticket touts, for whom there is no public sympathy, is folly. No one has a good word to say for them and MPs who are prepared to speak up for the unspeakable are unlikely to carry favour with the Whips.

Next, I decided on a piecemeal attack on public monopolies using Ten-Minute Rule Bills. My first target was the Post Office's monopoly on delivering letters; I called for the privatisation of the Post Office. The Post Office, prone to slow and restrictive practices, would no longer be able to hold the public to ransom. I recalled the time that they almost destroyed my business. For years, militant postal workers had staged lightning strikes in local sorting offices. Never a week went by without one somewhere in the country. By simply removing the restriction on delivering letters under £1, we would let the competition in. Nicholas Soames, the Conservative MP for Crawley, known in the tea-room as the Crawley butter mountain, announced that he would join Labour to scupper the legislation. He believed that post offices were a national institution and should not be touched.

Undeterred, I tried out another idea. Buying a house in England is a long and tedious business. The Scots do it better. But so, too, do the Australians, as I learned from my visit there. The Aussies have made it as simple as buying a used car. The idea for a MOT for houses has been adopted by Labour, although there is strong resistance from those in the conveyancing business. My bill would have cut out the chains, cut out bogus offers and brought a stop to endless haggling over a price. But that too was talked out.

I also sought to regularise relationships between cohabiting couples by bringing in a Ten-Minute Bill to make provision for the enforcement of contracts entered into between cohabiting partners. My bill sought to encourage people who share a home or property to make proper contractual arrangements about their joint possessions. It would set out the ownership rights to prevent family quarrels and bad feelings if the relationship breaks down, and give guidance to the courts when dealing with such cases. I pointed out that more than one million young couples between eighteen and forty live together without any formal arrangements, many involving children, who may not be protected if those relationships break down.

On a visit to St. Andrew's Hospital, Billericay, where there is an excellent burns and plastic surgery unit, I discovered that eighty-three patients were waiting to have tattoos removed. After making enquiries I discovered that there were long lists of patients waiting for tattoo removal operations in hospitals around the country and the lists were becoming longer as the fashionable tattoo rage gathered pace. You can have a tattoo from as little as £25, but to have it removed costs the NHS £2,500 or more. Prompted by this discovery, I devised a bill proposing that people who chose to be tattooed should first obtain insurance against the cost of removing it and a commercial tattooist should be required to see the insurance certificate.

Since I introduced the idea in 1991 the boom in tattoos has rocketed. Today, the tattoo has gone mainstream – suddenly everyone wants one. And tattoos have gone from dark art to fine art, from backstreet to high street; it has even entered high society. Despite this fact, the medical profession report a constant stream of people who come to bitterly regret being tattooed. But all they can do is swap it for a nasty scar. Why should the overburdened health service be responsible for this, or any other, self-inflicted damage?

By now, I was developing a reputation for being outspoken, with a good line in parliamentary questions and some bizarre ideas for legislation. This does not necessarily go down well with the all-important Tory Whips. There is, of course, a government Whip always on duty sitting on the front bench and taking notes of questions asked and answered. He will be the judge of a member's contribution. On many occasions I suspect that the note about me read, *'Teresa Gorman intervened and made an unhelpful contribution.'*

Within a few months of my parliamentary baptism, I was receiving attention in the press, but I also swiftly realised that my outspoken comments were not always appreciated. New members are best seen but not heard if you want to make progress on the path to promotion. I recalled Marcus Fox's words of advice to me when I applied to become a Tory candidate, stating that what the part really wanted was team players, not star turns. He continued, 'After people have achieved success in their own walk of life, the next thing they want is to be a Member of Parliament.' To judge from the record of people who have come into Parliament after highly successful careers, there is not a lot of point in becoming an MP. There is no getting away from the fact that politics is a game for team players. Apart from Archie Norman, I can think of few businessmen who have ended up on the front bench. Even prime ministers have to be team players. Margaret Thatcher was perhaps the only prime minister in modern times who was an exception to that rule. She was driven by ideology, but that upset her Cabinet and look what happened to her.

It is difficult for people who are used to giving orders to knuckle down to the disciplines of life in a political party. Later, John Major wrote of me, 'I seriously thought about making Teresa a minister but decided that she would be too unreliable.' He was probably right. However, I'd be less than human if I did not regret not having seen political life from that side of the fence.

The civil service have their own way of doing things, trying to achieve their goals through regulation and controls. As a result, people have become addicted to government handouts. Whitehall has its own way of dealing with a minister with radical views. I believe giving people encouragement to build their own businesses is far and away the best way forward. In Britain today, the state inhibits people; it doesn't trust people to use their energies wisely. My mind frequently goes back to America and their enthusiasm for individual responsibility. It is this that the Conservative Party needs to inject into our economy. Without a vision, a party dies

When the state ran most of Britain's major industries, such as coal, steel, housing, ship-building, airlines, buses and even the railways, they were all grossly inefficient. Twenty years on, Labour too has come to the conclusion that markets must be introduced into the public sector. Today, even education and the National Health Service are under review. Labour has stolen our clothes. They acknowledge that money alone cannot cure the problems. The missing ingredient is the lack of opportunities for individual enterprise which, I believe, is the quintessential element for success.

I know from my own experience in the public sector as a teacher, that the harder you work, the more your colleagues complain that you are making a rod for their back. As a way of increasing their benefit from work, absenteeism is high and go-slows are common. A 'golden backache' or some other mystery ailment will secure you an early exit from the job and perhaps give you the chance of a supplementary income. This route is commonplace in state-run industries: the fire service, the police, prisons, the health service and teaching. But it is an odd way to run a country.

Chapter Twelve

THE TEA-ROOM, TALK SHOWS AND THE TELLY

'But far too numerous was the herd of such who think too little and talk too much.'
JOHN DRYDEN

People complain to me and other MPs that apart from Prime Minister's Question Time, the Chamber of the House of Commons is virtually deserted. They accuse MPs of having a 'cushy' life and seem to imagine that we do little work, live a life of luxury and draw a good salary. If only this were true!

It is true that after PMQs the Chamber rapidly empties and many of us beetle off to the famous tea-room. This is the place that you hear about the latest news. Performances at Question Time are picked over and criticised. Hot gossip is chewed over, elaborated and passed on. But most of all, people bury their heads in the latest edition of the London *Evening Standard*. It is by far and away the most frequently read newspaper in the Commons. The latest editions of the *Standard*, fuelled by tittle-tattle from the House fed to them by lobby correspondents, pre-empts what the rest of Britain will learn about Parliament from Radio 4's *Today* programme next morning.

The members' tea-room is divided by the serving counter. Labour MPs sit at one end and Tories at the other; the Liberal Democrats sit round their single table, as do the Unionist members from Northern Ireland. Sometimes the Welsh Nationalists will bag a table to themselves and carry on their conversations in Welsh. It's a case of never the twain shall meet! In other words, neither party wants their gossip overheard in case it winds up in a diary column in tomorrow morning's newspapers, like the one Matthew Parris writes in the *Times*. And some members are notorious for leaking to the press.

Very occasionally, at the end of PMQs, the prime minister graces the tea-room with his or her presence. John Major was a frequent visitor. His arrival was almost unnoticed – unlike that of Margaret Thatcher, whose presence swept through the tea-room, like an advancing tornado. Accompanied by his bag-carrier, Graham Bright, John would suddenly appear at one of the tables. Graham would ask him what he would like to eat and drink.

'I'll have tea and crumpet,' was his standard order.

'Would you like anything on your crumpet, Prime Minister?'

'No thank you, just tea and buttered crumpet.' And off Graham would go to join the queue.

Every Tory MP knew the script, it never varied, although we waited with bated breath to see if for once he might order beans on toast – the most popular item on the menu – but he never did. Then those around him would open up the small talk, which usually began with someone ingratiatingly congratulating the Prime Minister on his 'excellent' performance at the Dispatch Box that day.

'Do you think so?' he would ask in his piping voice. 'That's very kind.'

Whenever John Major was short of small talk in the tea-room, he would tease me, saying that he kept a copy of my book, *The Bastards*, which tells the inside story of the revolt against the Maastricht treaty, beside his bed. And he would tell me that when he woke up in the small hours of the morning thinking about who to and who not to promote, he checked the list of Fresh Start members in the back of the book – and eliminated anyone who appeared on it. It was meant as a tease, but it indicates the degree of anger he felt at our attempts to prevent the ratification of the Maastricht Treaty, which gave away to Brussels the last remnants of Britain's power to govern itself. And it is true that the two dozen excellent and independently minded politicians on the list were never promoted. Politically speaking, this is a good example of cutting off your nose to spite your face. I recalled once more Marcus Fox's warning that the Party wanted team players. But I preferred Churchill's view – himself a 'bastard' in his day – that the first duty of an MP is to his country, the second to his constituents and only then to the policies of his party. Without his defiance of Party Whips, our country may have been absorbed into a greater Europe in 1939.

When Margaret arrived in the tea-room, the whole place became electrified. Even the Labour members looked up surreptitiously at her entrance. These royal visits were not for chit-chat. They were linked to some tricky piece of legislation that was not going down too well in the Chamber. Her PPS would advise that Margaret would do herself a lot of good if she popped into the tea-room to spike a few guns.

It was 1989 and she was having some difficulty getting the Football Spectators Bill through Parliament. The bill, based on an idea from David Evans MP, who owned Luton Football Club, was designed to curb football hooliganism by making supporters carry identity cards. Margaret arrived and sat down at the head of one of the large oval tables. I happened to be sitting at the opposite end, some six feet from her, enjoying a toasted teacake and a cup of lemon tea. She immediately got down to business. One by one she went round the table, asking each member what they thought of the idea of identity cards.

'Now what do you think, Charles?' fixing him with a beady eye.

'I think it's a splendid idea, Prime Minister. You have my one hundred per cent support' said Charles, metaphorically touching his forelock.

She moved on. 'What do you think James?'

'We should have done it years ago, Prime Minister, and put a stop to all this nonsense – disgracing the name of our country.'

And so on round the table. So far so good. She was getting the right feedback. And then it was my turn. Margaret peered hard at me.

'And what do you think – dear,' she said, with an emphasis on the word 'dear'. I had been in the House eighteen months, but I got the impression she could not distinguish me from the tea ladies.

'I don't think it will work, Prime Minister, someone will soon find a way to forge them. And we'll have the problem all over again.'

There was silence but for a brief but audible sucking in of breath. Margaret paused and screwed up her eyes.

'What did you say, dear?' she said, icily, but then, without more ado, moved on to the next person.

A few minutes later, when Margaret returned to her duties of 'running the country' as she was prone to say, my colleagues shook their heads in disbelief.

'You'll never get your promotion, Teresa,' said one.

Another said, 'I agree with you but why say that to her? Why not just agree with her? You know she's determined to get this through.'

'It's worse than that,' I said. 'I've tabled an amendment to exempt women from this daft idea. They never get involved in football violence except as victims.'

'But the men will simply turn up in drag,' someone joked.

'Yes. But you can always tell a transvestite – they have big hands and big feet.'

The bill met considerable opposition in the Chamber and was eventually dropped. But I had learned a lesson. The leader is always right – and there are no brownie points for disagreeing.

There is nothing more boring in the tea-room than a member who has held some junior office in government for a short time and failed to make it to the top. They subconsciously attribute their failure to the lack of foresight on the part of their superiors.

George Walden was one such, as was Peter Bottomley. George, who entered politics from the upper ranks of the Foreign Office – was given a junior ministerial role in Higher Education and forever more he expounded his views on the reform of education, especially comprehensive education, which most people around the table deemed to be a failure, but George considered a success.

Peter Bottomley, over tea and biscuits, told us over and over again that while he was a minister in Transport, he had reduced road deaths to 5,000 a year – the implication being that if Margaret had had the good sense to keep him in the job, who knows what wonders he might have achieved. Peter was very fond of statistics, as was his wife – the fragrant Virginia, the epitome of a well-bred Conservative lady – whose progress was aided up the greasy pole by Sir Geoffrey Howe, a family friend. With the right patronage, Virginia rose to the dizzy heights of Secretary of State for Health, still carrying in her handbag a little notebook in which she

kept a list of facts. At the despatch box, on TV, radio –
anywhere at all, she would bore on for hours about the
numbers of operations performed, the number of new nurses
recruited, the number of new beds, hospitals, bed pans – any
statistic. In political terms, the Bottomleys are a successful
couple. In tea-room terms, their conversation left a lot to be
desired.

You can guarantee that in the tea-room there will always
be a Whip or two in attendance, making mental notes,
picking up the gossip, judging the mood amongst the back-
benchers. I had written an article for the *Daily Mail*
defending Margaret Thatcher who was accused of failing to
promote more women. I pointed out that it was the Whips
who recommended MPs – good team players – whom they
think suitable to join the road to promotion. The Prime
Minister, of course, selects the secretaries of state, who head
up each government department. In my article I named
Tristan Garel-Jones, the Deputy Chief Whip, as the spider
sitting at the heart of this web of intrigue. I pointed out that
no one got promotion without their MOT – Mate of Tristan.
I was rather pleased with it.

As I sat in the tea-room that afternoon reading the article,
I looked up to see not one but four Tory Whips facing me. It
was extremely unusual; someone must have tipped them off
I was there.

'Did you get paid for that article, Teresa?' asked one of
them.

'I jolly well hope so,' I replied. 'Have you read it?' I asked.
No reply. 'Did you enjoy it?' I persisted.

Still he did not answer.

'How much did you get paid for writing it?' one demanded.

'The usual fee I imagine,' I said, without giving anything away.

'I would call someone who sells their services for money, a prostitute,' he spat out.

I was taken aback, deeply offended by such an outrageous insult.

'And I would call a Whip who would say that little better than a sewer rat,' I replied, echoing Enoch Powell's description of the Whip's office as the sewer of Parliament.

Later, Garel-Jones himself sidled up to me. 'I had no idea, Teresa, that I was so powerful,' he sneered. 'My constituents are amazed to learn that I am such an important figure in the party.'

'Really? Well now they know you pull the strings Tristan, we're just your puppets.'

Tristan Garel-Jones was not a man to be crossed. The perfect Deputy Chief Whip, he avoided the limelight but wielded his power behind the scenes. He would on occasions be prepared to bully you or even swear at you. In fact, do everything and anything necessary to achieve his objective of getting the party policy through.

He was also an enthusiastic European, something that would inevitably influence his views on promotions. His bullying technique could be ruthless. During the dramatic battle over the Maastricht Treaty, when tensions were running high in the party, I saw Walter Sweeney, a

Eurosceptic, pinned against the wall by Garel-Jones. He was arguing with Walter, who looked far from happy. Twenty minutes later, I returned to the lobby to find Walter still pinned to the wall, looking even more distressed – even close to tears. Garel-Jones's face was only inches away from Walter's as he continued to lambast him.

I walked up to the two men.

'Is he giving you a rough time, Walter? Just remember, you are a patriot and he is a European. There's a difference,' I said.

Furious, Garel-Jones turned on me. 'Why don't you fuck off? This is none of your damned business,' he spat out.

I liked Walter. He was a typical country solicitor – rather old-fashioned in his manner but scrupulously courteous. However, his parliamentary majority was only eighteen, and he was already under tremendous pressure from the chairman of his association to vote with the government.

'You see, Walter. He's not even a gentleman,' I went on. 'Why don't you just walk away? You don't have to put up with his bullying.'

Walter was a good MP, but he paid a high price for sticking to his principles. When he lost his seat at the 1997 election, he was refused permission by Central Office to reapply elsewhere round the country.

But it wasn't only the Whips who would, on occasions, pepper their comments to women colleagues with gutter language or smutty remarks. On one occasion, an argument took place in the Chamber between Edwina Currie and Nicky Fairbairn, the former Attorney-General for Scotland.

Fairbairn, a barrister, was a powerful debater, and a well-known womaniser but, on many occasions, he was the worse for drink.

Edwina, who was renowned as a bit of a nag, was the butt of one of his more outrageous, though funny, comments, when he told her, 'I would happily rather take poison than be spread-eagled on the floor of the House by her.'

If there was a woman present, Fairbairn would make distasteful remarks calculated to embarrass for no good reason. Standing next to me, waiting to be served in the tea-room, he once commented on my 'nice tits'. On another occasion he began a detailed description of female condoms, which he alleged he had seen in his local chemist shop at the weekend. Half a dozen men sitting at the table in the tea-room buried their heads in their newspapers. Eventually I could stand it no longer.

'Why are you carrying on about this? Can't you see you are only embarrassing your male colleagues?' I told him.

He stopped, looked down at the table and mumbled an apology. Not until he had gone did my male colleagues look up and express relief.

'Well done, Teresa,' said one.

'Poor Nicky – he's on his fourth claret,' observed another.

What does seem quite extraordinary, and breathtakingly arrogant, on the part of many male MPs, is the assumption that all women MPs and secretaries must always welcome attention of this sort and that women are game for subtle offers of amorous activity. One evening I was chatting in the Commons to an MP who was a well-respected lawyer and I raised with him a legal matter that was troubling me.

'Would you mind advising me on this issue?' I asked him.

'Not at all. Glad to be of help,' he said with a smile.

I began to outline details of the problem when he suggested that it might be better to meet later his office where we could talk in private.

Later, I knocked on the door and he opened it. He ushered me in, closing the door after me.

'Come in, Teresa. A glass of claret? Now, what is it that is troubling you?' I waited until he had poured two glasses of claret. I had hardly begun to explain my problem when he said, 'Do we need bother with all this?'

I was puzzled.

'That's what I'm here for,' I said.

He paused. 'Is that so? Do you mind very much standing up?' he asked.

I began to wonder whether he had taken leave of his senses.

'What on earth for?' I was beginning to feel apprehensive.

'I would rather like you to stand on the desk,' he said, perfectly politely. 'I rather like to get my fees up front.'

Then the penny dropped.

'You must be mad,' I said and made for the door but it was locked. He must have locked it to stop anyone coming in. Without a word, he came around the desk and opened it.

The incident was all over in a few minutes, but I was shaken. I was absolutely sure I had never given him any reason to think I might welcome this kind of attention.

I'd be surprised if other women were not propositioned. There are plenty of office romances – usually a secretary is involved. The House is full of rumours of members who have consummated their passion in the showers, in an upstairs corridor – or even on the woolsack in the Lords. Sooner or later, you hear about them in the tea-room. I can think of four Cabinet ministers who divorced their wives and married a woman from the Commons, usually their secretary. It is partly because of members' isolation from the world outside Parliament that family relationships break down.

On the outside, the House of Commons may appear oh-so-sober, but behind the scenes, it is a seething mass of sexual activity. The mere status of MPs gives some men the *droit du seigneur.* It has been my experience, through my varied career, that men with a high level of ambition are also high on hormones.

Cecil Parkinson is one of those high-octane politicians who ooze an almost magnetic irresistible charm. There is no doubt that if Mrs. Thatcher had fallen under the proverbial bus, he would have been high on the list to succeed her. Handsome, debonair with a very attractive voice, he had all the qualities of leadership displayed by his American counterparts Kennedy and Clinton.

I first met Cecil in 1982, at a selection weekend for the Approved Candidates List. In 1983, we met again when I was one of a crowd of people celebrating our election victory outside Central Office in Smith Square. Margaret and Dennis were at a window in Central Office, waving at the crowds below. We had a bottle of champagne, and all around us, everyone was happy and laughing as Cecil came through the crowd shaking hands. I offered him a glass of champagne, he grabbed the glass and me with it. We hugged. Our body language and the excitement made it one of those magic moments you always remember. I was high on the oxygen of proximity.

Once I was elected, I often bumped into Cecil in the corridors of Parliament, when he would tell me how lovely I looked. I didn't know whether this was his standard chat-up line, but it was very effective. On one occasion, as I was reading a list pinned to a wall in a small office off Members' Lobby, two hands slid around my waist. Before I could react, a voice purred in my ear.

'What are you up to now, Teresa?' he asked. 'What's so interesting?'

Of course, I knew it was Cecil, I recognised his voice instantly. His presence registered up and down my spine. My body, from the waist down, turned to jelly. I could have stood there all day. I didn't dare turn around to face him or I might have been in his arms. Instead, I muttered something trivial and after a long moment – not too long for me – he was gone.

I wasn't the only one who found him utterly seductive. Half the secretaries in the Commons fancied him. They wouldn't have minded swapping their bed jackets and hot water bottles for Cecil's electric blanket. In the enclosed world of Parliament, where there are 659 MPs – almost all males – and 5,000 women – mostly secretarial staff – it would be unbelievable if clandestine romances didn't take place.

* * * * *

There is only one radio programme that provides intelligent

discussion about women for women. It is *Woman's Hour* and its feisty presenter is Jenny Murray. It is regularly attacked by male listeners for its sexist content.

Whenever I turn on the radio – or less frequently, the TV – I am bombarded by male-dominated sports programmes and soap operas, male wildlife presenters, male chat show hosts and male academics presenting medical series or historical surveys. And lots and lots of gay male comedians sending up women.

There are a few opportunities for women to present the news or midday chat shows, so long as they are young and glamorous. And occasionally, late-night arts programmes when Germaine Greer appears – always Germaine Greer. Don't women have sporting talent? Play golf or team games? Are there no scientific brains? No ability to talk the hind leg off a donkey?

Tiger Woods dominates any tournament he graces with his presence, but his performance is not a patch on that of Kerry Webb, the Australian woman's golf champion. However, the majority of commentary surrounding women golf players focuses on their outfits, and how short their hotpants are rather than the quality of their game – and this kind of stuff comes from both male and female commentators.

TV is a medium that most politicians still need to master. It plays an important part in most people's lives. But again, in the Commons, few members have the time or the inclination to watch the programmes which are the stuff of workplace chit-chat. It matters that we have some indication of the interests of the people we represent.

Politicians may turn up their noses at the idea of such publicity, but a good appearance on television can boost your election result. It is important for all politicians, especially leaders, to learn the tricks of the trade. Appearing on TV is a splendid opportunity to talk to people when they are relaxing at home. But political parties still regard it as a threat. I opposed the introduction of TV cameras into the House of Commons. I thought it would distract us and turn us into a branch of show business. I was wrong. Apart from Prime Minister's Question Time, what goes on in the Chamber bores most people. The House of Lords gives the impression of being an old folks' home, which is unfair because the Lords often make better speeches and do more useful work than MPs in the Commons.

TV can make a politician into a star or even a megastar. Betty Boothroyd is better known internationally than many film stars. But it can also be your undoing. A party leader who cannot hack it on TV is doomed. No matter how many times you tell people that he or she is wonderful, they will be judged by the standards of the professional actors who are seen on TV every night.

Few people watch or listen to news programmes. They watch chat shows. These have huge audiences and consume celebrities at a great rate. MPs regularly receive invitations to take part – and most turn them down on the grounds that they are beneath their dignity. But there are times – election time, for example – when they can do wonders for your election results.

I try to time an appearance with the run up to an election.

The hugely successful *Mrs Merton* with 12 million viewers, made me a household name in a large area of Basildon New Town, which had recently been attached to my Billericay constituency.

Caroline Aherne wrote to me personally to say how much she would like to meet me. We had something in common: she is an Essex girl, from nearby my constituency, and we have both fought our way through male-dominated professions. Although I had heard that she was tough on her guests, I figured she wouldn't give me too much of a hard time.

Also waiting in the green room was Michael Winner, accompanied by a nymphet. Later, on camera, Michael complained to Caroline about the fact that she was asking him ridiculous questions. Caroline relies on sheets of prepared questions and keeps on until she provokes the right response for her captive audience. And that's the bit you see on the screen.

I did an hour on her couch, I came prepared with some lines of my own. I explained how much I admired her, but suggested that she might look a bit further than Oxfam for her frocks. I also asked her whether she had thought about getting her awful grey wig tinted. 'I'm supposed to be asking the questions,' she informed me tartly. At the end of the day, they record for hours and your best jokes end up on the cutting room floor. This is where I learned that you are there to make the star shine.

No matter. The weekend following the transmission, when I was shopping in the local street market, everyone seemed to recognise me. 'Saw you on the telly last night,' said a stallholder. 'What's Mrs. Merton really like?' Just as with soap stars, people treat these characters as if they were real people. They may not even share my politics, but they knew my name. And there was a chance that this might reflect in the votes cast for me at the next election. That one appearance put me on a shortlist of politicians who are instantly recognised by complete strangers. Once you appear in on a high-rating TV programme, your image changes. You become a real person. But it can cause jealousy. A constituent once stood against me on the grounds that I was using my parliamentary position to further my show business career.

Have I Got News For You attracts even larger audiences than *Mrs. Merton*. After some years of persuasion, I agreed to appear despite my reservations. But before deciding, I consulted other MPs.

Diane Abbot (Labour MP for Hackney North and Stoke Newington) warned me about the show. 'I wish I had never agreed to go on it,' she confided But then she had got off to a bad start with Ian. Ian Hislop, one of the regular panel members and the editor of *Private Eye*, had attacked me in print on more than one occasion. Paul Merton was my partner for the show and is famously left-wing. He made me feel uncomfortable; perhaps he meant to. But I was not to be put off. When he made a dodgy impression of Ringo Starr, only to be told that it was 'too musically accurate' by Angus Deayton, I replied that it was 'too musically horrible if you get it in your left ear'. The audience loved it, but Paul made it clear that he made the jokes, although I do not think he disapproved of me as a person.

The presenter, Angus Deayton is the star of the show. For weeks after my appearance, complete strangers would ask me what kind of person Angus was off-screen. Some months later, on a plane to Lisbon, the stewardess serving packed lunches in economy class could hardly wait to ask about him. The passengers on either side put down their newspapers and joined in. Even the people in the seats behind were listening. It was as if the whole plane wanted to get in on the conversation. I had become a proxy for the real thing.

The brothers Dimbleby monopolise the political chat shows. David is far more relaxed on TV's *Question Time* and treats it more as entertainment. But Jonathan, who chairs radio's *Any Questions,* is very politically correct even in the way he introduces you. He has succeeded in making me feel uncomfortable on more than one occasion

That said, Jonathan does not hold the monopoly when it comes to quips about guests in their introduction. When Edwina Currie appeared on *Have I Got News For You* in 1993, Angus introduced her by saying that she was due to star in a TV advert with a number of gameboys – later she found out that they were just computer toys.

Jonathan suffered from poor eyesight and wore thick glasses. On a trip back to London after appearing on the show, I filled the time by talking about the importance of eye contact on TV, telling him about my own experiences with contact lenses and that I had recently discovered an operation that can permanently correct your sight.

Some time later, as we again travelled together to an *Any Questions* destination, I noticed that he was no longer wearing his ultra-thick glasses.

'Have you had the operation?' I enquired as an opener to our conversation.

'How do you know?'

'Because I've had the operation too. Don't you remember? We talked about it the last time we met.'

He looked at me strangely.

'You've had a vasectomy?' he asked, incredulously.

'My God! I was talking about your eyes, not your ... er, um ...' I stammered.

Jonathan raised his eyebrows and explained earnestly that he had in fact had an operation, but not on his eyes. I thought it was quite funny, but he didn't seem to share the joke. The conversation dried up; I knew then that he would never learn to love me. He buried his head in the newspaper and we didn't speak again until we arrived at our destination. It was not the best beginning to my appearance on the show.

Some people may think that politicians who appear on these shows demean their office. I disagree. But I do acknowledge that it can cost you dear with the Whips – who are looking for team players, not MPs with stars in their eyes!

Chapter Thirteen

WOMEN IN THE HOUSE

'Whatever women do, they must do twice as well as men to be though half as good.'
CHARLOTTE WHITTON

There is a little-known room behind the Speaker's Chair called the Ladies' Room. I call it Heartbreak House. It is here that you see, in microcosm, the strains that our ridiculous working hours place on women MPs. The small, oak-panelled room is barely twelve feet square and is furnished with a Knowle sofa, an armchair and two small desks. Women of all parties pop in to read the newspapers, catch a news programme on the TV monitor or change their outfit for a speaking engagement. There is an ironing board and an old-fashioned iron for members who want to smooth out their creases, which dates from the days when all Conservative women MPs would automatically change into a dinner dress after 7 p.m., as they did when I first entered the House in 1987. In those days, Tory women MPs never dreamed of wearing trousers to the Commons. On the odd occasion when I rushed back to vote wearing a trouser suit, a dozen or more of my male colleagues would tut tut as if I had forgot to put on any trousers at all. Their eyes also popped when, on a rainy day I wore a bright red shiny raincoat or black shiny boots. To me it demonstrated the gulf between the old-fashioned world within Parliament and the progress that women were making in the world outside. It was the Labour women who broke the ice, led by Margaret Beckett with her huge wardrobe of smart trouser-suits and her taste for sexy high-heeled shoes. Her clothes belie her determination to succeed in a man's world. 'If you want to be taken seriously in politics,' she advised me, 'never smile and never make jokes.' Unfortunately, I did not heed her advice. She has one of the most successful careers within the Labour Party, and has held just about every political office in Parliament except that of prime minister.

Some women use the Ladies' Room for a brief after-lunch siesta on the sofa or a snooze in the evening. Men tend to take these short breaks in the library, stretched out on the long leather armchairs that were especially designed with them in mind. Sometimes, when we are voting late into the night, the windows in the library vibrate to the sound of their snores.

On their way to and from the Chamber, women use the Ladies' Room as a port of call, stopping off to powder their nose and use the telephones, the most important items in the room. There are hundreds of telephones all over the Commons, including rows of telephone kiosks for members who want to have private conversations. But remarkably, many women MPs seem quite happy to carry on the most intimate and personal phone calls when maybe four or five women from other parties are present. There is an unspoken understanding that this is a private place even though other women are present. By way of contrast, it is commonly acknowledged that the most important conversations between the men take place in the loos.

At 7 o'clock you hear women pouring their hearts out, dealing with family problems or just saying goodnight to their children. If ever there was a reason why we ought to change the hours that the House of Commons sits, this is it. Why should women – or men for that matter – who want to contribute to public life sacrifice their family because a committee of old fogies who control the Commons working hours, like to hang around in the House until all hours? The Leader of the House uses the excuse that there is so much legislation that it cannot be fitted into a normal working day. That's nonsense. Work expands to fill the time available, and the House of Commons is no exception. The work of the House of Commons Chamber is geared to the needs of men of a bygone age – mainly lawyers – who practise in the courts until 4 p.m. In those days there was less legislation. Governments did not try to regulate and control every aspect of people's lives.

The rivalry between political opponents evaporates as soon as you enter the Ladies' Room. There is a camaraderie between women from opposite ends of the political spectrum. You can chat with someone from the opposition about clothes, sport, holidays and even criticise your own side in just the same way that you would with one of your own colleagues. On the other hand, some people in your own party sometimes cannot bring themselves even to speak to you because they disapprove so strongly with your political views.

Women call their husbands or lovers, their mothers and their close friends. It is inevitable that it crosses your mind that while the hours are so long – sometimes mid-morning until midnight – and the Whips are so ruthless, this is a job that young women with young families should perhaps think carefully about before taking it up. The Whips make no exceptions for family mumps or measles. No matter what the problem, their role is to bring out the vote and even with a large majority, both parties are reluctant to treat women any differently from male colleagues. This conflicts with New Labour's demands for better treatment for women in the workplace where a sixteen-hour day would not be tolerated, and in most cases is illegal.

When you overhear the conversations taking place at around 7 p.m., the dramatic effect on children's lives is obvious. Sometimes you hear women MPs discussing family matters with their partners or the school day with children, or simply trying to send the young ones happily off to bed.

'How was your day at school?'

'What lessons did you have?'

'Have you done your homework?'

'Have you been good for nanny?'

'Did you eat your supper?'

'Are you going to go to bed like a good child?'

One by one the children come to the phone for a brief, intimate conversation. For a woman MP whose constituency is far from London, the chances are that she may not have seen her children for days at a time. This must surely be tough on the mothers, and doubtless makes them feel guilty. It is difficult to reconcile the fact that so much of their time in the Commons is wasted, buried in paperwork, or just hanging around in the evenings to vote at 10 p.m. or even later.

A former woman colleague, a Conservative MP, confided in me her dilemma. She had unexpectedly won a seat in a traditionally Labour constituency. Her family home was in the Cotswolds, where her two young daughters were looked after by a nanny. During the week she lived in a tiny flat in London and spent most of her weekends in her constituency in the Midlands dealing with a busy 'surgery' and other engagements. It cost her all she earned just to maintain the situation; eventually it cost her her marriage. 'It's hell,' she told me. 'I wish I had waited until the children had grown up.' Nor is she the only woman to find the situation intolerable. A number of women New Labour MPs have decided to quit after one term in the House putting their parliamentary career on hold.

Sometimes you hear women MPs having rows with their rebellious teenagers, trying to discipline them. Often the conversation ends with a demand to speak to their father and having a argument with him. MPs, like families all over the land, face teenage problems over drugs and alcohol, as even Tony Blair knows from first-hand experience. But if you are away from home and your partner also has a demanding job, inevitably, the chances are that problems will multiply.

Most young mothers in the Commons have one or sometimes two nannies looking after their children. The nannies are a vital part of their lives – without them even more younger women would probably resign their seats, unable to juggle two impossibly demanding lives.

All governments are intent on getting their legislation through and on some occasions, even the sick are forced back to vote. But when I overheard a junior woman minister talking to her mother, who was obviously extremely ill, I seriously wondered whether it is necessary to continue such inhumane practices.

'Mummy, did you try to eat something today?'

'You must do as the doctor tells you, you really must try to eat. I'm sorry, but I just can't be with you. I have to do a debate tomorrow. The Whips won't let me off.'

When she put the phone down, she had tears in her eyes.

'Is your mother very ill?' I asked her. She nodded.

'She's dying.'

'Isn't there anyone else who can be with her?'

'I'm the only child.'

'Why don't you tell the Whips to go to hell?'

'I can't, I have a debate tomorrow and I must prepare my speech.'

'Let someone else do it. What does it matter?'

Women do face special problems in those circumstances. A man would probably have a woman in the background who would cope. If women ask for special consideration – especially if they are aspiring ministers – they are in danger of appearing to put their families before their parliamentary duty. It is fundamentally wrong that MPs – men or women – should be made to feel their jobs and their future depends on them being in the Commons, day and night if necessary, even when clearly their heart and their sense of duty screams out that they should be somewhere else.

* * * * *

At the 1997 general election, over one hundred Blair Babes arrived in Parliament, quite a number of whom had not expected to win a seat. Some of them won their seats because they were on women-only shortlists. And some of them have lived to regret their election. None of this means that we should put up with so few women in the Commons. It makes a powerful case for adapting Commons procedures to the demands of this century.

I made two attempts to amend our electoral laws to enable more women to be elected, and I think there is a role for older women like myself – freed from domestic duties – to play a much bigger role in the way our country is run. Our experience of life – and our common sense – can inject some more down-to-earth thinking into the corridors of power.

I get sick and tired of seeing those gatherings of international politicians – smiling smugly and not a single woman in the picture since Margaret's departure. A Martian tuning in to TV Planet Earth would assume that the world is run by creatures in grey suits – and that the creatures in skirts only take part in entertainment.

It has been over eighty years since women got the vote in Britain and the first woman MP, Lady Astor, arrived at the House of Commons. Few women have made it into the Cabinet in that time, not because they weren't good enough but because they didn't stay long enough to get their feet on the ladder that leads to promotion. Many women MPs have been elected for only one term of Parliament, because they are rarely selected for a safe seat. Betty Boothroyd tried for sixteen years, and Shirley Williams fought four seats before being elected. Few women have the resources to spend the time needed to nurse a constituency that may be miles from home.

Does this really matter? In the old days, Parliament assembled to raise taxes to fight the monarch's wars. Today, most of the money goes on social services. Women who manage homes and bring up children know where the shoe pinches, and keep an eye on the price of everything. The Blair Babes may not have performed miracles, but they changed the atmosphere. Women are no longer an oddity in Parliament and some have plenty of useful things to say.

Women today are more educated, articulate and able, and display the potential for high office.

Of course, there are ineffective women just as there are ineffective men, but acting together, they could do wonders to break the taboos in all areas of public life – not least in the law courts and other professions that are dominated by men.

When it comes to policies that matter to women, Parliament is completely myopic. The things that concern a woman most – housing, children, shopping, and healthcare for her family – are all tied up in laws in which women have hardly any say.

* * * * *

If ever there was an example of the need for more women in the House, it occurred during the debate on the CSA (Child Support Agency) set up by the Conservative government to reduce the burden on the taxpayer of supporting the children of divorced parents. The divorce courts were in the habit of deciding that child benefit and housing benefit could take care of most of the financial need; as a result, government spending in this area had reached crisis point. The unenviable role of the CSA was to assess the means of the father not only to support his children, but also their mother, if they were in her care, until the children left school

Fathers claimed that many women did not inform the CSA of a change in circumstances, for instance taking a new partner or a new job, for fear of losing support for their children from their estranged husband. That may well have been true in some circumstances but it seemed to me that most male MPs were using this pretext to bring so much discredit on the new law that it would eventually be scrapped.

I was desperately keen to state my views during the debate. The House was packed. Every member had a story to tell about one or more of their constituents. Raising matters in the House can result in a report of the speech in the local papers. This subject touched a remarkable number of people across the social divide and across the entire country.

There is a tradition in the House that a member who wants to speak in a debate drops a note to the Speaker's clerk 'hoping to catch the Speaker's eye'. I put in a request. Senior members of the House are given priority in the speaking order, and these are overwhelmingly men. One after another, Betty Boothroyd called them to speak despite the fact that a number of women, including myself, were trying our damndest to be called. The debate was in danger of becoming a one-sided argument. Of course, Betty was following tradition, but, as the time wore on, not a single woman had been called. I appealed to the Speaker, who was not best pleased.

I pointed out that although the debate had been running for over one hour not one single woman had yet been called to speak. All the men called had been pointing out how unfair the legislation was towards fathers and not one male MP had by then said a single word putting forward the woman's point of view. Betty was clearly angry at my intervention and rebuked me for daring to criticise the way that she was conducting the debate.

Being ticked-off by the Speaker is a chastening experience for any MP. There is no other higher authority to whom a member can appeal. My intervention had little effect. The debate continued roughly along the same lines, with more men going over the same ground, all speaking on behalf of disgruntled and angry fathers. It seemed to me that the male MPs on both sides of the House strongly empathised with the fathers and some were absolutely hostile to the woman's point of view. I hardly heard a word said on behalf of the mothers.

Towards the end of the long debate, Betty Boothroyd did call one or two women, including myself. This was a debate in which gender was of paramount importance, but it was hopelessly unbalanced.

This was a prime example of a situation in which if there had been more women MPs in the House, the whole tone of the debate would have been more balanced and rational.

Thankfully, the debate to change the legislation was lost and millions of women bringing up children on their own were finally financially safeguarded.

* * * * *

Even though I had several spats in the chamber with Betty Boothroyd, there was never any animosity between us. I had campaigned for her to become Speaker despite the fact that she was a Labour MP. Indeed, on occasions during a slow night in the Commons, Betty would beckon me over to the Speaker's Chair and compliment me on something I was wearing. Betty loved clothes. Whispering, she would ask, 'Where did you get that? It looks really lovely!'

On one such occasion, I had just returned from the

International Menopause Conference in Seoul, South Korea, where a number of internationally known dress-makers were having their clothes manufactured. 'You could pick up some terrific bargains there,' I told her. 'And, we stopped over in Hong Kong on the return journey and visited the famous Stanley Market, where lots of model clothes were going for a song.'

Betty seemed excited at this bit of news. 'You must tell me the next time you're going. I would love to go with you.' I was quite taken aback. It would never have occurred to me that someone in her position would enjoy rummaging through the street markets of Hong Kong.

On more than one boring night in the Chamber we would chat about this and that – hairdos, expanding waistlines and whether we took enough exercise. Betty confided that she always did her own immaculate head of hair and we both agreed that we found the parliamentary gym boring. Instead, Betty told me she kept her joints moving with a regular massage in the privacy of her Commons flat – much nicer than rowing machines.

* * * * *

When I started out in life, women were still regarded as the property of their husbands. They could not borrow money or raise a mortgage without a man to guarantee it – a problem I encountered when I first went into business. The attitude that women are somehow not up to the job still prevails in the nooks and crannies of Parliament, witness the criticism levelled at the so-called Blair's Babes. The difficulties of pushing yourself into the debate are daunting enough for experienced politicians, so it was not surprising that – as a whole – these women did not make an impact. But then, neither do men.

From Plato to John Stuart Mill, people have been critical about the subjugation of women. But the Christian Church believed that in marriage a man and a woman became one person – with the man on top. There are still many in the Church who believe it. This became obvious in the ferocious debate in the Church of England over the appointment of women priests.

John Gummer, one-time Conservative Party Chairman and a former Secretary of State for the Environment, liked to boast of his membership of the Synod of the Church of England; he paraded his Christian views in the Chamber. When the debate on women priests was raging in the country, he took a high profile stand against it. One night, as we lined up in the voting lobby, I asked him casually, 'Why do men who love God hate women?'

He exploded. 'How dare you say that! It's not true! I love and cherish my wife but I do not want a woman preaching at me from the pulpit.'

Eventually the Synod capitulated. Women were admitted to the Church of England as priests. I am not religious, but I went to Church that Sunday to witness the swearing in of the first woman priest in my constituency.

Soon after, I again found myself in the voting lobby next to John.

'Now that we know that men who love God don't hate women, where does that leave you?'

John was beside himself with rage. Later, I bumped into his delightful wife, Penny. She gave me a flea in my ear for criticising her husband. 'Of course he respects women. He's a wonderful father and husband,' she insisted.

'But does he regard us as equals?' I asked her. There was no reply.

There are plenty of men in the Commons who still think like John Gummer. They sit on both sides of the House, making lewd remarks about women on the benches opposite. They block all attempts to change the working hours to make it easier for women to participate as if politics were their fiefdom instead of the jury of the country where women have a proper place. They object to special arrangements for women, who, on rare occasions, need time off to attend to a family crisis while at the same time legislating for these concessions from employers.

I am not a raging feminist, but I believe that it is essential that women play a full part in government. There is only one way to achieve this. We must change the franchise.

The Tories are not the only chauvinists in the House. Far from it, as I discovered when I made my maiden speech soon after arriving in the House. This ordeal is a bit like the first audition for a play. It is given before a sparsely attended chamber and is traditionally heard in silence, apart from a few hear-hears from members on your own side of the House, who are there to give you encouragement. As I rose to speak, I noticed, side-by-side on the Labour benches opposite, Dennis Skinner MP and his sidekick Brian Sedgemore – Labour's answer to Laurel and Hardy. No sooner had I opened my mouth than I heard the cry from the opposite benches:

'Here she comes, Harvey Procter in drag' – a reference to my predecessor. Dennis Skinner has always denied that he made that remark, and he was not in the habit of denying authorship of any of his quips, but if he didn't, he must be a ventriloquist as well as Parliament's stand-up comedian. Whichever one of them said it, or if it was someone else, it was designed to put me off my stroke and it succeeded. And now I had to overcome another problem. It is traditional for the new MP to praise her predecessor. As I attempted to regain my composure and carry on, there came another comment from the same direction.

'She's got more hormones in her than a Christmas turkey' – a quip lifted from *Private Eye*.

This was turning out to be less of a dignified contribution to Parliamentary tradition and more like a Victorian music hall act.

'Order, order,' shouted Mr. Speaker Weatherall, in the role of Master of Ceremonies, 'the Honourable Lady must be heard in silence.'

On another occasion, I watched as Edward Heath rose from his favourite corner seat on the front bench like a bear from a pit and began to speak. Dame Elaine Kellett-Bowman, who worshipped Margaret Thatcher, always made sure that she was sitting behind him. As soon as he began his speech, she started to heckle him. I didn't know what, on this occasion, made him rise to the bait, but he paused in mid-sentence and turned towards her.

'I have been heckled by the Honourable Lady for twenty years, Mr. Speaker,' he said. 'Will someone get this woman off my back!'

Elaine Kellett-Bowman also seemed to have a grudge against me, ever since her husband failed to get selected as an MEP for Essex, for which she possibly blamed me. I too was given the Heath treatment. Every time I rose to speak, she cried, 'Silly woman, silly woman,' like a parrot. But I was not as brave as Heath – I moved my place to another part of the Chamber. In true Tory fashion, Elaine was in due course, created a Dame of the British Empire. If only I had kept my mouth shut!

There is very little room in politics for people with strong convictions. Most Conservative MPs and most prime ministers are pragmatists averse to changes in society. They prefer not to disturb the status quo, but rather to try to make it more tolerable. John Major was in that mould; Margaret Thatcher was the exception to the rule.

It is not only MPs, but also lobby correspondents, who manifest a streak of chauvinism. Matthew Parris, who swapped his job as a Tory MP for one in the Press Gallery, once wrote in his *Times* column that whenever Emma Nicholson addressed the Chamber, 'her nipples stuck out delightfully'. Emma was not amused. But the adrenaline rush when you rise to speak, which doubtless brought about Emma's predicament, also affects men – a fact that I have never seen mentioned.

It was probably his affair with his secretary, which was all over the newspapers at the time, that made Paddy Ashdown extra nervous at Prime Minister's Question Time on one particular occasion. Instead of the ritual barracking that usually greeted his performance, the House fell silent, riveted not so much by his remarks as by ... more obvious, pressing events. Next day I scoured the gossip columns in vain; no mention of his predicament appeared.

On another occasion, as I sat patiently waiting for the opportunity to speak in a debate, a senior colleague, sitting behind me – a man with great experience of the Chamber – rose to speak. Obviously nervous, his hands clasped behind his back, he swayed back and forth to as if to emphasise the points he was making. As I listened, I became aware of something lightly tapping the back of my head. I turned and what I saw made me quickly adjust my position, sliding sideways on the bench so as the avoid the distraction.

Fortunately perhaps for him, the Press Gallery was nearly empty and the Hansard writers, the people who compile the daily record of the House's proceedings, report only what is said in the Chamber. But occasionally, the record does mention 'interruptions' and sometimes records that 'a member rose'.

Not all Parliamentary members are chauvinists   far from it. One of my favourite people was James Douglas Hamilton MP, second son of Duke Hamilton and a Minister in the Scottish Office. It wasn't his title or his stately home that fascinated me. It was his upper-class lisp and his impeccable manners that I found so endearing. Unbeknown to either of us, we both travelled to Edinburgh on the same train, he in first class on government business and me in standard on my way to address the students at Edinburgh University. As I was wandered along the platform, waiting for my student escort to appear, Lord James, as he was always called, spotted me.

'Teresha,' he said, 'How nish it is to see you. May I ashk what you are doing here alone on thish platform?'

'I'm waiting for a student from Edinburgh University to give me a lift – he's a bit late.'

'Then I will give you a lift, I inshisht.'

'It's kind, but not necessary,' I replied, enchanted nevertheless.

'Then I will wait with you until your lift arrives, I can't leave you here all alone. It might be dangeroush.'

Surrounded by his flunkies – who were waiting to escort him to his official car – he absolutely insisted on remaining with me until my escort, in a battered old green VW, arrived to collect me. Not many ministers would have done that. Power usually goes to their heads. When they acquire the government car and the paraphernalia of office, they forget all about the likes of back-benchers. Late at night, when you are hurrying from your office to the Commons to vote, they swish past you in their chauffeur-driven ministerial cars – even honking their horns for you to get out of the way. They never stop to give you a lift. Only James Douglas Hamilton was a shining exception to the rule. His courtesy was not reserved for women MPs. Whenever he left the ministry for an engagement, he made a bee-line for the driver's door, and opened it for his female chauffeur, before climbing into the back seat.

Chapter Fourteen

SECOND AMONGST EQUALS

'We are here to claim our right as women,
not only to be free, but to fight for freedom.'
CHRISTABEL PANKHURST

Anyone who thinks that the law treats women fairly should try reading Jill Saward's book, *Rape*. She describes her hideous ordeal, which occurred just after her twenty-first birthday, at the hands of three thugs who broke into the family home, a vicarage in Ealing, intent on theft. Jill was a quiet girl who had little knowledge of men. Her family life had brought Jill a different perspective on life to that experienced by many teenage girls of the time. The intruders threatened Jill's family with knives, and as if as an afterthought, two of them subjected her to the most revolting sexual assault.

At their trial, the judge gave the perpetrators five years for buggery and indecent assault; according to the judge, Jill's trauma was 'not so great'. The sentences caused an uproar at the time and Jill's MP, Harry Greenway, presented a Bill to the House of Commons calling for anonymity for the victims of rape, who are put through an additional ordeal at the trial.

In the foreword of her book, Jill writes: 'Rape is totally and utterly destructive, striking right at the roots of a person's sense of self and worth. I would not have believed that the events of one hour on 6 March 1986 could have such devastating effects.'

I read newspaper accounts at the time but it was not until 1990, when I read Jill's personal account of her ordeal, that I was spurred on to examine the whole area of crimes against women. What I learned made me angry. Clearly nothing had happened to improve things or to curtail the inappropriate comments and sentences handed down by judges.

It was not until some years later, after another spate of rape trials, more inappropriate comments by judges and more totally inadequate sentences, that I raised the subject during questions on the floor of the House. 'Does the Home Secretary deplore the soft sentences doled out to rapists by geriatric judges and would he agree with the view of most women – that we should cut off their goolies?' I demanded.

The House gasped – my intention was to shock, and I succeeded. The reaction of the men in the Commons was an indication of the effect that such a measure might have on potential male offenders. Since my remarks – but not necessarily because of them – major changes have taken place in the way rape cases are handled, to give more respect to the victim, although we still have some way to go.

The subject of violence towards women continued to interest me. Nearby my constituency was Bullwood Hall Prison – an all-woman prison – where ninety high-security prisoners were held. They included a number who were serving life sentences for murdering their husbands or partners after years of abuse. Women in abusive relationships rarely kill in anger – in which case they could plead manslaughter. They are too busy trying to stay alive as some evil brute batters them. They wait for their chance to rid themselves of their tormentor and often kill while their partner is asleep in a drunken stupor.

Southall Black Sisters, an organisation that specialises in helping women caught in this kind of dilemma, wrote to ask me to intervene in two cases that were coming before the Court of Appeal. Kirangit Ahluwalia poured fuel over her abuser and set light to him while he slept; her appeal was eventually upheld. In another case, Sara Thornton stabbed her husband. Her case was brought to my attention by Justice for Women and she too won her appeal. This may seem – indeed, it is – an horrific act, but Kirangit's actions would not have been an uncommon way of dealing with abuse in her country of origin.

I arranged to visit the prison where I met the two women and thirteen other inmates serving sentences for murder. We met, without prison guards at their requests, in a locked room. I listened in despair at the ordeals that some of them had endured. One Asian woman, with nine children, had made several attempts to escape from the family home, where she was regularly beaten. Each time, members of her community returned her to her tormentor. Over the years, she had almost every bone in her body broken: she showed me facial and body scars from her wounds and most of her teeth had been knocked out. And now she found herself in prison with a life sentence. Of course, not all of these women had killed after years of abuse, but those who had made enough of an impression on me for me to decide to see the then Conservative Home Secretary John Patten.

Together with a small group of MPs, both Labour and Conservative, we discussed a change in the law so that women in this dilemma could plead manslaughter. John Patten was not sympathetic. 'I can't believe you approve of people killing in cold blood, or that the law should be changed to accommodate them,' he said to me. 'Why don't they report the abuse to the police?'

'Have you any idea what it feels like to crouch in a corner while someone kicks the daylights out of you?' I replied. 'Do you really think you can dust yourself down and storm off to the police station? Some of these women are never let out of the house without an escort. Some do run away and are returned by members of their own community. Some can't even speak English.'

I was infuriated at his dismissive attitude. He clearly thought the case we were making was not of any great importance. Later, we again raised our case, this time with Lord McKay, the Lord Chancellor and head of the legal profession, who listened with great sympathy. His response was very different.

'I do realise that women could find themselves in an impossible situation,' he conceded. 'We must review the law – and we must also look for other ways to help.'

There is no need to incarcerate these women for life. Many have no history of crime or violence. On the contrary, they are driven to act as their only means of self defence – or even survival. They fear for their children and that is why they stay in the relationship so long, despite the violence.

The law in this respect still awaits amendment. A few women, with the support of outside bodies, manage to mount an appeal against their sentence. This is not easy or cheap. It requires acute legal brains to make their case convincingly. Only the most educated and the most articulate are likely to succeed in even bringing an appeal.

Women are generally not involved in serious crime and they very rarely kill other adults. I believe that women would get a more sympathetic response over a whole range of issues if we had more women judges. Even today, only eight out of the 105 High Court judges are female. These posts, at the top of the legal profession are invariable filled by men with thirty to forty years' continuous service in the law. Women usually take career breaks for family reasons. I have argued that domestic experience is likely to make them even better judges. Once again, women are required to play the game by the rules laid down with a man's career structure in mind. Judging is not just a matter of knowledge but of experience of human behaviour. Women judges could also be recruited from the ranks of experienced magistrates. With technical support from their clerks, they could be just as good as their male counterparts. Yet with more and more women entering into the legal profession, mainly as solicitors, we still wait for a Lord Chancellor who will lob a grenade into the antediluvian, male-dominated legal profession, and blow it out of its past and into the future.

As a result of the publicity that my parliamentary question attracted, three young women solicitors wrote to me on the subject of 'common law wives'. The had written a book called *Living Together*, in which they explained the problems facing women who were not married to their partners. They outlined the case of two policemen who were killed while working as divers. One was married to his partner, so his wife had full rights to his pensions and their joint possessions. In the other case, the relationship was not a formal marriage, so the woman got nothing – no pension, no house and no possessions.

A more recent example is the family of SAS trooper Brad Tinnion, who was killed not long ago in Sierra Leone. His long-term partner was refused a war pension, even though she is named the chief beneficiary in his will. His daughter was granted a pension until she is seventeen. This was not a casual relationship. The two had lived together all of their adult lives. A formal contract between two people (of whatever gender) should be allowed by law to cover these examples of injustice.

Many people wrongly believe that the law confers the same rights on women in a long-standing relationship that apply in marriage. This is not the case, and all hell can break loose in a dispute if the male partner dies and his family choose to claim not only their joint property but even the children of the relationship.

I was not aware of this. I imagine many of my colleagues were ignorant of the fact too. So I arranged for the solicitors to visit Lord McKay in his apartments in the House of Lords. These are the rooms since made famous by the extravagant decorations installed by the high and mighty Lord Irvine. But James McKay was a very modest man – a lovely man – with a delicious soft Scottish voice and a delicious sense of humour. Even the 'speak your floor' lifts in the House of Lords developed a Scottish accent. His sympathetic response led eventually to a clause to legalise relationships other than marriage being included in the Family Bill going through Parliament. But it was not to be. Several women on the Conservative benches, led by Elaine Kellett-Bowman, objected violently to condoning 'living in sin' and threatened to hold up the legislation. The clause was eventually dropped.

I tried again to raise the subject in a Ten Minute Rule Bill, which I called the Cohabitation (Contract Enforcement Bill), but this is gesture politics. And there the matter rests. It is an area of the law that could have been reformed if a sufficient number of Blair Babes had insisted on it. A possible revolt by a hundred members would be more than enough to force the government to act. It is on these occasions that you realise how important it is to have a larger number of women prepared to act jointly to improve the position of women in society as a whole.

* * * * *

There is a tendency for the Conservative Party to insist on supporting an idealised modern family in which the parents are married with two or three children, who will be encouraged to stay together if the government gives them sufficient support through the tax structure. This media myth of the 'cereal box' nuclear family hides the varied reality of what people describe as family life. One-parent, reconstituted, foster, communal and cohabitation families are only some of the variations, giving proof of the family's durability through social, economic and historical changes.

One in three marriages may end in divorce, but that leaves two-thirds successful. Marriage statistics however, are not the most reliable indicator of the family's existence. Behind closed doors, families juggle an incredible variety of arrangements, adapting to changing circumstances. Mothers who go to work, or look after grandparents, fathers faced with redundancy, and children struggling with adolescence are just some examples of the variety of set-ups that fall under the umbrella of the word 'family'.

They may represent havens of safety and refuge from the world, but some families also breed the very violence from which they are supposed to protect their members.

A high percentage of violent crimes – particularly those against children, wives and the elderly – are more likely to be committed by other members of the victim's family than by anyone else in society. These troubled families are the staple diet of councillors, therapists and children's homes.

Conservative policy needs to adapt to these variable circumstances. The way to do it is not through tax breaks, family allowances and other financial bribes, but by leaving people with their own resources to manage their own affairs. Before 1939 you had to earn the equivalent of £40,000 a year before income tax was deducted from your pay packet, now taxes begin at £5,000. Instead of cultivating a universal dependence on the state, we should encourage families to be self-reliant and self-sufficient. Not the begging bowl, but the power of the market will deliver the services they require. But first, politicians must resist the temptation to provide everything for them. They must be left with enough money in their pocket to pay for it. And this should be the guiding principle of a future Conservative administration. It would put clear blue water between us and Labour.

* * * * *

It was inevitable, of course, that I would find myself at the epicentre of the abortion debate that has raged, off and on, for years in the Commons. If there is one thing which raises my heckles at 7 o'clock in the morning, it is someone from the Society for the Protection of the Unborn Child [SPUC], usually a man, on the *Today* programme, telling women that they have no right to control their own fertility.

Simone de Beauvoir, the left-wing philosopher, said that the free market had done more to liberate women than the State – and the contraceptive pill is, in my opinion, its greatest gift.

Before this century, women were very lucky if they lived beyond fifty, worn out with endless child bearing and the incredible drudgery of trying to put food in the mouths of their children. The attitude of women of an earlier generation was summed up for me when, as a young teacher, a mother of six was called in by the headmistress about one of her disruptive children.

'Why do you let him do it to you?' the headmistress asked sympathetically, referring to her obvious pregnancy, 'You can't even manage the children you have.'

'Oh Miss, if it wasn't for the disgrace of it, I'd rather be single like you,' she replied.

So when bachelor David Alton MP decided to introduce a bill to turn the clock back twenty-one years, it was a foregone conclusion that I would oppose him. It was the most serious challenge yet to a woman's right to obtain a safe and legal abortion, which is already made difficult and sometimes dangerous by the complicated rules laid down by the government.

The original bill introduced by David Steele in the 1960s was heavily supported by the Home Office, primarily because of the concern for the number of young women all over Britain who were dying as a result of botched-up backstreet abortions. Alton's bill sought to reduce the length of time allowed for a woman to make the vital decision whether to have a termination. He wanted to reduce the number of weeks from twenty-four weeks down to fourteen weeks.

Even under the current legislation it is not easy to get an abortion in Britain. The law decrees that a woman must have the consent of two doctors, a process that sometimes take several months not weeks. It often involves women facing sanctimonious criticism from doctors critical of the whole process.

Because of my opposition to Alton's bill, I had no hesitation in becoming part of the large group of women MPs, mainly Labour members, who were dedicated to thwarting him. What did he know about the terrible dilemma facing women who were pregnant against their wishes? Will he ever face a partner who says he just won't support more children? We formed a cross-party *ad hoc* group, mainly composed of women, to fight and defeat the bill. Even Dennis Skinner, whom many women MPs wrongly regarded as the House of Commons tame male chauvinist pig, joined the committee and became our chief bother boy, filibustering where necessary to prevent Alton from pushing the question to a vote.

I hope that my speech demonstrated the insight that women can bring to public life and which is so lacking in the Commons: 'For centuries theologians have equated sex with sin and celibacy with grace. They have regarded women as little more than flower pots in which future generations of children, preferably boy children, are reared. I believe that the great majority of women in this country – and throughout history – would agree that they should have the right, as a man has, to enjoy their sexual nature. Women are grateful for the opportunity that progress and science has given them to control their fertility. If the men in this House, and some of the women, are mindful to deprive women of the benefits of this progress, they should think carefully about their motivation.'

I was also determined to tell the men in the Commons that they must not presume to control women's lives: 'I hope that the majority of my colleagues, perforce mainly male, who do not have to bear the responsibility of an unwanted pregnancy and birth, and who are not faced with this dilemma, will not have the temerity, arrogance, inhumanity and insensitivity to seek to make those decisions for women. As sure as night follows day, women will continue to make these decisions for themselves – if not in this country, then somewhere else. The grand delusion of the House is that we can legislate to force people into different patterns of behaviour. We can indeed make life difficult, but that should not be our business.'

In that speech I was talking from the heart about a subject that I believed was one of the most fundamental problems facing Britain – unwanted pregnancy. I became bolder: 'If I were to take a hand count in the House of people who believe that a woman has a right equal to a man's to enjoy her sexuality, I should probably have all hands up. But if I asked whether a woman had the right to deal with the unforeseen consequences of the overwhelming passion which consumes her, as it does a man, it would be a different story.

'There would be talk of social abortions – when women conceive without being properly prepared, as it is usually described. We are told by the preachers of the pro-life movement that in those circumstances a woman has, to all intents and purposes, sinned and must bear the consequences. They may not use that old-fashioned biblical language, but that is what they mean.

'If the pied piper of Mossley Hill [David Alton] had his way, he would lead the House and the country back to the time when women were the victims of their sexuality – perpetually pregnant, physically worn down, old before their time, unable to find time to develop the other talents with which they were born and always subservient to a man and the demands of an ever-increasing family.'

Claire Short, born and raised in Liverpool, made a particularly impassioned speech about the days of back-street abortions and the awful experiences of women in the community in which she was raised. Listening from the bench in front of me was a minister in our government.

'That old slag would know all about that, wouldn't she,' he said, loud enough to be heard by me and others around him. I was angry. I knew that I should have instantly called the Speaker's attention to the remark. But I also knew that to do that to one of my own colleagues would be considered beyond the pale. If I had complained that, 'My honourable friend is using unparliamentary language,' it was possible that the Speaker would have asked me to repeat the insult.

By doing so, the entire House would have been privy to this insult. It would then have appeared in Hansard and been reported in every national newspaper.

As the debate wore on over months, I became more and more friendly with women on the Labour benches, some of whom in other circumstances regarded my right-wing views as anathema. Stories began to appear in the press of the unlikely friendship between myself and Claire Short. We were dubbed 'the odd couple'. In politics you have to dismiss these pot-boilers for what they are – a way to fill up newspaper columns on a thin weekend. Whenever Claire and I appeared together on a platform, she was determined to distance herself from my views on everything but abortion – and she gave me hell.

As is often the case, the House compromised. But the debate was raised again – in the case of women in Northern Ireland. Abortion remains illegal there, and women have to come to the mainland whenever they feel that they just can't go through with an unwanted pregnancy. The pro-choice lobby, which I support, is making progress. And Labour is inching its way to a more liberal stance, by making the 'morning-after' pill available over the counter.

With two women colleagues, Harriet Harman (Labour) and Jenny Tonge (Lib Dem), I travelled to Holland to inspect their arrangements. Why is it that the Dutch – so close to us in many ways – are so much more grown-up in social matters? There, teenagers are given specific information on birth control – and the 'morning after' pill is easily available. The Dutch pregnancy rate amongst school girls is a fraction of ours. We continue to tolerate an intolerable situation in which young women, hardly more than children themselves, marry the state and raise 'dysfunctional' families. Parliament causes the problem and so far it refuses to face up to the solution.

Chapter Fifteen

MARGARET'S DEMISE

'[Margaret] was a tigress surrounded by hamsters.'

JOHN BIFFEN

It was just three years after my election that Margaret Thatcher's premiership was ended by the men in her own Cabinet. They just could not stand working under the leadership of such a powerful woman, and the economy was in a mess. The chief assassin was Michael Heseltine. He had been after her blood – and her job – since he stormed out of the Cabinet in 1985 after a dispute over a contract for helicopters – the so-called Westland Affair.

Since then, Heseltine had toured the country on the

rubber chicken circuit – ingratiating himself with the grass roots in the constituencies and biding his time. His opportunity came when Margaret left the country on 19 November 1990 to attend a minor conference in Paris, which lasted for three days covering the crucial period when her leadership had to be reaffirmed. This was usually a routine matter, but this time, Heseltine had announced that he would challenge her.

It was the duty of Margaret Thatcher's Parliamentary Private Secretary, Peter Morrison, to keep her informed about what was going on amongst her back-benchers. They were mainly Thatcherites, but they needed encouragement and reassurance about the direction in which she would be leading the country in the run-up to the next election. But by now the Iron Lady had become a remote figure, more interested in international affairs than what was happening in her own backyard.

When Margaret and Nigel Lawson fell out over Alan Walters and the ERM (European Exchange Rate Mechanism) – the prelude to joining the Single European Currency – he resigned and made a bitter attack on her from the back benches. John Major got his job.

Then Sir Geoffrey Howe was removed as Foreign Secretary and made Leader of the House, which he regarded as a demotion. He vented his anger in another bitter resignation speech, allegedly written by his wife, Elspeth, who sat in the box at the side of the Chamber, a smile hovering around her lips as she witnessed the knife going in. Throughout both acts of treachery, Margaret sat on the front bench, her face expressionless.

Geoffrey was an unbelievably boring speaker. In my opinion, his only useful contribution to politics was when, as Chancellor in Margaret's first Cabinet, he abolished the exchange controls, which restricted people to £50 of currency for trips abroad. He, too, had occupied the highest offices under her patronage – and the perks of the job – including the use of a series of grace and favour houses and vast country estates. But there is no gratitude in politics.

Margaret was not without blame for her difficulties. She was barely seen in the tea-room or around the bars of the House of Commons – she had lost contact with her street-fighters on the back benches.

'Why did she go to Paris before the first ballot knowing that her leadership would be challenged while she was away?' asked a colleague in the tea-room.

'It must be the only election contest in her political career she's not personally in charge of,' observed another.

It was a sign of a loss of contact with reality that Margaret seemed so distant from what was going on. Yet she knew the rules. They had been tested the year before, when Sir Anthony Meyer, a complete non-entity, was the stalking-horse who challenged her. She knew it required more than a simple majority to hold on to the leadership and Heseltine was snapping at her heels.

Nick Jones, a BBC lobby correspondent, said that he had never known the Chief Whip to leak information. Normally Whips did not talk so openly with lobby correspondents but now some were intent on spreading black propaganda, saying that Margaret couldn't survive on this occasion. Their blatant feeding of misinformation to journalists was an unprecedented breach of the secrecy that they usually maintain.

It was the umpteenth time I had been on television or radio in the space of a few days in an attempt to defend her reputation. Apart from Cecil Parkinson and Norman Tebbit, the people close to her were all 'unavailable' to the media. They were already distancing themselves from her.

It was almost 8 o'clock when I left the breakfast television studios in the basement of Norman Shaw North, the old Scotland Yard building in Whitehall, and the whole country was transfixed, awaiting Margaret's decision on whether she would continue the fight for her job. The cold, drizzly morning matched my mood of anxiety and deep pessimism. Margaret had the skids under her after failing to win a large enough majority in the first ballot of the challenge to her leadership. Now she was fighting for survival.

I stood in the courtyard outside the TV studio, wondering whether to go back to my office, when Nicholas Bennett, a junior minister, came hurrying across the courtyard towards me.

'She's gone.' The stark remark stung me like a slap in the face.

'She can't have. I've just been on breakfast television sticking up for her.'

'She decided to go at half-past seven this morning,' Nicholas replied.

'We have to stop her,' I insisted.

'We can't. She hasn't got enough support in the Cabinet. Too many of them have ratted on her.'

'Surely not Michael Portillo and Peter Lilley?' I said in amazement.

'No, not the No Turning Back people or Kenneth Baker. But most of the rest.' Nicholas, a combative, pugnacious character, was himself one of the loyally Thatcherite No Turning Back group. 'Some of the group went to see her last night. They had to fight their way past Tim Renton [the Chief Whip]. They stayed for ages, trying to talk her out of her resignation, but I think her mind was already made up. They were almost in tears when they came back.'

The group had been having dinner together when a call had come from Michael Portillo, who was in Downing Street. He wanted them to come around urgently to talk to Margaret, who was still considering what to do. Cabinet colleagues such as Tim Renton and John Gummer were telling her that she could not win a second ballot; they were knocking down every argument her supporters put up.

'They went back this morning at six-thirty but Charles Powell [her Private Secretary] refused them admission – they were told it was too early to see her. They waited downstairs but by seven-thirty she had already asked Powell to make an appointment with the Queen. She had decided to go. They couldn't save her.' It was this information that Nicholas was hurrying to convey to the breakfast news audience.

'Is there nothing we can do?'

'Nothing. She's gone. Now we have to act quickly to make

sure we don't get landed with the wrong person. I'm going back to the Commons to start canvassing.' And with that, he was gone.

As he walked away, I stood paralysed by feelings of despair, anger and total inadequacy. How could they do this to Margaret after everything she had done for the country? Little did I know that the anger I felt would soon be a drop in the ocean compared to the rage that was about to engulf the Party.

I walked quickly, I wanted to get home to hear what was being said on television. In a daze, I crossed New Palace Yard, where Margaret's friend Airey Neave had been murdered when his car was blown up by the IRA just before she became prime minister. It was almost deserted at that hour in the morning, except for the security men. I nodded briefly to the policeman at Members' Entrance and moved quickly through the members' cloakroom, which is just like the ones in infants' schools: we each have our own peg and we are still issued with a pick sash at the beginning of term, in which to place a sword – presumably for stabbing into opponents' backs.

As I passed a group of telephone boxes at the end of the gloomy corridor, I stopped. I decided to phone Jim to tell him the news. As I pushed open the wooden door and stepped inside the phone box, David Evans, came around the corner.

'She's gone,' he said, his plump face sad and droopy.

'I know. It's terrible. What are we going to do?' David, a staunch Thatcher supporter, put his arms around me. That was too much. Suddenly I was sobbing uncontrollably.

'The bastards. They all owe their careers to her and now they've torn her down.'

'I know. I know. But she's gone now and we've got to think quickly about who will follow her.' I replied.

'I'm backing Heseltine,' David announced.

I was taken aback. Heseltine had challenged Margaret in the first ballot. I had him down as the villain of the piece.

'Heseltine! You can't possibly. Not after what he's done to her.'

'But he's our best performer. Look at what a mess the economy is in. We need someone who knows how to run a business.'

'I wouldn't vote for Heseltine if he was the last man alive,' I told him.

David produced a large handkerchief and started to dab my cheeks. 'Do you want me to take you for a cup of tea?' he asked, kindly.

'No, I'll stay here until I've calmed down and then I'm going home for some breakfast.' My tears under control, I made my way across the vast expanse of Westminster Hall where members of the Royal Family lie in state and where Charles I was tried and condemned to death. As I began to descend the steps that led out to the street, one of the policemen stopped me.

'Have you heard the news?' he asked. 'Is it true? Is the Prime Minister going?' He sounded shaken.

I nodded and looked up. The tears began to pour down my face once again.

'I can't walk out of here like this,' I said in exasperation.

'Why don't you come into our rest-room till you get a grip of yourself?' said the policeman guiding me through the side door. 'Here, have a bit of chewing gum. That might help you.'

'You have some. You're crying too,' I said as two large tears rolled down his cheeks. 'The bastards,' I added.

'You're right. They are bastards,' he agreed, emotion choking his voice.

It emerged during the leadership challenge that two of Margaret's most vociferous opponents were women, both of whom owed her their career: Edwina Currie and Emma Nicholson. Edwina was appointed Minister of Health by Margaret. And Emma's attempts to find a Conservative seat were boosted when Margaret made her the party's vice-chairman with responsibility for women. Emma later defected to the Liberal Democrats and was rewarded by them with a seat in the Lords.

Angela Rumbold, a minister in Margaret's government, suggested we should have farewell lunch as a mark of sympathy. Margaret was asked if she would accept the invitation. She replied that it was a lovely idea but that neither Emma or Edwina were to be invited.

The lunch took place in a private room at L'Amigos in Horseferry Road, a favourite watering-hole of MPs and not far from Westminster. The lunch was long, relaxed and friendly and for once there was no necessity for Margaret to rush away. For most of the fifteen Tory women MPs this was probably the only time that we had enjoyed a proper, friendly, relaxed chat with the leader whom most of us had previously held in awe. She was laughing and joking in a way we had never been seen. It was as if she was one of us, one of the girls.

'Congratulations. That was a good lunch.' I said to Angela.

'If only Margaret had spent more time talking to her back-benchers instead of rushing around the world playing the international statesman, she would still probably be Prime Minister,' she replied.

As pressure increased to find Margaret's successor, you could hardly pass someone in the corridor or sit next to them in the Chamber of the tea-room without being canvassed. Three candidates emerged: Michael Heseltine, John Major and Douglas Hurd. Despite her distress, Margaret went in to bat for John Major, whose career she had accelerated to the point that, in a short space of time, he had occupied two of the highest offices of state: Foreign Secretary and Chancellor.

Shortly before the ballot for party leader I went to see John Major. I told him that many women in the country were openly grieving for Margaret and I thought it would be disastrous if there were no women in his front bench. I also told him that many male Tory MPs were going around openly boasting that they were pleased to be rid of her.

John Major looked at the large brown envelopes on his desk, stuffed with official papers, and, wanting to be rid of me, diplomatically suggested I go to Number 11 and have a chat with his wife, Norma. I decided to take up the offer. A bit of pillow talk might be more effective than my direct remarks.

'Congratulations, it looks as if John will win the ballot,' I said to Norma when she greeted me with a warm smile, as though we were close friends.

'Oh, I don't know about that,' she replied looking somewhat glum.

'Why?' I asked, surprised, 'It's wonderful news.'

'I'm not so sure about being wonderful,' Norma replied. 'If he wins I doubt I'll ever see him. It was bad enough when he was Foreign Secretary. I hardly saw him much then. And the ghastly ambassadors' wives who think they're God's gift to womanhood and the British Empire.' I was taken aback; I had supposed that she was looking forward to a role as the nation's second most important hostess.

She went on, 'At one stage I felt that we didn't have a marriage. Sometimes I felt like throwing in the towel but, of course, I couldn't for John's sake. But I came close to it on a few occasions. And now, if he does become Prime Minister, I'll never see him.' I was surprised. It was a side of life with a top politician that I had hardly thought of. I tried to cheer her up. Then to my surprise, she invited – almost insisted – that I stay for lunch. 'I have some chicken legs in the fridge and enough salad for two,' she went on. 'The trouble with living in official residences is you never have any proper food. I try to leave meals ready in the fridge for John but he usually arrives home too late and too tired to eat anything at all.'

During lunch Norma seemed to want to keep clear of politics and the prospect of being married to the Prime Minister, so I turned the conversation to other topics, and what she would wear if and when he won the ballot. There was hardly enough time to go shopping.

'I've just come back from a conference in Korea – with a case full of beautiful blue suits. Would you like to try them?' I offered. Later I did send them round to Downing Street, but in the end, Norma opted for a favourite old blue suit for the traditional photograph of the Prime Minister entering Number 10 for the first time.

* * * * *

The parliamentary party was divided into two factions, the pro- and anti-Europeans. Both groups were hungry for power and when Margaret began to falter, the battle was on to choose their champion and get him or her into the job. The irony was that both groups appeared to light on the same man. Was that because nobody really knew John Major? Or had he played his cards close to his chest? Both groups thought he was 'their man', but one group was obviously mistaken.

Some unkind souls called the Euro-sceptic No Turning Back Group 'Margaret's Kindergarten' and its members certainly had a head start in government. Michael Forsyth, Francis Maude, Eric Forth and Angela Rumbold were already in the government. John Redwood, Peter Lilley and Michael Portillo were tipped for Cabinet jobs under Major. But their resistance to John's soft policies on European Monetary Union led him, later, to describe them as (that word again) 'bastards' in an on off-the-cuff remark recorded after a television interview. It was pretty certain that all of them were sceptical of further integration with Europe, and in particular, the forthcoming Maastricht Treaty, the first treaty to be negotiated by John Major after he became leader.

The Blue Chip group represented the other side of the European debate, and was formed in 1979 when five new Conservative MPs found themselves sharing an office in Dean's Yard, behind Westminster Abbey. They were William Waldegrave, Chris Patten, John Patten, Tristan Garel-Jones and Richard Needham. It was Needham who, years later, while a minister in the Thatcher government, was overheard on his car telephone describing Margaret as 'the old cow'. The Blue Chips were friends, they were gregarious and they were out of sympathy with Thatcherism. They met two or three times each term at Tristan's house in Catherine Place, where his Spanish wife, Catali, cooked for them. One of the most popular, but least conspicuous members of this group was John Major. 'The Blue Chips' had not been their idea for a name. It had been coined by the Whips, who were amused by the number of earls, marquises and old Etonians involved. But the group's members were happy with it, just as Margaret rather liked to be called the Iron Lady.

By 1990, Tristan Garel-Jones was firmly rooted in the Whips' office, a key position in selecting back benchers for promotion. Chris Patten was marked down as their first choice for the future leadership of the party, but he wasn't in a position to make a bid at the time Margaret was ousted. He had a marginal seat in Bath and the chances were that he would lose the next election – which, of course, is exactly what happened.

Everyone in the group benefited under the change of leadership. Those members of the group who were not promoted under Margaret's leadership were rapidly drawn in when John Major took over. William Waldegrave and Chris Patten were already in the Cabinet when John became Prime Minister, and when Chris lost his seat in 1992, he was rewarded with the governership of Hong Kong.

John must have been privy to some of the scheming that went on against Margaret among the Blue Chips; he had shown no interest in Thatcherite groups within the parliamentary party. In Margaret's terminology, he was not 'one of us', yet she seemed to have been completely taken in by John, and his promotion from back-bencher via Chancellor and Foreign Secretary was rapid. It was another example of the fact that she was not always a good judge of the opposite sex.

It was by no means certain that John Major would win the contest to succeed her. Michael Heseltine represented pro-European views and Douglas Hurd was the Establishment candidate. On election day, Heseltine's supporters held back from voting until the very last minute, knowing that their candidate had little chance of an outright win. In exchange for their votes, Heseltine would be offered the deputy leadership of the party.

John's views on Europe did not become clear until after he was elected leader. In a speech shortly after the Maastricht Bill completed its committee stage in the House, he described

Euro-sceptics as 'Defeatists who make your flesh creep.' John Major's nice guy mask had slipped, but it was too late. Margaret had gone, and Major was now in the driving seat. Under his leadership, we would move closer to Europe. It would be left to a small group of Conservative MPs to continue the battle to resist the ever-closer involvement of Brussels in our domestic affairs, and the inevitable weakening of our parliamentary democracy. That group was called Fresh Start, and I was a founder member.

Chapter Sixteen

MAJOR AND MAASTRICHT

'A poor workman always blames his tools'

ANON

It must be one of the worst experiences for a former prime minister to return to the Chamber as a back-bencher. Edward Heath came regularly, and did it on purpose to annoy Margaret. But she looked ill at ease when she rejoined us for the speech John Major made before he left Britain to travel to Maastricht in order to negotiate the next step on our integration into the European Union. Her speech etched itself into my memory. It was poignant and painful to watch her looking awkward in her new position on the back benches, where she had not set foot for thirty years. She was sitting at the end of the third row to the left-hand side of the Prime Minister and was looking down at the front bench where she had sat as prime minister for so long. Now John Major occupied the place. Next to him sat Norman Lamont, his Chancellor, and Tristan Garel-Jones, Minister for European Affairs.

John Major spoke first and then the leader of the opposition, Neil Kinnock. As soon as he sat down, Margaret rose to speak. Dressed in one of her famous dark blue suits, she looked uncharacteristically nervous. I could have sworn that her hand, clutching some prompt cards, trembled slightly. I was sitting near her, willing her on.

Margaret put the case the simply and succinctly: 'Our authority comes from the ballot box and we are talking about the rights of the British people to govern themselves under their own laws made by their own Parliament ... it is about being British and about what we feel for our county, our Parliament, our traditions and our liberties. Because of our history, that feeling is perhaps stronger here than anywhere else in Europe ... We should not make a massive transfer of power to the Community which is not accountable to our electorate.'

Because of our system of government, where the leader has to reconcile different points of view within the cabinet, the prime minister cannot always express his or her true sentiments. In office, Margaret had signed up for all the previous treaties including the Single European Act, which set us on the road to full integration. Now she revealed herself as one of us, but too late to stop the rot. Later, when Major returned from the conference, the compromise he arranged was that he had refused to accept the Social Chapter, which would impose enormously expensive burdens on employers. He had also refused to agree to the requirement to move to full integration of the currency.

When the Maastricht Bill came back to the House for approval, it precipitated one of the epic battles in our recent political history. The Fresh Start group fought the bill clause by clause, determined to prevent its adoption into British law. With a majority of only twenty, John Major was in a very vulnerable position. But to the Euro-rebels, this was a heaven-sent opportunity; even though it would mean voting in the same lobby as Labour, we could ditch the bill once and for all.

For me, the experience was exhilarating, it was the first time I had been included in any group in Parliament acting together to achieve a political goal. I became an honorary chap. At one stage, Sir Peter Tapsell confided to Michael Spicer, the chairman, that he realised for the first time that I had a brain as well as a body. The media labelled us a party within a party.

From that day on, the fourteen Whips had their work cut out. Their task was to get the legislation through and they would use every trick in the book. They are as secretive as the Masons and as ruthless as Rottweilers. They look for the most vulnerable part of your anatomy and sink their teeth in.

The chief bully boy was David Lightbown. Six feet tall and

three foot wide, he had a walk like a bull elephant. At one stage he picked up a member by the lapels to get face to face with him – a terrifying experience. Others were offered the prospect of a knighthood if they were prepared to sacrifice their principles. Even parliamentary wives were leaned on to persuade their husbands to toe the line. It is often said that Whips know more about MPs' sex lives than they know themselves and are prepared to use this information when necessary.

During the weeks and months that the bill was debated, people came and went from the group. Ex-ministers, including Norman Lamont and Norman Tebbit, lent their support. But on the final, critical, vote – the paving debate – several failed to support us in the lobby.

Towards the end of the Maastricht debate, I was standing in Central Lobby when one MP came up to me, his face red with anger. I thought that he may have had a little too much wine with his meal, as he demanded to know why I wasn't supporting the party line. I found his manner threatening but I brushed him aside saying, 'You have to live with your conscience and I have to live with mine. I can make up my own mind and I don't need any help from you.'

I went straight to the Chamber to listen to the debate, and sat next to another member. The first followed me and sat on my other side. He immediately addressed himself to my neighbour.

'You know she's talking about voting against the government?'

'I always said we shouldn't let women in here in the first

place. They're a thundering nuisance,' he replied.

Neither man was a fan of Margaret Thatcher; both were ardent Major supporters, and were furious at our opposition to the treaty.

'A woman's place is in the home,' said one.

'Yes, flat on her back,' said the other.

I realised they were trying to provoke me, but I ignored them. I was beginning to feel uncomfortable and angry. I felt trapped. I sat still, my back pressed hard against the seat, staring ahead, wondering what to do. Should I get up and leave? Should I say something? But that would only give them the satisfaction of thinking they had riled me. Their conversation continued. And it got worse.

'Do you think Teresa would be any good on her back?' asked one. And then, after a pause, 'I wonder what kind of knickers she wears.'

My mind was racing. This was sexual harassment directed at me for political reasons. And the more offensive the comments became, the more vulnerable I felt. It seemed unbelievable that two colleagues, allegedly civilised men, could act so despicably.

After a few more remarks I exploded, 'Why don't you go and badger someone else! I'm here to listen to the debate.'

'I thought you'd be enjoying it,' said one, insultingly, 'I thought that's what you liked about this place: plenty of men.'

I felt angry and humiliated. But decided not to be provoked.

'Women should be barefoot and pregnant,' said one. 'They

should never have been let in here in the first place.'

I lost my temper.

'Margaret ran rings round the men in this place,' I retorted. I immediately realised it was a mistake.

'That old cow,' said one of them, whose dislike for Margaret Thatcher was matched by his affection and support for John Major. 'She would have lost us the last election, stupid bitch. John Major is bloody marvellous. He won us the election. And you're trying to undermine him,' he spat out.

I'd had enough. I left my seat and hurried out of the Chamber. It was one of the worst half-hours I have ever spent in my life. Nothing quite like it had ever happened to me before, and – thankfully – I have never experienced anything like it since.

* * * * *

Towards the end of the nine-month long debate, the government lost a critical vote. This could have meant the resignation of the government, but the Prime Minister responded by calling for a vote of confidence. Now, if we failed to support him, he announced that he would resign and call an election. But John Major's determination to adopt the treaty was bought at a heavy price. At the end of the long debate, one of the longest in the history of Parliament, he made the speech to a packed House recommending that the Maastricht Treaty be adopted. Sitting around me were several of our colleagues from the Fresh Start group who, like me, fought against it for nine months through days and nights of parliamentary debate. To my astonishment, first one, John Carlisle, and then another, Michael Lord, rose to praise the Prime Minister for his handling of the negotiations. This looked like an attempt to wipe their slates clean, and perhaps a sign that they hoped to be forgiven when the honours came around. I was disgusted.

'How could they do this? They are undermining everything that we've fought for,' I whispered angrily to Sir Peter Tapsell, who was sitting beside me on the green benches.

Suddenly, I was on my feet. 'Will the Prime Minister give way?' I cried, as I attempted to make my feelings known.

A roar of approval rose from the benches opposite. They clearly anticipated that I, too, was about to do a U-turn. Suddenly, Dennis Skinner was on his feet.

'This lady's not for turning,' he yelled, jabbing a finger in my direction.

I made my feelings known. The cheering was tremendous, drowning out the Speaker's calls for order. When the House calmed down, John Major rose to continue his speech.

'I was rather hoping that the Honourable Member for Bolsover [Skinner] was right – and my Honourable friend from Billericay was about to rejoin the Party,' John said to much laughter.

Major's government did not fail because of the rebellion over adopting the Maastricht Treaty from the so-called Fresh Start group or the bastards within his Cabinet. He failed because he lacked the commitment to our right to run the

251

country without interference. Maastricht symbolised the onward march of this encroachment. He may have negotiated two opt-outs, but there was no guarantee that they would last.

A favourite technique in politics is to advance, withdraw, and then attack again when public interest had been exhausted, but Major's government did not last long enough to employ this technique. In 1997, the incoming Labour government moved quickly to introduce the so-called Social Chapter, re-imposing old-style socialist impositions on employers, but they are biding their time on abolishing our currency. They know that the strength of the public support for the pound could well defeat them.

* * * * *

The Maastricht battle may have been the political high point of my time in Parliament. But the rebellion that took place two years later, against increasing the EU budget, was a publicity triumph.

For years, MPs of all parties complained about the waste and fraud in Brussels, but time and time again, they held their nose and voted for it. Few MPs are prepared to risk their seats or their careers on a point of principle. Not so the eight of us who became known as the 'Whipless Wonders'.

Things had begun to settle down after the bruising encounter between the Prime Minister and the Fresh Start group. It was now 1994. Ken Clarke, then Chancellor of the

Exchequer, wrote to all members warning us he would be introducing a bill to increase our contribution to the EU budget. To soften the blow, he reassured us that although we were already the second-largest contributors, the deal would cost other member states much more than the United Kingdom.

What the Chancellor called a small net increase of £75 million – rising to £250 million by 1999, however, did not tell us the real cost. The Chancellor's Departmental Report showed our gross contribution rising from £7.4 billion in 1994/5 to 10.25 billion in 1996/7. It was this gross amount that counted, as this is what the taxpayer had to find from his or her pay-packet.

I tried to work out what this might mean to the average taxpayer. A price rise here. A tax increase there. Petrol up. Pension contributions reduced in value. One man's small increase is some taxpayer's last straw. But I doubted whether any of the Brussels mandarins would notice – or care. Their already considerable incomes were boosted by free tax and massive expenses. But the man in the corner shop, or the housewife on a tight budget, does notice these things. In addition to £28 a week added to food bills, Europe's agricultural policies keep cheaper food out of Europe. How much more could we be expected to pay to fund European industries and road construction?

It is often hard for people to realise the significance of the huge sum of money we were already paying into Europe's coffers. If we refused, we could have reduce the basic rate of tax by about 3.5 pence in the pound. We could abolish VAT.

And we could have paid every pensioner an extra £7 a week.

After his last encounter with his back benches over Maastricht, the Prime Minister decided to try to defuse another potential battle by inviting likely rebels, one by one, to meet him in 10 Downing Street. When my invitation arrived, I was apprehensive. I had no idea what the invitation was for – but I doubted that the Prime Minister had decided to forgive and forget. The meeting was a disappointment for both of us. The Prime Minister was clearly not amused when I turned down his request for a commitment to vote for the increase. I left knowing that there was no way of mending the rift between us; we just did not share the same views on whether Europe was worth the money.

The Fresh Start group was reconvened to discuss tactics. Of the twenty-three present, only eight were prepared to push a protest to a vote. John Major's majority was small, and even eight members known to be unhappy might be significant enough to change his mind. He could hardly risk another crisis.

Led by Richard Ryder, the Chief Whip, the Whips got to work on us. We were threatened with losing the Whip, which meant that we would be thrown out of the parliamentary party. The speaker called the vote at 10 p.m. Only seven of the original group were prepared to go through with it: Teddy Taylor, Nick Budgen, Tony Marlow, Richard Shepherd, John Wilkinson, Christopher Gill and me.

'Ayes to the right, noes to the left.'

Our group of seven sat huddled together on the green leather benches, abstaining from voting, while 310 of our colleagues obediently streamed past us, into the government lobby. There was no possibility of the government losing the vote or calling a general election, but that didn't stop some of our colleagues vilifying us for our actions.

The Liberal Democrats voted with the government and, much to his relief, John Major secured the Commons approval to increase our contribution to the EU budget – but he was furious with the way the situation had been handled. After the vote, he stormed into the Whips' office and ordered Richard Ryder to sack us by withdrawing the Whip, which meant we were banished from the Parliamentary Conservative Party.

To sack even one member was rare. To sack seven (soon to be eight when Dick Body resigned as a token of his support) was a disaster. Nothing like this had happened in the history of the party before.

Richard Ryder handed me a letter:

Dear Teresa,
You took a deliberate decision not to support the Government in the Division Lobbies tonight on what you knew to be a vote of confidence. A general election would have taken place if this vote had been lost. Consequently, the Conservative Party Whip has been withdrawn from you.
Yours, Richard

I later discovered that some senior colleagues had urged John to 'sleep on it before shooting your own foot off' – to no avail.

Now what? I had no idea what being whipless entailed. Would we be ostracised by the whole party? Would we be given our marching orders? Get our P45s? I went home to bed apprehensive. Perhaps this was the end of my parliamentary career.

As it turned out, being cast out into the wilderness wasn't half as bad a punishment as we expected. After the sleaze, the public seemed relieved and delighted to find a group of politicians – however small – prepared stick to their principles.

Free from party discipline, we were able to give our full support to the 'Save Britain's Fish' campaign, for one thing, which the government was reluctant to support. The livelihood of Britain's fishermen had all but been destroyed as a result of Edward Heath's decision to allow EU fishing boats free access to our traditional fishing grounds. Britain has the best fishing waters in the North Sea, with some of the world's largest spawning grounds, such as the Dogger Bank. Christopher Gill (MP for Ludlow and a fellow rebel) took to organising our support like a duck to water. Tom Hay, of the Fishermen's Association, and a natural orator, organised meetings for us. We travelled the country 'like an ageing pop group trying to resurrect their careers', to quote Boris Johnson of the *Daily Telegraph*.

In the Commons, not all MPs with fishing ports supported the fishermen. They placed party loyalty above the interests of their constituents. Sebastian Coe, MP and Olympic gold medallist, represented the fishing port of Falmouth. But he was notably reluctant to support their call for the return of their fishing grounds. At the next election, the fishermen took their revenge.

'Don't stop training and don't stop running,' they told him. Seb lost his seat in the 1997 election and became special advisor to William Hague after he had won the leadership, and as a reward, has ended up in the Lords.

During our exile, no longer subject to a three-line Whip, we were able to defeat an increase in VAT on fuel imposed by the Chancellor, Kenneth Clarke, simply by abstaining from the vote. In doing so, we did the party a favour. The policy was strongly resented in the country, and widely believed to have cost us council seats. The Whips were angry, but they had no hold over us. As for the rank and file Tory voters, there was great relief, particularly amongst pensioners.

Six months later, the Whips capitulated. Richard Ryder wrote us each another letter.

Dear Teresa,
I am writing to confirm that, as from today, the Whip has been restored to you, I am pleased to enclose this week's copy.
If you do not wish to receive the Whip in future, then you should let me have your formal resignation of it in writing.
Yours,
Richard.
We were back in the fold, but our opposition to government

policy meant that we would never be forgiven; never promoted. We were not the team players that the party needed. We were outcasts for defending the rights of Parliament against the encroachment of European law.

* * * * *

Not all my experiences with John Major were quite as acrimonious. His quiet way of speaking was a relief after the hectoring that Margaret developed by the end of her premiership; it even grated on me, her biggest fan. Some time had passed since our falling out over Maastricht when he invited me to tea at 10 Downing Street to try and persuade me to support a large increase in our contribution to the European budget. There was no way I could bring myself to bail out Brussels with £75 million of our taxpayers' money. Our contribution was already running at £10 billion a year. In the frosty silence that followed, I had tried to change the subject to be helpful to him.

Prime ministers' speeches on key issues are circulated to MPs – and as I had tried to plough through a recent one to the European Forum on the role of the state, which consisted of sixteen closely typed pages, it had occurred to me that John could do with a new speech writer.

'Who writes your speeches?' I asked.

'Why do you ask?'

I explained that I thought that the last one was wooden and overlong – about three-quarters of an hour too long, I guessed.

'An audience concentration span is about three minutes, after that, they begin to nod off.'

He laughed. 'Well, if that's what you think, why don't you have a go at rewriting it?' he replied.

This was not the response I had been expecting. The speech lay on my desk well into August, like a plate of cold cabbage that your parents insist you eat before you leave the table. Each time I sat down to read it, I gagged. I decided to abandon the project and write to him:

15 August 1994

Dear John

When we met at the end of July, we talked about the speech which you had recently made, to the European Forum on the 'Role and Limits of the State'. I said I thought it was wooden and you challenged me to look at it and come up with something better. I hope you won't mind me being frank. I've attached some suggestions.

It was too long and too detailed, your audience couldn't possible take it in. A speech must first grab the attention of your listeners; a little humour helps.

The contents must relate to the interests of your audience. This means couching it in language which is familiar. And as for your style, as far as possible, speak in conversational tones.

It should leave in people's minds a visual picture. This is the secret of the biblical speechmakers; and why we all remember their message. If you achieve these elements, you will come alive to your audience and seem like a real human being.

Avoid using I, we or one! You are talking to a group of people so use you over and over again.

To do an important speech, sit down with the person who is helping you, decide on a storyline and talk about it between yourselves to get the colloquial flavour.

I've got a hunch that when you made your remarks on the death of John Smith, you were speaking from the heart, that those remarks were not written for you. It showed in the way the House responded.

I'd be happy to help or even run my eye over something which someone else has prepared for you.
With Best Wishes,
Teresa

The Party Conference, at which the Prime Minister gives a keynote speech setting out his agenda for the coming year, was looming. I guessed that, even now, John's speech writers would be making notes on what to include. Whatever he says, the Prime Minister is guaranteed a standing ovation from the party faithful, but the impression he makes on the media can have a crucial effect on whether he gets good or bad press.

At the conference, the great and the good are arranged on a high platform like a politburo gazing down at the hoi polloi. As each Minister speaks, an absurd lectern rises up in front of them, cutting them off at the armpits and giving a new meaning to the term 'talking heads'. The invisible teleprompter, a magic invention which allows the speaker to read their lines without appearing to, drains the last vestiges of spontaneity from the performance. Bearing this in mind, I sat down and wrote John another letter.

2 September 1994
Dear John
The Party conference is coming up and I imagine your speech writers will be planning something for you. Conference speeches are so contrived – and so boring. I doubt whether the audience takes in more than a fraction – and most of them nod off at some stage.

The platform, the lectern, the teleprompter, they all come between you and your audience. Forget about them.

Get close to the audience. Abandon notes. Just talk to them. They will be fascinated by you – so tell them about your background, your ambitions for the party and the country. Keep it short and snappy. You are best when you speak off the cuff.

And don't forget to talk to them and not at them.
Best wishes
Teresa

I heard no more and almost forgot about the whole episode. I imagine that most correspondence sent to Downing Street disappears into the letter answering machine – or at best – is looked at by the Private Secretary before being binned.

In October, I went to the Conference as usual, and left early on the last day to avoid the crush that leaves Blackpool once the Prime Minister's speech is over. When I arrived home and I turned on the television for the Conference coverage, I couldn't believe my eyes. As I watched, John left the platform, walked down towards the audience and began talking about his childhood, his early struggles, his hopes for the future of the party and the country. It was a brilliant performance. The audience loved it, and I was ecstatic. At last, someone in the party was actually listening to what I had to say.

I didn't expect him to acknowledge my contribution; a good idea has a thousand fathers. But I was wrong. John hadn't forgotten. After the Conference, he wrote to me.

19 October 1994
Dear Teresa,
Thank you for your letter of 2 September.
It was kind of you to take the trouble and write and I was most grateful for your comments and suggestions which were most helpful.
I am sure you will agree with me that the Conference was a great success and that we sent our supporters home in good heart with a clear message.
See you soon!
Yours ever,
John
In his memoirs, John has something quite nice to say

Despite John Major's pleading, I just had to say, 'No, Prime Minister!'

Above: My first hug with Cecil, on election night in 1992.

Below: Victory! The day Jim and I triumphed over Mr. Mudd, fighting our way through the crowds outside the law courts.

Above: 'Vulcan launched from Gorman's bosom'. The picture that allegedly scuppered Redwood's leadership bid.

Below left: With my good friend Norman Tebbitt at the RAF Club, where he addressed the Billericay Businessmen's club.

Below right: One of my favourite pictures, waiting to hear if I'd been accepted as the Tory party candidate for London Mayor. I put my hat into the ring after Jeffrey Archer had to withdraw.

Banging Drake's drum on Plymouth Hoe for the *Save Britain's Fish* Campaign. My red mac drummed up a storm in the voting lobbies and with the fishermen in the West Country.

Above: Regaining the whip, wearing my lucky yellow jacket.

Below: Turning the turf with Fatima Whitbread, former Olympic Athlete, during an opening ceremony for a new old people's home in Billericay.

Above: Our house in Orsett made famous by the porch fiasco!

Below left: The original plastic door on our fourteenth century house that we were condemned for replacing.

Below right: Restoration of the house well under way.

Above: Before…

Below: …and after!

With Glenda Jackson and Liz Lynne, celebrating the 75th anniversary of the women's franchise.

about me, in contrast to the other members of the Fresh Start group. He says that he almost thought of promoting me – and then changed his mind! He said I was too outspoken, too unreliable. In other words, not a good team player.

Chapter Seventeen

HRT

'Youth is a blunder;
Manhood a struggle;
Old age a regret.'
BENJAMIN DISRAELI

On my arrival in the House of Commons, I lost no time in spreading the news about HRT (Hormone Replacement Therapy), which I regarded as the one of the greatest advances in preventative medicine for women this century, second only to the pill.

I hosted a supper for the wives of politicians at my house in Lord North Street. Over forty attended – a stream of

Cabinet ministers drove them – my drawing room was packed. They listened avidly to one of London's leading HRT specialists. And when their husbands came to collect them, they had difficulty in getting them away.

Then I set up a cross-party committee of MPs on the health needs of older women to raise the profile of menopause amongst members. But my big chance to introduce this taboo subject in the Chamber came when Edwina Currie, then a junior health minister, arranged a Friday morning debate on women's health. This was an unique occasion not only because of the subject matter but because the green benches were lined with almost every woman MP in the House. A sprinkling of men joined us in the Chamber to listen.

As I got into my stride, Bernard Braine, the Father of the House, suddenly rose from his seat and hurried out, his head bent forward muttering to himself. Later when I left the debate, the doorman who controls entry into the Chamber, stopped me.

'What were you saying in there to upset Sir Bernard? He went past here muttering that he had never dreamt that he would hear such matters discussed in the Chamber.'

That was not untypical of people's reaction to any public mention of the menopause. It was this attitude that I set out to overcome. Going through such a traumatic change in your life could be bad enough without being made to feel guilty – even ashamed – about it.

As my public association with HRT grew, I became a kind of agony aunt for my male colleagues. They would sidle up to me in the tea-room and tell me about changes that their wives were going through that they found difficult to cope with. 'When I go home at the weekend, she's either screaming at me – or crying,' one said. 'Do you think your pills would have a beneficial effect?'

Barbara Cartland had written about HRT in the Sixties. She once told me that in her eighties, she had fallen on a concrete floor in a supermarket and hadn't even chipped a bone! I don't know what surprised me the most, the image of Barbara pushing a supermarket trolley wearing one of her feather-decked hats or her spread-eagled on the floor in one her exotic pink dresses.

But despite the fact that it had been around for some time, HRT was still hardly talked about in the UK by the 1980s. In the US, it had been in use since the 1940s, although American women prefer to talk about ODS (Oestrogen Deficiency Syndrome) rather than the menopause; a deficiency syndrome is acceptable but any indication that old age is creeping on is not. In Sweden, HRT has been taken for granted for many years. Any woman at menopause is offered this therapy. Women in Britain were missing out because no one was talking about it.

The menopause brings many frightening changes to a woman's body. Bones become thinner, more brittle and liable to fracture. Blood vessels become less elastic. Women over fifty have a higher rate of heart attack than men, and with it, often comes a stroke. Perhaps the most obvious sign of change is the memory loss, the irritating feeling that you have something on the tip of your tongue but just can't make your brain produce the information. The latest research from the USA shows that HRT can make a considerable impact on Alzheimer's in women.

And as your energy fades, so does your ambition to continue an active a life much less begin a new career outside the home. Just as the family has grown and women have more time to spend outside the home, they lose their energy and their drive, which would enable them to make the most of new opportunities. Earning money outside the family home gives them more control over their lives. Yet this is also a time when many marriages fail, as mood swings and depression can make women impossible to live with. I often say that HRT can keep you out of hospital, out of the madhouse and out of the divorce courts. It can add years to your life, but more importantly, it adds life to your years.

I was in my late forties when I suddenly I began to think I was cracking up. The first thing I noticed was my joints. My ankles were so painful that I could barely manage to climb the stairs from the kitchen in the basement to the bedroom on the third floor of our London house. My wrists hurt so badly that I couldn't cut the bread and my ankles were killing me. My usually tidy desk looked like the wastepaper basket had been emptied on to it and I could no longer remember the names of the familiar plants and animals that formed the basis of the educational products we manufactured. By 7 o'clock, I was dozing in the armchair. If this was getting old, I thought, I'd rather be dead. I was in charge of a successful business that relied on my energy, my memory and time travelling abroad. I think the memory loss worried me most. I knew enough about human biology to suspect an early menopause. I had heard of HRT from an older colleague whilst living in the States, so I took myself off for a check-up. The tests showed that my hormones were on the blink. I was given hormone replacement therapy and within days I was back to my old self again. It felt like a miracle cure.

I figured that many more women might be suffering the same symptoms – in silence – when help was available if only they knew about it, and so decided to do something about it. The first problem was finding a neutral name that would not embarrass everyone. My pal Daphne Macara came up with Amarant, an obscure plant, symbolic of beauty and eternal youth. With the support of leading specialists from King's College Hospital, the Amarant Trust was born. At first, the charity was run out of my business offices. All the women on my staff volunteered to help, as did the people who did the publicity for my teaching products. Soon other journalists and actresses weighed in with support, including Agony Aunt Marjorie Proops of the *Daily Mirror*, the actress Kate O'Mara and the writer Fay Weldon.

I put time and personal resources into it. With some financial help, we laid on meetings around the country and instruction courses for practice nurses. Ann Strutt, the granddaughter of one of my neighbours, Lady Davidson, staged a mass meeting in London, which was packed to the rafters. Women came from all over the country. One coachload had come down from Scotland, leaving home at three in the morning to arrive on time. Ann was a brilliant organiser, and went on to set up our first charitable clinic without a penny from the government.

I had not imagined when I decided to set up the Amarant Trust how much suffering I would uncover, nor how much callous indifference there is towards women who were experiencing the effects of the menopause. Nor did I realise that lives could be redeemed and marriages saved by the application of this simple treatment.

It is amazing how many people thing that women over the age of fifty are over the hill. As women grow older, their ability to have children fades, and they lose vital hormones which kept their bodies in good condition. As far as nature is concerned, once you are no longer fertile, you are not much use.

The thousands of letters I received painted a picture of human misery on a huge scale, which women endured ignorant of the cause. Terrible migraine headaches. Awful cramps in their leg muscles. Breaking out in a sweat without warning, so badly that they had to get out of bed and change not only their nightclothes, but their bed linen as well. One woman said that she had slept in a towelling robe for seven years. All of these symptoms could have been prevented if only women knew the treatment was available.

The first article I wrote in the *Daily Mail* about HRT brought a deluge of letters – 10,000 altogether – and the paper had to employ two of its staff for three weeks just to deal with them. Almost every letter was a cry for help. That's when I knew the Amarant Trust would fill a real need for women facing the menopause alone.

For as long as I can remember the menopause has been one of those subjects that nobody likes to talk about. Women refer to it in whispers, euphemistically, as the 'change of life'. Most men, even married men, couldn't bear to mention it at all, except to make jokes about it and usually very unsympathetic ones at that. It was barely two years after establishing the Amarant Trust that public opinion began to change. I rarely went to a party without the subject being raised, usually by the man sitting next to me.

By the spring of 1988, the Amarant Trust was receiving over 1,000 letters a week, and interest in the Trust's work continued to grow. Within hours of an appearance by myself and Claire Rayner on 'Richard and Judy', we were besieged with calls from women desperate for help. That's when we decided to set up the first Amarant Centre in London, a clinic offering counselling and treatment to women who had been refused treatment locally. It was the prototype, we hoped, for many more centres, but still today, there are only a handful and hardly any are funded by the NHS. Doctors specialising in women's medicine have to raise money from pharmaceutical companies and even so, in major cities, some clinics can only afford to open one day a week.

Middle-aged women often come to my surgery, their skin grey and tired, and it turns out that they are younger than me. They are usually experiencing problems – often marital – and as they talk to me, I can define in them obvious symptoms of post-menopausal depression that is affecting their relationship with their family. I advise them to talk to their GP and failing that, the Amarant Trust.

HRT is a natural substance, not a drug. Organisations that attempt to gain publicity for their own causes by linking it to breast cancer are irresponsible and do women no favours. The research they rely on does not bear out their claims. However, we still need to reassure some GPs that HRT is safe and the benefits immense. I know from my personal experience that it can do more to improve the quality of your life, your appearance, your energy and your happiness than pots of expensive cream, a holiday in Spain or a complete new wardrobe of clothes. I could not possibly maintain my incredibly busy schedule without it.

When I entered Parliament, the NHS spent less than £1 million on prescriptions. Today, it spends £150 million. In time the NHS will need to spend less and less on mending broken bones in women over fifty, or helping them to recover from heart attacks and strokes. HRT can protect women against memory loss and other symptoms of mental decline.

When she was Junior Health Minister, Edwina Currie once pointed out that the single largest number of NHS prescriptions were for tranquillisers prescribed for middle-aged women who had complained of 'feeling under the weather'. Women simply do not know enough about their biology. I have tried my best to persuade Government that a chain of women-friendly health centres would save the NHS a fortune.

Menopause undoubtedly plays a part in the phenomenon known as the 'glass-ceiling' which seems to prevent women in their late forties and fifties from making that final spurt to the top of their profession. They seem to fade, or as the Victorians put it, 'go into a decline'. In other words, your body is letting you down. Traditionally, women over fifty were thought to be 'past it', yet I began the most strenuous time of my life at fifty-seven. A Member of Parliament has a sixteen-hour day, seven days a week.

Fay Weldon wrote an article that tells a wonderful story about her mother, who also used to be a writer. When she was in her seventies, her health and her memory began to fail, and she moved to a nursing home for her own safety. Seeing her mother's distress, Fay requested her doctor to prescribe HRT. What harm could it do? Within weeks, her mother's whole personality was restored. Her memory improved to such an extent that she was able to leave the nursing home and live independently. She even began to write again.

In my time in Parliament, on several occasions, I have taken delegations of medical specialists – including the country's leading authorities on HRT – to meet the Ministers for Health – from Ken Clarke to Virginia Bottomley. We explained the huge value to the NHS of this protective treatment and the need to promote it. We were listened to sympathetically – but nothing much came of it. The spread of information has been left almost entirely to charities like Amarant.

When, in 1987, I unexpectedly joined the ranks of Conservative candidates, I was interviewed by journalist Peter McKay. For want of something better to write, he dubbed me the 'Queen of HRT'. He went on to speculate about whether Margaret Thatcher's phenomenal energy could owe something to the treatment, especially as women of 'her age' – then sixty-two – were reckoned to be over the hill. I didn't do much to deny the possibility.

I didn't dare ask Margaret if it were true – she was after all, the Prime Minister. Whenever I bumped into her in the voting lobby, she would compliment me on the quality of my skin. Lots of people do. But Margaret also had a good skin and perhaps this was a clue that something other than adrenaline was responsible for her phenomenal energy and mental alertness. I found it astonishing to think that HRT might have had more to do with her spectacular career than any amount of political commitment.

When Margaret was deposed and had more time to talk to ordinary mortals like me, I went to tea with her in her temporary home in Eaton Square. She had become a legend in her lifetime. Such was her status that she became an icon – a two-dimensional character – in the mould of some heroine in a Greek tragedy. In truth, she was a woman with a family and all the ups and downs of family life: difficult children, running the home and keeping her husband happy. Dennis was always there in the background, but shunning the limelight. The media image of him is as two-dimensional as that of his wife. But the surprising insight into their private life dispelled the caricature portrayed in *Private Eye*, and made me realise that Dennis still had lead in his pencil.

As soon as we settled down with a cup of tea and a biscuit, I summoned up the courage to steer the conversation towards the subject I had really come to talk to her about.

'I've never liked to ask you before,' I ventured, 'but do you use HRT?' My object was to persuade her to become Amarant's President – It would have been a great coup.

'Yes, dear, I have a patch,' she replied, tapping her bottom – as if to indicate that it was in place. (HRT can be taken in the form of a pill or absorbed through the skin as a patch; another option is an implant, which lasts for six months.) She paused, as if remembering. 'But I've only had it for eighteen months.' She paused again. 'You see, no one told me to come off the pill.'

I was startled. Women usually give up the pill in their fifties, but Margaret was sixty-five.

'The pill?' I repeated. 'Well, HRT is much the same thing.'

'Yes,' she went on, 'you see, Dennis and I agreed that I could not risk having more children once I became leader of the party – it was a full-time job. And in those days, I don't think the country was ready for a prime minister on maternity leave. Of course, it might have been acceptable in Scandinavia, but not in Britain, at least not when I became leader in 1974.'

This was an amazing revelation. Most women of her age – then 65 – would have stopped taking the contraceptive pill in their fifties at the latest. Did someone forget to tell her? I can imagine people being to timid to broad the subject with the Prime Minister. A curious kind of deference develops between people in high office and those who serve them.

I had always suspected that she was on HRT, and even hinted at it during my first election campaign. I worried a bit that she might have been made aware of my remarks and possibly resented them. But as I began to understand the workload of a prime minister, I realised that a casual reference to her in a popular newspaper was unlikely to find its way into her red boxes.

But this insight shed new light on her reaction to Mikhail Gorbachev, the Russian President who visited Parliament in 1989. A side effect of HRT is that your libido revives – you feel more sexy, and Margaret showed all the signs of a woman who is sexually attracted to a man, albeit unconsciously.

I talked a bit more about the work of the Amarant Trust, with the hope of interesting her in becoming our President, but I didn't succeed. Her mind was still on politics. What she really wanted to know was the talk in the tea-room.

Later, she inscribed another of my books, *The Bastards*, which tells the inside story of the battle over Maastricht. She described me as a 'Bonny Fighter'. I hope she meant it. It's just about the nicest thing anyone has said about my political career.

When, in 1975, Wendy Cooper published her classic book on menopause, entitled *No Change*, the foreword was written by Sir John Peel, the gynaecologist to the Queen Mother. He wrote, 'I am convinced from experience that Hormone Replacement Therapy can be of immense help to a great number of women ... [the book] should do much to educate women about themselves and stimulate them to seek medical advice instead of putting up with unpleasant and at times disastrous symptoms in the belief that they are the inevitable consequences of being a woman who must grin and bear it all.'

I have good reason to believe that the Queen Mother has indeed benefited from hormone replacement therapy. This could account for her amazing energy and health into old age. If only information about HRT was more widespread, many other elderly women might benefit, instead of being left to deteriorate in old people's homes.

It is not the quantity of life that matters, but the quality. HRT has given me twenty years of trouble-free health and energy and enabled me to pursue my hectic life. That's the message I want to send to all older women. Don't grow old gracefully like women of an older generation. Keep going and make the most of your later years.

* * * * *

It is common knowledge that when I first applied for my constituency, Billericay, I knocked ten years off my age. People often ask me how I got away with it and I tell them it was down to HRT. When I was forty-seven and hit the menopause, I looked sixty and felt seventy-seven. But by the time I was fifty-seven and had become an MP, I looked forty-seven and felt twenty-seven. I have lost count of the number of women who have told me that finding out about HRT transformed their life – at a time when they had begun to feel that it was not worth living.

Beauty is only skin deep. One of the early signs of ageing is the first appearance of wrinkles. Anti-ageing cosmetics are a multi-million pound business, including a whole range of organically correct, magical ingredients, from royal jelly to monkey glands. According to dermatologists, they are all worthless and exorbitantly expensive. The most such creams can do is to shield the skin from the sun and trap moisture temporarily in the upper layers to putt it up. Personally, I have never spent more than the bare minimum on cosmetics. Every morning and every night, I wash my face with soap and water and apply a tiny drop of the finest baby oil to my face. That is all I do – apart from take HRT – and all of my skin is in the same condition – no wrinkles.

Life is harder for older people these days. Gone is the respect for age. The harsh epithets of 'wrinklies' and 'crumblies' underlines the bias against employing older people in immature trades such as television and air hostessing. Things are worse for women than men. Men are often considered to look more interesting with wrinkles. Even so, I can recall several occasions on which a male colleague sidled up to me in the tea-room or even the Chamber itself to ask if there was an equivalent of HRT for men.

Belief in an elixir for youth is the oldest example of wishful thinking. In 1512, Ponce de León set sail from Spain to find the Fountain of Youth and, in 1513, discovered Florida instead. With its attractive climate, Florida has become the retirement state for older Americans, where women, in particular, live longer, not because of the climate, but because so many of them take HRT. Much of the research on the effects of HRT on ageing is carried out on the population of Florida, and it has come up with some very encouraging results.

Falling in love does more than biotechnology for a youthful appearance, but short of that, HRT can do as much for your skin. It slows down the collapse of the dermis, the skin's scaffolding layers, which begin to collapse as their elastic fibres deteriorate. And it is the collapse of these underpinnings which brings on the wrinkles. As the body gets older, the outer sack gets looser, drier and thinner and your skin looses its youthful glow. But nowadays, you don't have to put up with the worst nature throws at you. With a bit of exercise, a dab of make-up and your HRT, you can beat the clock!

Chapter Eighteen

JOLLIES

*'I have been travelling around the world – on your behalf
and at your expense – visiting some of the chaps with
whom I hope to be shaping your future.'*
PETER COOK

Parliament is not all hard graft. We have a wide selection of opportunities to travel abroad on 'goodwill' visits or fact-finding missions. From Australia to America, West Africa to the West Indies and the Mediterranean to the Arctic, there is hardly a spot on the globe that has not been graced by a Parliamentary delegation. These 'jollies' – in parliamentary parlance – are, of course all free, include club-class travel, first-class accommodation, fine wines and food, and the occasional day off sight-seeing.

My first jolly was a three-week trip to Australia, a visit from British parliamentarians in conjunction with the Commonwealth Parliamentary Association for the summer recess. There are usually a few of these visits each year. Personal contacts between Commonwealth nations is important, an effective way of diffusing potential disagreements. That is the serious point of the visit and some very hard work was put in, with meetings from dawn to dusk.

On arrival at your destination, you begin a round of meetings. The first meeting of the day is at breakfast and the last at dinner, with an outing such as a trip to the local sewage works thrown in as a special treat. But the jolly to Australia was to be much more enjoyable.

Our group of six MPs – three Labour, three Tory – was led by the Tory MP Alan Howarth and included the elegant Lady Patricia Hollis, a tall, willowy, redhead who had been elevated to the Lords by the Labour Party.

My husband Jim always insists on driving me to the airport hours before a flight. This time, my early arrival paid off. When our party boarded the Quantas Jumbo flight, I was the only member to be upgraded to first class. In terms of protocol, this was a blunder. The seat should have been allocated to the leader of the group, and I made a half-hearted offer to give it up. But the steward insisted that I take it. Having settled down in my stretch seat, with my own miniature TV set fitted to the arm rest and a tray of canapés at my side – I decided to bow to the inevitable. I didn't want to cause a fuss.

Shortly after take-off Lady Hollis appeared in the first-class cabin, ostensibly for a chat and to see if there were any magazines in first class that might interest her. But she took the opportunity of pointing out that by right the first-class seat should have been reserved for the group leader.

After chatting to me for a few minutes she moved forward and began to shuffle through the selection of magazines that had been placed on a table in the centre of the cabin. She had only been checking them for a matter of seconds when a first-class cabin steward came up to her, told her that she was not permitted to be in first class and asked her to return to her seat. This did not go down too well. Patricia looked daggers at the steward, turned on her heel, and all but marched out of the cabin.

When we arrived at the luxury Perth Hotel, her title bagged her the best suite. Throughout the trip, she was treated with far greater deference than the rest of us, although she was the only unelected representative. Patricia was always given the most impressive accommodation in all the hotels and we would all troop along like peasants to see how much better her grand accommodation was than ours.

I had heard from some cynical MPs that many of these parliamentary jollies are really excuses for MPs to have an overseas holiday at the expense of the taxpayer, perish the thought. Stories abounded of brief affairs, partying, high-living and too much drinking. MPs disappeared into the night to find other company of either sex. It seemed that all tastes could be catered for on these overseas jaunts.

Our trip to Australia was no exception. Patricia and I, perhaps because we were the only women on the jolly, eventually became good friends and spent time together. Despite the fact that we belonged to opposing political parties with different ideals, we found we also had much in common. A few days later, I sensed that Patricia and Alan, both academics, had struck up a friendship. They appeared to be getting on famously.

It was not long after we returned home that Alan Howarth quit the Tory party and joined Labour, where he was given a safe seat in Newport East. Who fixed this up? I always thought it surprising that a sophisticated middle-class English intellectual was shoe-horned into a working-class seat in Wales. Did Alan's conversion to Labour begin in Australia? Was Patricia the *femme fatale* responsible for turning him?

But Australia also had its more serious side. For one thing, we visited Aborigines in the Maralinga Lands, the site where the British tested some of their earliest atomic weapons in the vast aboriginal areas of South Australia. We met a delegation of Aborigines in a ghost town – all that was left of the atomic trials which took place there in 1963. They were seeking compensation from the British and Australian governments. We left Maralinga promising to see the two governments press ahead with further decontamination of the area. That kind of work was where we earned our keep as a parliamentary delegation.

But our trip very nearly ended in disaster. We flew from

Adelaide to the remote mining town of Coober Pedy, the opal capital of the world in the Great Victoria Desert. The surface temperature is 120 degrees in summer and everyone lives underground in large, cool caves hewn out of the red sandstone.

As we approached the airstrip, the pilot of the six-seater Cessna, told us through our crackly headphones, that the plane's undercarriage appeared to have locked and he couldn't release it.

'I'm going to have to circle around for a while to get rid of nearly all the fuel because I'm going to have to crash land this thing,' he told us, calmly.

We looked at each other and one or two of us turned white. We all knew that crash-landing a light plane on a dirt track could be dangerous, even, God forbid, life threatening. I took hope from the fact that the pilot seemed hardly affected by the prospect of making such a landing on the dusty, red track. It was as though this was his preferred way of landing the Cessna. But others felt that we were heading for possible disaster.

'There will be six good by-elections if he doesn't pull this thing off,' I said to my companion. He gave me a sickly grin.

Labour MP Ian McCartney, who was sitting in the suicide seat next to the pilot, turned round and looked at me. It was down to me that he was sitting next to the pilot at all. At each flight, there was jockeying for position at the front of the plane. Originally Ian had refused the seat, deferring to our group leader Alan Howarth or Lady Hollis. But I had insisted he take it.

As we circled overhead, I looked out of the window to see an ancient Land Rover, which had three large plastic dustbins on top, charging along the runway in a cloud of red dust. This turned out to be Cooper Pedy's excuse for a fire engine.

The pilot told us to check our seat belts and brace ourselves for the crash landing. 'There'll probably be a bit of a bump, lots of dust and the old crate will shake and rattle like a hell,' he informed us, casually. 'But we should be OK.'

He wasn't exaggerating. We hit the dirt with a tremendous crash and the whole plane felt as if it would break into a hundred pieces. Then it leapt in the air and crashed down again, though this time the bang wasn't so hard. 'It's down, it's down,' shouted the pilot into our headphones, meaning that the first bump had unlocked the undercarriage. Within a couple of hundred yards, we finally came to a halt, engulfed in a huge cloud of choking red dust.

The fire-engine hadn't even bothered to follow us down the runway. The pilot explained later, 'The tubs are filled with water, which is more expensive than fuel or whisky. Water is too precious to waste.'

At the end of the trip, I arranged to stay on to meet some friends and visit the Barrier Reef. However, the British Embassy received a call from the government ordering us home. The currency had collapsed and the Chancellor, Norman Lamont, had taken Britain out of the ERM (Exchange Rate Mechanism). Black Wednesday had occurred. John Major ordered an emergency debate and all MPs were called back to Parliament. It didn't matter that it was summer recess. No matter how much you plead, or how far away you are, you have to obey a three-line Whip.

* * * * *

Party Conferences are all about sucking up to the right people. If you are in government, then the media, banks, businesses and everyone else wants to suck up to you. They attend in droves, throw lavish parties, and give away lots of samples – British Airways used to give out lovely china mugs. They pay astronomical prices for display stands, and smile, smile, smile!

At evening functions they fight to get the star turns: lots of ministers, preferabley cabinet ministers, and of course the ritual arrival of the leader. Hoi poloi like me are invited to make up the numbers. The rest – including the 'delegates' – try to gatecrash. Some beg you for the invitations that are beneath you, but which will provide them with a free drink and canapé.

At almost every conference for the past twenty years, I have been part of a fringe meeting or lobby group. It began in the 1970s, before I was elected, when we stood outside, handing out leaflets about the plight of small business. I continued as a new MP when I helped in the forlorn would-be Conservatives from Northern Ireland. It culminated in two terrific meetings on a Parliament for England. If only William Hague had deigned to attend, he would have felt the real passion of politics – a love of country which could still propel us back to power.

I have always attended Conference. I think we owe a duty

to be there and touch base with all those grass-root Conservatives who work like hell to get us elected. We get paid for the job. They don't. They go to spot the star turns and pack the Conference Chamber, applauding the speeches. Wannabe MPs. If they are lucky, they take the stage for three minutes in the limelight, hoping to make the same kind of impression that propelled William to power.

For those at the top of the pecking order, there used to be the ultimate invitation to a reception in the private suite of Alistair McAlpine. The millionaire builder and Party Treasurer provided 24 hour seafood – you ate so much of it that you risked turning into a lobster. But when Alistair retired and Jeffrey Archer took over, it was meat and potatoes – shepherd's pie and Krug – and much more difficult to gatecrash. I was never grand enough to be invited, but I always managed to get in.

The conference culminates in the Leader's speech, which is only as good as his or her speechwriter. Margaret had a superb speechwriter. John Major needed a bit of help...

* * * * *

Norman Lamont only lasted a year before John Major sacked him. He nursed a grudge against Major who, he felt, had left him to carry the can for a policy that Major himself had developed. What followed could have been his revenge.

Midway through his term, John Major decided to throw his hat into the ring. He was tired of the sniping over his policy on Europe from Conservative members and launched his 'back me or sack me' campaign. The next day, as I prepared breakfast for Jim in the constituency, I received a call from Alan Clark. Not for the first time during our Parliamentary in fighting, he suggested – tongue in cheek – that I take up the challenge and face John Major in the leadership contest. Before I had time to give it serious thought, Norman Lamont phoned me to ask me to second his bid to compete for the leadership.

No one would have taken me seriously, so I agreed – to tell the truth, I was relieved. Norman and I shared the view that we should pull out of Europe and I had just got used to supporting his campaign when he telephoned again. John Redwood had taken up the gauntlet, and offered Norman the key position as his second in command so he absolved me from my obligation to support him, but suggested that I might like to join the John Redwood camp.

On Monday morning, I hurried back to London to attend the press conference at which John Redwood would announce his decision to bid for the leadership. When I arrived, the room was already packed. The police were advising latecomer MPs to squeeze in behind the table prepared for John and his entourage. By pure chance, John took a seat immediately in front of me. I was rather pleased at the time. It didn't occur to me that my position would be perceived as the ruination of his campaign.

Next morning, a photograph of Redwood appeared on the front of the *Times*. I was standing behind him dressed in bright green. The caption read 'Vulcan launched from Gorman's bosom'. I would have laughed it off, but his campaign team were appalled. The word went out to keep Gorman away from the campaign altogether. If one picture is worth a thousand words, that was a thousand words they could do without. I was a prominent right-winger and John's campaign team were terrified that he would be tarred with the same brush as me, and that he would not be able to secure the all-important support across the party. Internal elections do not focus on winning votes from the people, but the MPs.

John Redwood's campaign did not succeed, and John Major continued as Prime Minister. I dare say that there are those amongst Redwood's ardent supporters who believe to this day that if only I had slept late that morning, it might have changed the course of history.

Chapter Nineteen

ORSETT

'An Englishman's house was his castle.'
JIM GORMAN

People expect their MP to be an expert in just about everything. Most of us have a good general knowledge, but we mug up the details if and when necessary, such as when a constituent has a problem or you are put on a select committee. And so it is with planning laws. Jim and I had no idea how much they had changed since we had extensively restored our London house – a Grade I listed building – with the full co-operation and agreement of Westminster City Council and English Heritage.

The guiding principle of the 1970s was *restoration*: we were encouraged to remove later additions. But by the 1990s, that had changed. I was not aware that *conservation* was now the fashion and everything that was in place when the building was listed in the 1960s was 'protected' and could not be altered without consent. But there is nothing more satisfying than bringing an old house back to life. It was against this background that Jim set out to restore Old Hall Farm, a derelict farmhouse in the village of Orsett, and a Grade II listed building. It was a labour of love that turned into a nightmare and became a national cause célèbre. It scandalised the press. It infuriated English Heritage. It aroused hopes in the breast of households driven mad by officious planning officers. And it secretly delighted Thurrock Council, an old-style Labour council – who saw in it the chance to claim another Tory scalp for the Labour Party. There was something in it for everyone – except Jim and me.

We had been looking around for somewhere secluded to settle, when we came across a derelict farmhouse set well back from a country lane. When we first saw the property, standing forlorn in the middle of a few acres of tall, overgrown grass that reached to our waists, it was like approaching something out of an historical horror movie. The doors creaked eerily. Huge cobwebs draped every corner. It was not hard to imagine that Miss Haversham was in her armchair in one of the rooms. One of the house's principle charms was its isolation; privacy is a precious commodity for someone in the public eye. But for me, the main attraction was the beautiful ancient mulberry tree just outside the back door. It was July and the tree was loaded with berries. The hedgerows were overgrown and full of bird's nests and there wasn't a telegraph pole or a pylon in sight. It was just perfect.

The former inhabitant was a small tenant farmer, a man by the name of Dick Martin, who had lived in the house for nearly a century without spending too much time on maintenance, though he had carried out some 'modernisation'. The centuries-old front door had been replaced with a modern, white plastic-coated one from the local B&Q store. The huge open fireplaces had disappeared behind small modern, tiled surrounds, which did not need so much coal. The mullioned windows were boarded up to reduce heat loss and the inside walls were lined with plasterboard in an attempt to keep out the draughts. The fourteenth-century building had been turned into a pastiche of a 1920s villa.

Before we finally bought the derelict farmhouse, we invited the Thurrock Chief Planning Officer, Paul Shelley to view the place with us. We had him round again after buying it at auction, before work began. So, bit by bit – over a period of two years – Jim carefully restored the dilapidated building, turning it into a beautiful home in an idyllic setting. Only one more thing needed to be done: to inform Thurrock Council that the house they had dubbed inhabitable was about to be occupied.

I was delighted with his work. Jim had painstakingly researched fourteenth-century buildings, consulted Essex

Archives (where we discovered that the house had once had a porch) and sought guidance from the Weald and Downland Museum, which rescues and restores buildings of this period that would otherwise be destroyed. In fact, he did everything he could to ensure that the ancient parts of the house were restored in character. We did not set out to defy the law – on the contrary.

It took Jim the best part of two years' hard labour, with the help of local craftsmen: carpenters, masons, bricklayers, plumbers, plasterers, tilers, and the local blacksmith, Mr. Theobold. He recreated the latticed windows, rebuilt the fire baskets and designed, especially for us, his own version of a mediaeval light fitting for the hall! They made a splendid job of the restoration. I was proud of what Jim had done and so were our new friends that we met at the Foxhounds or the Wentworth Arms in the evenings.

It was only when the farmhouse was almost complete that we received a visit from Ms. Reeves, the Conservation Officer. From the minute Jim set eyes on her, he could see she was beside herself with rage.

'Stop. Stop work at once. You cannot continue.

At first, Jim, and the lads who were finishing off some pointing at the back of the house were taken aback.

'You must be joking!' said one of them.

But Ms. Reeves was not joking. Far from it. She was in possession of all the powers granted to her by planning regulations and she was here to exercise them.

'This house must not be touched until further notice – from me,' she cried.

'We are moving in at the weekend,' said Jim, 'and you can like it or lump it!'

Even though I was the local MP, the planning committee failed to make us aware of their intention to prosecute. We were in Portugal for a Christmas break when we saw our house on Sky TV and later, plastered all over the newspapers. The council refused to discuss the matter – or even consider retrospective planning consent. It was obvious that they had every intention of throwing the book at us. While we were still on holiday, they produced a council agenda alleging thirty-four separate offences. Each carried a maximum penalty of £20,000 and a six-month prison sentence. And what of Paul Shelley, the planning officer who had already visited the property with us before we'd even bought it? 'Mrs. Gorman should be prosecuted for carrying out irreparable damage to Old Hall Farm,' he announced.

Looking back, I should have been more aware of the pitfalls when we bought the house, but they simply didn't cross my mind. With hindsight, we all have twenty-twenty vision. MPs are very vulnerable to publicity. The media lap up stories that can seriously affect your reputation. And your opponents are only too happy to co-operate with the press.

The media went wild. The sleepy village of Orsett was besieged with reporters and cameramen down from London, all searching for Old Hall Farm. George, our handyman, tried to fight them off with a pitchfork as they swarmed over the fields to get within snapping distance of the house. By lunchtime, the village shop had run out of sandwiches, while the regulars in the Foxhounds arrived to find their favourite stools at the bar occupied by strangers. For good or ill, Orsett would never be the same again.

Overnight, our house became the best-known building in the country, after Buckingham Palace. It was publicity that the stately homes business would have died for, but we could have done without.

We later learned that the media coverage of Old Hall Farm did indeed reach Buckingham Palace. Some years later, the Queen and the Duke of Edinburgh came to Essex to celebrate the 50th anniversary of the creation of Basildon New Town, part of which was in my constituency. At lunch, I sat next to the Queen's new Private Secretary, Sir Robin Janvrin.

'Didn't you have a little problem with your house some time ago?' he asked. I expressed my surprise that he remembered. 'We followed the whole episode with bated breath, we could hardly miss it. What happened to the porch?'

Was that the 'royal we'? Had Her Majesty sat in front of her television viewing Jim's restoration and my interior decoration? Had Sir Robin briefed the royal party as they drove down the A13 in their limousine? 'We had to take down the porch.' I told him.

'Shame, I thought it looked rather nice,' he replied.

I congratulated him on the wonderful restoration of the fire-damaged Windsor castle which we had recently visited. 'I hope you didn't have too many problems,' I said.

'The Queen has a number of listed properties and she takes a keen interest in their upkeep,' he said with a smile.

I thought we were getting on famously as he changed the

subject to safari trips to Africa – on which I am a bit of an authority – having visited most of them during my time in business.

A council spokesman commented later, 'Retrospective consent cannot be given in this case. That leaves us with two options. We can either prosecute for criminal damage, which normally results in a fine, or we can apply an enforcement notice to reinstate to the original condition. That is always our preferred choice, for the obvious reason that we are not here to get people fined, we are here to get the building as close to the original as we can.' Which is exactly what Jim had achieved.

It would indeed have been absurd to return the interior to a pastiche of an Edwardian villa. But that was not the Labour council's intention. They thought a high-profile scandal could damage the Conservative Party. Jim and I had come up against the same red tape that engulfs the lives and undermines the liberty of millions of home owners. We were dragged before the Magistrates' court and threatened not only with a fine but a prison sentence.

The stipendiary magistrate, Mr. Mark Romer, said the Court accepted that the Gormans were motivated by 'a desire to find somewhere peaceful to live and to restore the building to a habitable state. It is not a willful defiance of the planning law.' He went on, 'Some alterations had affected the character of the building. It is perfectly clear that the purpose of the Act is to preserve what is left in this country of fine, original buildings ... and this was and still is a fine building.'

Nevertheless, as a gesture to the council, we were made to remove the front porch – which had existed on the original building. And we were fined £3,000 each for failing to obtain planning consent, although I personally had not been involved in the work. The moral victory was ours. Our only regret was that a quarter of a million pounds of ratepayers' money had been wasted in pursuit of a political vendetta.

In its advice to local councils, the Department of Environment states, 'A well-publicised, successful prosecution can provide a valuable deterrent to willful damage of a listed building.' But it can also deter people from trying to save them.

Chapter Twenty

BOGUS SCIENCE

'Science is built up of facts, as a house is built of stones;
but an accumulation of facts is no more a science than
a heap of stones is a house.'

HENRI POINCARÉ

Before becoming an MP, I spent my life as a biologist and for
twenty years, I manufactured teaching materials related to
microbiology. I knew a great deal about the culture of
microbes and how they spread.

In Britain, we are regularly gripped by scare stories
involving microbiological events such as salmonella, mad
cow disease (BSE) and foot-and-mouth, which seemed to

paralyse our natural scepticism and throw the country into spasms of anxiety. When politics and science clash in the House, science usually suffers. Parliament's response makes a mountain out of a molehill and an animal health problem into a national crisis

On 3 September 1988, the Junior Health Minister, Edwina Currie, uttered twenty words in a television interview that sparked off a food scare crisis of unprecedented intensity, I was keenly interested. The salmonella crisis was to bring an industry to its knees and eventually cost the government and egg producers nearly £4 million per word. This was all on the basis of twenty-six outbreaks and 460 cases of food poisoning in a population of 60 million people. A relatively minor matter.

'We do warn people now that most of the egg production in this country, sadly, is now infected with salmonella.' These words were prepared by the PHLS (Public Health Laboratory Service). Salmonella food poisoning is not a contagious illness; indeed, it is scarcely more serious than the common cold. Edwina's remarks about salmonella in eggs in December 1988 triggered huge attention from the media and anxious interest among the general public.

I knew something about the use of eggs in the culture of germs. My instinct was that this was not a farmyard crisis but a kitchen hygiene crisis. An undamaged, complete egg is an hermetically sealed unit designed by nature to protect the developing chick. It is not easily penetrated and its internal 'atmosphere' would not support the growth of salmonella bacteria, which requires a good supply of oxygen. This only happens when the egg is broken and its contents left lying around, uncooked, as happens, for example, when making fresh mayonnaise.

A number of outbreaks took place in hospitals coinciding with the large-scale introduction of pre-cooked and chilled food. There was considerable political opposition to this move from trade unions, who saw it as an attack on their jobs. Other outbreaks were associated with bar mitzvahs and wedding breakfasts where food was prepared in advance and left unrefrigerated for days.

We even had an outbreak in the House of Lords. A total of eighty-five people were affected by salmonella arising from the consumption of food produced by the House of Lords' kitchens. Foods containing mayonnaise were implicated in the first outbreaks. The mayonnaise was prepared by staff two or three times a week. At the end of each day, unused mayonnaise was returned to the kitchen, where it may have been mixed with a new batch, providing the opportunity to contaminate subsequent batches.

The egg white surplus from the mayonnaise was stored and later used to bind raw minced chicken for lamb en croute, which was served at a private dinner on 6 May. And taramasalata was implicated in the final outbreak, which was most probably caused by the inadequate cleaning of piping bags that were used for a number of soft foods including mayonnaise.

The potential mixture of political pressure and poor hygiene triggered a massive slump in the market for eggs and chickens. Within days, egg consumption had slumped by an unparalleled fifty per cent overall. Hospital and school sales fell by ninety per cent. Nine days later, newspapers were reporting a mountain of 300 million unsold eggs. Sales a year after the event were still down by about ten per cent. Cumulative losses of income were estimated at £70 million.

The crisis hit businesses and farmers in my constituency, which included a number of small holdings engaged in the intensive rearing of poultry including one of the largest egg packers and distributors in the country. I decided to put my case to the Ministry. I had the devil's own job to get even a meeting with David Maclean, Parliamentary Secretary in the Department, who was standing in for Edwina, despite the fact that I reminded him that I knew what I was talking about. I think he only agreed to see me on sufferance. Senior civil servants and scientists from MAFF (Ministry of Agriculture, Fisheries and Food) listened with barely concealed irritation. They had targeted poultry and eggs as the cause of the outbreak and my views undermined their advice to the Minister.

'I hear what you say, Teresa, but I'm afraid we will have to differ. The Public Health Laboratory Service doesn't share your view.'

As a result of their advice, over a million birds were killed, and the livelihood of hundreds of small businesses were destroyed. But the amount of salmonella food poisoning was not reduced; the policy was shown to be misguided and futile. We could not eradicate salmonella and other food poisoning bacteria from the environment, but we could advise people to refrigerate food containing raw eggs – and particularly fresh mayonnaise.

Edwina's statement was the beginning of the end of her

career. She was held responsible for the crisis – and never forgave her boss, Ken Clarke, Secretary of State for Health, for leaving her to carry the can.

Later when John Major moved into Number 10 Downing Street and there was much clamour, from myself and others, to put some women on his front bench, he sent for Edwina. She knew how to milk a situation for publicity and turned up to Downing Street with the press all cameras blazing. They expected her to emerge triumphant, accepted back into the ministerial fold. Instead, she emerged tight-lipped and grim-faced. 'He offered me Minister for Prisons,' she recounted in the tea-room later. 'That's bad enough, but under Ken Clarke as Home Secretary. Talk about a lack of sensitivity.'

Edwina never recovered politically. She remained on the back benches, championing the outlandish cause of Outrage and writing her first sexy novel allegedly based on the goings on in Parliament, raunchy enough to be serialised in a national newspaper. In the tea-room, we speculated on whether this was based on her personal experiences. If so, there was more going on in the House than we were aware of. I too indulged in a spot of writing – an account of the egg disaster that I called 'Chickengate', after Watergate, the botch-up that cost President Nixon his job in the White House; unfortunately, it did not make the best-seller list. In 1992, Edwina lost her seat.

* * * * *

Ten years later, I would again find my constituency involved in a new agricultural crisis. This time concerning cattle, which appeared to have developed a new disease: BSE, or mad cow disease. The largest abattoir in the south-east, Cheales, was situated on the borders of my constituency and its business was devastated. Once more, I would clash with MAFF and the then Agriculture Minister, Nicholas Soames, delegated to deal with the crisis in its early stages. For centuries sheep suffered from a disease called scrapie and MAFF contested that this had entered the cattle through eating processed feed, including sheep remains. On a scientific basis, I disagreed with this hypothesis.

As long ago as 1946, a House of Lords committee chaired by the famous biologist Sir Solly Zuckerman warned against the dangers to human as well as animal health from the excessive use of chemicals derived from the nerve gases developed for use in warfare. These substances, called OPs (organo-phosphates), were widely used pesticides. During an epidemic of warble-fly, a particular OP called phosmet was recommended to kill the pest, which burrows into the hide of the cattle to lay its eggs. In Britain, MAFF ordered an excessive dose – three times that recommended by the manufacturers, and it is possible that this increased dose could have triggered the epidemic.

Margaret Marr, the Countess of Marr, a sheep farmer in Scotland, developed serious health problems as a result of using sheep dip that also contains OPs. She has fought long and lonely battle in the House of Lords to have its damaging effects recognised. But she has received little support from the manufacturers or from MAFF.

An increasing number of sheep farmers develop severe

depression, even to the point of committing suicide, which could be brought on by the toxic effects of these substances. And it is also possible that others working in industries which use pesticides on a large scale in horticulture or animal husbandry including horse and dogs could be at risk, due to the potential damage to their nervous system.

A group of back-bench MPs, led by Paul Tyler, is fighting to have this whole area investigated but we are up against government-funded organisations such as SEAC (the Spongiform Encephalopathy Advisory Committee), on whose recommendation the theory of the scrapie connection is based. Moreover, representatives of the manufacturers of these products sit on the government's Medicines Committee, which hands out advice on the relative safety of products that could affect health.

It is difficult to understand why the infective feed theory was embraced so quickly and emphatically, despite the misgivings of many in the scientific community. But so much can be explained by looking at how science is conducted in the UK, and indeed, most of the rest of the world.

There is a certain mystique about scientists. The boffin image still predominates, conjuring up images of eggheads with awesome intelligence. Non-scientists assume that the scientists know what they are doing, and rarely question their more eccentric ideas. In truth, real genius is as rare in science as it is in many other fields.

Scrapie has been known of for about 300 years, with no suggestion that it is a threat to humans. When BSE emerged, it seemed natural to pass the research to the scrapie scientists, and endless research money appeared to facilitate the process. Scientists rely on grants to work. Without grants, salaries are low, and no chemicals can be purchased, no technicians can be employed and no work can be performed. It is the way that the grants are allocated that may have had the biggest detrimental effect on the course of the BSE disaster.

It is extremely difficult to achieve preliminary results without a grant, but no grant will be given without preliminary results. This is the catch-22 situation whereby larger companies are best placed to achieve results. Many good scientists have been thwarted in this way, despite the fact that they may be amongst the most gifted. The general public will never hear any complaints – after all, the scientists must still earn a living and life is precarious for whistleblowers.

The recipients of the biggest grants are often members of SEAC. Due to their membership of this exclusive club, these are the scientists turned to by the media in their quest for information. They are generally well funded in their research areas, though not always.

The media were quick to embrace the theory that BSE could be transmitted to humans through eating 'infective beef', although there is no scientific evidence to demonstrate that this could occur. They merely reported the gloomy predictions of individual scientists that we could lose a whole generation of young people. Whenever diseases are newsworthy, the same high-profile scientists are interviewed. And in this way, the theories of scientists are turned into facts by the media, causing hysteria amongst the public.

In a similar way, both the National Farmers Union officials and the *Farmers Weekly* – the journal devoted to farming matters, have shied away from any suggestion that OPs were connected with the crisis, although farmers are increasingly inclined to believe that there is a connection. The farming press relies heavily on advertising for their survival, much of which is filled with details of new or currently used pesticides. Rather than bite the hand that feeds it, it appears to be at best non-committal in its consideration of alternative theories.

After more than a decade of intensive study and an inquiry lasting more than two years at a cost of £27 million to the taxpayer, what have we learnt about the BSE crisis? Very little. The nvCJD epidemic he warned was inevitable is still to emerge. Millions of healthy cattle have been slaughtered and many farmers have been ruined. The costs of the BSE crisis are enormous, and must be measured not only in economic terms, but also in terms of their effect on society.

* * * * *

The latest crisis to hit the beleaguered farming industry – the spread of foot-and-mouth disease – is linked to policies implemented by MAFF in response to BSE. They forced the closure of hundreds of small abattoirs around the country, which dealt with local farmers. This meant that pigs and sheep had to travel long distances for slaughter. Now these animals must be transported long distances with the risk of spreading the disease round the country – which is exactly what has happened. Ironically, the current outbreak was first identified in pigs brought to Cheales abattoir in Essex from the North of England.

MAFF, once again, fell back on its policy of slaughter of infected and uninfected animals, running into millions of animals, at a cost of £3 billion. Foot and mouth is a mild disease that does not affect human beings and could have easily been controlled by the use of vaccine, large quantities of which were already available in the country. The Dutch wiped out a similar outbreak months ago using vaccine. MAFF's argument was that if we vaccinated, we would lose our export markets for pig and sheep meat, valued at £500 million a year. But we import more meat than this from other parts of the world.

Whenever a problem arises, the government panics, largely because the politicians handling the crisis have no knowledge of whom to consult other than the government advisory bodies. Under pressure from the media to come up with an instant solution, they fall back on the crude policy of extermination. It is inconceivable that such a policy could be applied with the outbreak of diseases in the human population. The use of vaccination and inoculation is widespread in agriculture for a variety of problems. It is entirely the demands of the European Union that forced us to adopt measures that no humane person would advocate.

Carl Popper, one of the most brilliant philosophers of science, whose lectures I attended years ago at the London

School of Economics, pointed out that no hypothesis can be proved beyond doubt; it can only be disproved. Organisations that have built their reputation around a hypothesis have a vested interest in ignoring contradictory evidence or of extending their hypothesis to include the new information. In this way, the policies which may have caused the problem go undiscovered.

To avoid similar errors of judgement in future, the government must obtain a wider spectrum of scientific opinion and extend its field of information to scientists working in the independent sector, including universities. It must resist the pressure to act precipitously. Within the Palace of Westminster is POST (the Parliamentary Office of Science and Technology), independent of Whitehall and with no particular axe to grind. It could undertake this role by compiling a database of scientists and their specialities. Instead of inevitably falling back on the same narrow group of those working in the ministry or in state-funded bodies, not only the government, but also the media would have instant access to a broad field of top-quality scientific opinion.

Chapter Twenty-One

KYOTO

'Eighty percent of air pollution
comes from plants and trees.'
RONALD REAGAN

The Japanese political system is very different from ours, with a number of political parties forming loose coalitions and a strange way of acquiring votes – by a system of giving presents to voters – that in Britain would be considered bribery.

In 1997, when I was offered the chance to take part in a delegation to Japan, I jumped at it. The Japanese were still a mystery to me and I was keen to learn about their political and domestic institutions. You can often learn more about a country from the inside of their homes than from the inside of a conference hall. So I contrived to visit a few.

The standard Japanese house seems very small to us – just one room and a tiny kitchen and bathroom. No wardrobes, no beds and not much in the way of a kitchen – no saucepans, just rice bowls, a microwave oven and an old-fashioned twin-tub washing machine.

But their toilet technology knocks spots off ours. When I ventured into the loo in my hotel bathroom, I had no idea that I would be in for a new experience. The loos have centrally heated seats and a choice of built-in bottom washers, everything from a jet to a spray. I tried the jet – it almost propelled me from the seat. The spray was nicer, but still leaves you with a damp bottom.

But where was the toilet paper? Everywhere you go, the toilets are immaculate, but however expensive the venue, there is no toilet paper. Japanese department stores have a whole section selling small towels, the size of a face cloth, some beautifully finished and very expensive. Japanese women always carry one of these in their handbags. Apart from the odd bidet that you find in a posh, Barratt-style house in a new estate, we have nothing to match it. I'm surprised that the Japanese haven't tried exporting them to the West.

We arrived in the week before the Kyoto Conference, when not only the Japanese economy was in a mess, but so too was its government. Kyoto was all about castigating industrial countries for their emissions of carbon dioxide gas into the atmosphere.

In the run-up to the Kyoto Conference, Tony Blair, pledged to encourage business in the search for ways to deal with the threat posed by climate change. More alarmingly, Chancellor Gordon Brown has adopted the proposed Climate Change Levy – a tax on the use of energy – which would be a nice little earner for the Treasury. Meanwhile, John Prescott was due at the conference to make pronouncements on global warming fed to him by the Green Lobby and its devotees in the Department of the Environment. He would pledge our industries to a reduction in CO_2 emissions by twenty per cent. I doubted whether he understood the science behind these proposals or the economic cost.

Not everyone believes in global warming; the Japanese and the Americans have their misgivings. I took the opportunity of asking the Japanese Minister for Trade and Industry, whom I met on an official visit to the Diet (parliament), if he endorsed the Kyoto target. Any such policy would play havoc with their car industry, a mainstay of the increasingly shaky Japanese economic miracle. 'We are thinking of five per cent, as a good compromise,' he said through the interpreter.

'Tell the Minister that his sensible views are music to my ears,' I replied. A broad smile lit up his face. I winked. We had an Anglo-Japanese understanding; but I knew his views would not go down well with Mr Prescott.

I am as interested in the politics of climate change as in the science behind it. Global warming is the latest in a string of apocalyptic predictions that began in the 1970s when global cooling and a new ice age was being forecast.

The scientific evidence is second rate, but the political implications could be disastrous for our economy. The Kyoto

Conference was the latest in a string of international junkets, beginning with the Earth Summit in Rio, Brazil in 1992.

The aim was to impose a system of environmental regulations, including onerous taxes on energy fuels on the population of industrialised countries. US President Bush Senior was advised by NASA and other scientific bodies that the evidence for CO_2 reductions was too weak to justify the economic costs. Nevertheless, he signed up to the reductions demanded, though without committing the US to a specific timetable.

As the strength of the World Green Movement increased in the 1970s and 1980s, the UN began to take an active role in environmental affairs, calling for 'sustainable development'. Sustainable development sounds reasonable, but is and was easily distorted by those who want private economic activity to be subordinated to a centrally planned strategy – with large-scale transfer of resources from Western countries to the Third World – in other words, socialism.

The predictions on which the politics are based are made by organisations such as the IPCC (International Panel on Climate Change) who are only as good as the quality of the statistical evidence available on the principle of 'garbage in garbage out'.

Industry is again under attack by non-governmental organisations such as Greenpeace and Friends of the Earth and their friends in the media. Every BBC report on climate change will feature a green guru, often Jonathan Porritt or George Mambiot. When did you last hear from a scientist who takes the opposite view?

Massive forces completely out of our control dictate climate. The unpredictable level of radiation from the sun; volcanic activity, which spews gases into the upper atmosphere and is notoriously difficult to forecast; and the vast ocean currents controlled by gravity and the phases of the moon. In other words, climate is dictated by the law of physics – not the laws of man. The argument of the NGOs is that industry, and in particular the motor car, is responsible for building up a blanket of greenhouse gases that prevents heat from escaping from the earth's surface. But the evidence suggesting a discernible human influence on global climate is replete with uncertainties and dismissed by many reputable scientists. In 1991, Channel 4 bravely produced an excellent programme called *The Greenhouse Conspiracy* featuring many prominent scientists from the UK and the USA, pointing out the flaws in the accepted view. But nothing came of it. It did not start a national debate. Other channels and most of the press ignored it, overcome by the power of consensus thinking.

Carbon dioxide, demonised as 'greenhouse gas', is a trace element in our atmosphere – less than 300 parts in a million or 0.003 per cent. Evidence that it has increased by a small amount in the last 150 years is questionable, but in any case, the amount has varied throughout geological time, long before motor cars and factory chimneys appeared on the scene. Carbon dioxide is the essential ingredient of plant growth – they can't get enough of it – and it is also very soluble in the oceans that cover three-quarters of the earth's surface.

Attended by John Prescott, Deputy Prime Minister and

Minister for the Environment, the Kyoto Conference has set a target of a reduction of 20 per cent in our CO_2 output. I sat on the Select Committee on the Environment and listened in despair to a whole raft of new measures, including a Climate Change Levy; a new tax on industry, and proposals for a complicated market in tradable emissions that would allow Western economies to buy the CO_2 allowance of Third World countries. The mind boggles. These stringent controls can only have one effect – an unnecessary and unjustified attack on fossil fuel industries, which produce CO_2 as a waste product – and, ultimately, on the competitive position of industries.

There is another sinister aspect to this problem. It is the tendency for climate change scientists to talk up the dangers of environmental problems. It brings attention to their work and a flow of funds to support their research. There are few funds available to the scientists who say it is all nonsense. To contradict a fashion amongst scientists is an invitation to vilification and abuse. Galileo was forced to recant when he suggested that the earth revolved around the sun and not the other way around, and Darwin was given a pretty rough ride when he challenged the orthodox views on creation. By 1992, the global warming industry was already worth over £1 billion a year, despite the fact that only 19 per cent of scientists believed that the warming of the atmosphere was induced by humans. But of course, it would not be in their interests to say so in public, because there is no capital in saying that the emperor has no clothes.

The scientists' dire warnings are communicated to policy makers and to the public via the media. There has been a systematic brainwashing of our school children, who can all trot out the evils of industry (i.e. Western capitalism) that are destroying our planet. This in turn generates pressure on politicians to do something about it. Those politicians who refuse to be stampeded into action are few and far between and, like President George W. Bush, are bound to be ridiculed or attacked, as he had been at the Kyoto Conference. But one politician of his stature is worth a dozen John Prescotts and his advisors, who are driven by the ranks of the NGOs.

I once went to discuss my views with the then Secretary of State for the Environment, Michael Howard, who is an excellent lawyer, but to the best of my knowledge has no scientific background. I wanted to bring to his attention an important research paper produced by the George Marshall Institute in Washington, which had a significant bearing on the beleaguered coal industry – one of the fossil fuel industries under attack for its alleged contribution to greenhouse gases. Representatives of the GMI were in the country and I helped to arrange a meeting with MPs in the Commons to present their views. I thought it would be useful for Michael to meet them too. But I was wasting my time. At his elbows sat his chief advisor, Peter Burke, formally the director of Greenpeace. I knew before I opened my mouth that I was wasting my time. I leave to your imagination the conversation that took place between them as soon as I left the conference room. I heard no more from the Secretary of State. I am sure my views were dismissed.

I brought my concerns to the attention of the Prime Minister. This is his reply.

Dear Teresa,

I very much respect the vigour and certainty with which you hold and argue your views, but I fear we must agree to disagree.

The government must, of course, be careful not to follow slavishly the latest scientific fears and fads. That is why it is our fundamental aim to obtain sound scientific advice on environmental issues as a basis for our policy decisions.

Your aide memoire raises many points of detail which you may wish to pursue directly with the two focal points of the UK research in these areas, the Hadley Centre for Climate Prediction and Research at Bracknell, and the EC/EFTA Ozone Layer Research Co-ordination Unit at Cambridge. Both of these facilities are supported through the Department of the Environment's Research Programme and Michael Howard's office would be pleased to put in hand arrangements for visits.

Yours Ever, John

It is up to politicians to keep an open mind when faced with evidence produced by scientific bodies with a vested interest and to obtain a wide spectrum of views. The history of science is replete with examples of theories, believed in explicitly by scientists of the day, only to be disproved later. Global warming is such a theory. And yet we are penalising industries and risking jobs in pursuit of this false hypothesis.

Chapter Twenty-Two

MY VISION FOR ENGLAND

*'There is a forgotten, nay, almost forgotten word,
which means more to me than any other.
That word is England.'*

WINSTON CHURCHILL

Patriotism is the great driving force of national unity. It should be meat and drink to the Conservative Party, which prides itself on being the party of the Union. We had no power to prevent Labour from fragmenting our country into separate administrations, but we could make a stand on a parliament for England. There was support for the idea amongst my Conservative colleagues, but William Hague rejected it.

In January 1998, I put forward a private member's bill, supported by seven Conservative colleagues, calling for a referendum to ask the people of England if they want their own parliament. Then, at the 1998 Conservative Conference, a packed meeting of party workers also agreed. This idea appeals to all shades of political opinion within the Conservative Party and beyond. Many of Labour's natural supporters would, if asked, rank patriotism above their party's plans of regionalisation, for which there is little or no demand.

I received thousands of letters of support for the parliament for England idea from ordinary Conservative voters. At the two Tory Party conferences following the 1997 election we held fringe meetings that were packed with people standing around the room, so great was the interest. We had to open the back of the room to accommodate all those keen to support our idea. At one stage, William Hague, accompanied by his entourage, walked past looking into what was obviously one of the most popular events of the conference. No leader can afford to ignore that amount of enthusiasm from the party faithful.

People standing in the polling booths at the 1997 general election may not have realised it, but the Labour Party already had big plans for the way Britain was to be governed. These policies will involve changes more drastic than anything that has happened since the seventeenth century, when Oliver Cromwell ousted the monarchy and established his Commonwealth – his new republic. Cromwell started out as a democrat but ended as king in all but name. If Labour's plans go through, Tony Blair will be the 'President of Britain', just as his good friend Bill Clinton was in America.

Tony Blair has already sent the majority of the hereditary peers packing, and plans to replace more of them with his chums. Half of all government ministers are unelected members of the Lords with another variation on the MOT certificate – Mate Of Tony. To keep the Liberal Democrats onside, he talks about changing the voting system to proportional representation – a system that spawns a mob of minor parties and produces a legislature too weak to resist a powerful leader. But, with a parliamentary majority as large as the Labour Party's, there has been no need to put these plans to the House.

To strengthen their grip on the Celtic fringe, the Blair government, through a series of referenda, has given Scotland, Wales and Northern Ireland a degree of autonomy denied to the people of England. The English are not to have their own parliament to regulate their affairs. Instead, we are to be fobbed off with nine regional assemblies, centred around industrial cities, run by Blair appointees. It doesn't take a genius to work out why the English are denied a referendum and its own parliament; England is where most Conservative voters are to be found. An English Parliament representing 48 million of our 58 million people would provide a rival power base to the Westminster Parliament – and its leader. So long as the present plan survives, the Westminster Parliament can rely on a large posse of Labour MPs hailing from the provinces, which will no doubt receive favoured treatment under the national budget.

The idea of a parliament for England – almost unthinkable just 18 months ago – is catching on. According to a *Sunday Times* poll in the last Parliament, half of all Conservative MPs, including two members of the Shadow Cabinet, expressed an interest in it.

Scotland has established its own parliament with 129 new SMPs controlling its domestic affairs and invested with tax-raising powers. Wales, with sixty members in its assembly and Northern Ireland with 108 members, will surely not long be content with less in the years to come. Yet English taxpayers are expected to bear the lion's share of the costs of these new assemblies, with no say about how our money is spent. Westminster members have no voice in matters devolved to the regions whereas the Celts will be free to pontificate in Westminster on English affairs.

They have the right to join the debate on setting the national budget, including the amount allocated to regional 'parliaments'. This cannot fail to foster keen resentment among English MPs, conscious of the fact that their constituents are subsidising the Celtic fringe. In brief, the Scots and Welsh are enjoying power without responsibility while the English, once again, draw the short straw – responsibility *without* power.

Scotland receives a subsidy of £7 billion a year from the taxpayer, equivalent to £1,000 for every man, woman and child, despite the fact that the average incomes in Scotland and England are neck and neck. Each time their MPs vote for more government spending, the true cost is not fully felt in the back pocket because the English pick up the lion's share of the bill. The stock response of the Scottish Nationalists to the accusation that their countrymen are heavily subsidised by the English is that an independent Scotland would receive ninety per cent of revenues from taxing North Sea oil and gas and that this would easily compensate for the withdrawal of subsidies. However, a study by Alex Kemp, Professor of Economics at Aberdeen University, commissioned for *The Economist*, rejects the claim of the SNP. Apparently, the bonanza days for Scottish oil and gas lie in the past, when oil prices were much higher, but even then, the Scottish share of these taxes would not have made up the deficit with England. In future, the Scottish tranche of oil and gas revenue could dip as low as forty-five per cent of a declining total. In 1998, when oil prices were low, the total tax revenue was £2.6 billion, of which the Scots would have received two-thirds. Unhappily for the Nationalists, the position is deteriorating because the new Scottish oilfields are in deep and distant waters and are therefore expensive to drill.

If the provinces had to raise all their taxes directly from their own electorates, that would be a different story. If the Scots and Welsh lost their present subsidies, their income tax would double. If the question had been put like that, there might have been different results in the referenda that have so far taken place. Admittedly the Scots were enthusiastic, but Wales was touch and go. In the Mayor of London referendum, the first of England's regional assemblies, barely a third of Londoners bothered to vote at all. What a hollow victory for Labour when less than twenty per cent of those entitled to vote in our capital city give two hoots for the idea. By manipulating our constitution, with England receiving a dog's breakfast of rigged regional authorities, Blair may think he has served his party well. Yet, as Scotland and Wales demand more powers for themselves, the people of England, thus far merely passive spectators, will be driven to ask what's in it for them.

Few people realise that the creation of these regions is the final move in the piecing together of one of the most ambitious political projects of all time, designed to change the United Kingdom so dramatically that it will soon be scarcely recognisable. The master plan is to carve up the UK into twelve administrative regions – including Scotland, Wales and Northern Ireland – to bring Britain into line with the EU's vision of a 'Europe of the Regions'. This ideal has been taking shape since the Blair government came to power in May 1997.

A significant step in the last parliament was the Regional Development Agencies Bill. This sets up agencies for each English region. They are truly the regional governments in the making and part of Brussels' plan for the whole of Europe. Each agency has its own 'chamber' of unelected government appointees plus representatives of the CBI and TUC. The revolution will then complete the bonfire of our liberty. A Trojan horse to lock us into our new centre of government in Brussels.

It adds up to a constitutional revolution as far reaching as any in our history. The astonishing thing is that this vast project has been put into place so secretly that almost no one has noticed what has been and is happening. When will Conservative politicians stir up the British people to what has been done to their country? But Labour's hope is that soon there will no longer be a British people to care: we will all be Europeans.

The Nationalists in Scotland and Wales want to defect to Europe. If Labour appears to be less than enthusiastic about this, it is because they want to retain control of the new devolved assemblies in order to maintain control of the Westminster Parliament. Portugal had a referendum on whether to adopt the European Regional Plan and firmly rejected it. The Portuguese are sticking to their traditional geographical boundaries – the equivalent of our counties – just as the English would do if asked. But England has not been granted a referendum on any of the legislation that is fragmenting our unity at great historical cost, because Blair has a shrewd idea that the answer will be no, they do not want regional assemblies.

The Conservative Party has, in the past, bent over backwards to appease the Celts and keep the Union going. It was a Conservative Prime Minister, Lord Salisbury, who set up the first devolved government in the form of the Scottish Office in the 1880s. It was Churchill who first created the post of Minister for Wales, and gave Wales a seat at the Cabinet table. Even at the most testing of times, we have made compromises to keep the Union one happy family. When Mrs. Thatcher was struggling to keep government spending under control, she kept the preferential treatment of Scotland and Wales firmly in place.

It has not always been in our interest to stick by the Union. Twice since the war, in 1964 and 1974, a Labour government had been let in with the votes of members of Parliament elected in Scotland and Wales. This was despite the fact that the Conservatives had won a majority of the seats in England. Never have we suggested changing the political system for our own political advantage.

The harmony that citizens of the United Kingdom have established over the centuries cannot survive if it is permanently biased against its largest component – England. The only party with a powerful interest in championing England and demanding that it should have the same political rights as the rest of the United Kingdom is the Conservative Party. If we don't demand fair treatment for England, if we continue to sit back while it is broken into competing regional authorities, we shall betray the people's trust and will not deserve the support of the English voters.

To put it bluntly, Labour's plans are a conspiracy against the 48 million people who live in England to cheat them of their birthright. Labour knows that England is the Conservative heartland and is likely to return a Conservative Parliament, with a Conservative First Minister. What powers would be left for the Westminster Parliament and its prime minister? Only Defence, Foreign Affairs and the Budget, including a fair debate on the allocation of funds to the devolved parliaments.

The spirit of the Union has largely disappeared and shows precious little sign of returning. Conservatives cannot bury their heads in the sand and proclaim their loyalty to the UK, only to allow England to be cheated of its constitutional rights. If the Scots want their own parliament, good luck to them. They have chosen to run their own affairs without English interference. Let us accept that with good grace. But the quid pro quo is that the English, too, must be able to run their own country without interference from north of the border. And like it or loathe it – we can't do that unless England has a parliament of its own.

Labour's rush is to dismantle the constitution has one good aspect: it has given the Conservative Party a rare opportunity. The English may be a fair-minded and conservative people, but with the Welsh and Scots throwing their weight around, they will be very responsive to a party espousing their cause.

England is presently run by the Scots. They dominate the Cabinet and the House of Commons. How long before the guaranteed way for a speaker on the hustings to get a cheer from an English crowd will be by declaring that the Scots are 'over-represented, over-opinionated and over here'? How soon before we hear the first explosion of grass-roots English anger against the growing tax burden imposed by a Scottish Chancellor?

Labour's game-plan is to soft-sell the single currency as a commercial advantage to British firms and a boon to foreign holiday-makers. However, the real significance of it is that, by losing the pound, we would lose the last significant barrier to full incorporation into the European Union and the end of our parliamentary democracy. Labour may still be riding high in England as well as Scotland and Wales (although it has lost ground to the Nationalists in both these countries), but Conservatives can, if they wish, ensure that Westminster will be in a ferment over the shameful treatment of the English majority. Many Labour MPs support this view and sometimes seem more patriotic than we Tories are.

England's stability, her history, institutions, laws and traditions have long been celebrated, even eulogised, by the Conservatives. This cannot be said for the Labour Party, which was born of discontent. Though nowadays seeking the middle-class vote, it finds it is leaving behind its class-war reflexes and even its senior members make use of its punitive attitude to private healthcare and the grammar schools. But it still has the itch to radicalise our government institutions – moving towards the socialist policies of the EU.

Whilst the vast majority of Conservatives believe that Labour's devolution policies are destructive, they have accepted that the Celtic provinces will go their own way. The Scots and Welsh Nationalists will try to keep feelings of hostility to England on the boil, but it is a fair bet that, when the true cost of independence is spelled out, the majority of people in Scotland and Wales will recoil at the final break with the Union. Even so, we still shall be left with a federal state.

A parliament for England would revive English patriotism. Nothing is wrong with that. But far from pouring fuel on the flames of nationalism of the negative kind, it would give England the right to express pride in its achievements. It would be okay to be English again. We may even be able – like the Scots and the Welsh – to celebrate our national day, our national saint, our national traditions and even our language without being accused of chauvinism. At present we make do with a few sentimental songs, sung once a year on the last night of the Proms, 'Jerusalem' and 'There'll Always Be An England', but they remain some of the most popular songs in the English language.

As long ago as the 1970s, Tam Dalyell, Labour MP for Linlithgow, pointed out that devolution to Scotland would drive a coach and horses through the traditional equality of powers enjoyed by all members of the Westminster Parliament. How, he asked, could Scottish MPs at Westminster continue to legislate on domestic matters affecting England, whilst English MPs no longer had the right to do the same in Scotland? That question has still not been answered. Labour's plans certainly do not include any reduction in powers of Scottish MPs in Westminster or in the subsidy that Scottish voters receive from English taxes.

Leaving aside the fact that Tony Blair is already discussing with Europe the possibility of a Euro-wide defence force and foreign policy, these issues, though of vital importance to national survival, nevertheless occupy a relatively small amount of parliamentary time. With separate parliaments flourishing in all the regions, what would their Westminster MPs have to do? Certainly there would be no way they could claim it as a full-time job.

The eventual use for the House of Lords could be for an elected second chamber from all parts of the United Kingdom to deliberate on the reserved powers of Defence and Foreign Affairs. They could share the chamber with the

Law Lords, who would carry on as our Supreme Court. The English parliament – with 529 members – would occupy the present House of Commons. Whitehall, except for the Foreign Office and Ministry of Defence, would implement its policies. There would be no need for an extra layer of bureaucracy, as some people fear. On the contrary, with the House of Lords replaced by surely no more than 109 elected representatives – one for each county – the cost and the workload of the Houses of Parliament would be greatly reduced.

A lesson we could learn from Spain is that you meddle with basic equality of a constitution at your peril, and once the principle of equality is breached there is no real limit on the powers that politicians in that part of a country will demand for themselves, or the civil strife that it can cause.

A parliament for England would leave us in a much more coherent position, if not as a Union then at least as a federal state. Everyone within it would know that an increase in the powers and responsibilities of one of the parliaments or assemblies would mean an increase in the powers and responsibilities of all. No one part of this Union would enjoy any privilege denied to the rest, or be forced to subsidise the others against its will.

Malcolm Rifkind, who remained a most powerful Tory influence in Scotland despite losing his seat in the 1997 election, held to the view that the Tory Party should not do anything that might imperil the chances of the Tories making a comeback in Scotland. However, the 2001 general election proved that Scottish Tories stand very little chance of returning any MPs to Westminster in the current political climate. Should we sacrifice our chances in England simply to try and revive the party's Scottish corpse?

Following the 2001 Blair election victory, this is surely the moment when the Tory Party should aim its policies at those voters who will propel the party back into government. By pushing for a parliament for England the Tories will once again awaken the spirit of patriotism, a characteristic that was sadly missing during the 2001 election.

Even the English Tourist Board supported the idea and were so keen that they staged a full-blown reception in the Commons to push the idea. They believed it will aid the tourist industry. Scores of Tory MPs attended the reception and queued to pose for a photograph with an actor dressed as St. George, which they proudly sent off to their local newspapers, knowing it would produce the right message in the constituency.

One of our staunchest supporters was David Davis, who had been Minister for Europe in the last John Major administration, and who threw his cap into the ring for the party leadership following William Hague's resignation. He told the meeting, 'In my job as Minister for Europe I have seen maps of the Britain Isles drawn up by Brussels in which the British Isles have been divided up into regions. On those maps the name of England does not exist, obliterated. And that I cannot accept.'

Here is an opportunity for the Conservative Party to re-establish its contact with its natural supporters. Margaret Thatcher's huge majorities did not rely on natural supporters. She drew support from people of all political persuasions because she represented that sense of patriotism and a love of country that stirs people in a way no other policy or sentiment can. Will the next party leader take up the challenge?

Chapter Twenty-Three

LABOUR'S SLEAZE MACHINE

'The power of the press is very great,
but not so great as the power to suppress.'
LORD NORTHCLIFFE

The great Lord Denning, Master of the Rolls, once said that something should be done to stop the trafficking in scandal for reward. MPs are not meant to be plaster saints. Ideally, they should be a representative cross-section of the population, with the same natural urges, the same weaknesses and the same temptations as ordinary people. But it does make them vulnerable to salacious articles in the tabloid press; mud sticks, and people will say there is no smoke without fire.

Once you have been elected as a Tory MP, you become a Labour target. To start with, I believed, like most Conservatives, that I would be a target solely for attacks on my political beliefs. And for my first Parliament, this was true. But it became apparent from 1992 onwards, when our majority was reduced to 21, that Labour and many on the left of politics, including left-wing newspapers and trade unions, were targeting Conservative MPs with a view to creating an impression of sleaze. Most of these revelations were about their private lives, but it was enough to create a bad impression. Labour were now focusing on the government's slender majority, and took the view that each and every Tory MP they could dislodge brought them one step closer to power.

This work still goes on, although I sometimes think that Conservative MPs have no idea of the methods Labour uses. The operation is now computerised and the so-called 'Labour rebuttal unit' is not so much involved in political rebuttal as in the production of personal abuse and attacks. Labour learned this new style of politics from studying the methods of former US President Clinton's main rottweiler, a political consultant called James Carville.

Alistair Campbell and Peter Mandelson are masters at the art of exploiting scandal. Campbell, Blair's personal guru, spent years as a lobby correspondent for the *Today* newspaper and then the *Daily Mirror*. He hung around the Commons all day, hoovering up the gossip and converting it into sleaze stories, most of which concerned the private lives of members. Mandelson specialised in spreading rumours.

He would sidle up to members in all parties spreading his scandalmongering.

I discovered that Labour researchers kept files on all of us. Every aspect of our background was being researched to see if a scandal could be manufactured. This was not an idle, amateur operation, but highly professional, and one which was to damage my reputation when I fell out with the local branch of the Fire Brigade Union (FBU).

In 1990, a representative of the Essex Fire Officers Association came to my surgery seeking my help in dealing with the local branch of the FBU. They were attempting to create a closed shop, refusing to sit on committees or attend meetings and generally being bloody minded. The fire service, he said, was in urgent need of modernisation, but the government and the chief fire officers were frightened of the FBU, which has a record of militant activity. It was easier to bow to its demands for fear of repercussions.

It is a brave MP – or a foolish one – who is willing to take on a major trade union, let alone one as militant as the FBU. I had lived through the campaign mounted by the print unions in the 1970s and seen what they were capable of. The trouble with dealing with the firemen was that the public believed the picture painted by the TV soap opera *London's Burning*.

My constituency had one of the most militant branches of the FBU in the country. In one year alone, they staged twenty-one lightning strikes, which are held without any warning, causing a serious risk if a fire did break out, as there is no back-up team to carry out their job. Essex Fire

Authority were forced to hire in Green Goddesses from the army at enormous expense. The idea was that the cost would force the council to accede to their demands.

In reality the cost of firemen's pensions is a huge drag on the fire budget. Throughout Britain there is a constant battle between Fire Service Authorities trying to keep within their budget and the militant firemen from the FBU, determined to resist all modernisation, which required a loss of manpower.

I did not go out of my way to antagonise them – on the contrary. But after another strike threat when I received a letter from their local TU representative asking for support for more industrial action, I blew my top, I wrote back: 'Britain's fire services are far too overstaffed. It is one of the last of the dinosaur industries clinging to feather bedding, using shroud waving and blackmail to prevent the modernisation of the service.'

I had obviously raised a sensitive issue and it wasn't long before a campaign of harassment, threats and abuse was mounted, not only directed at me but also at the councillors who served on Essex Fire Authority.

To prevent the retained firemen – who work part-time – from taking out the fire engines during the strike, FBU members sealed the locks with super-glue. Council members serving on the fire authority were deluged with unsolicited mail, including brochures from funeral companies sent to a councillor whose wife was known to be seriously ill. Members' cars, parked in their driveways, were mysteriously damaged in the middle of the night. Of course, this may have been the work of mavericks, done without the knowledge of the officials or leadership.

But not all fire-fighters attacked me. Writing anonymously for fear of reprisals, some were full of praise for my stance, supporting my statements that fire-brigades were 'grossly over-manned'. Some wrote of fire stations having recreational facilities second to none, complete with licensed bars and barmaids. Others wrote of firemen working only three days a week; while former firemen complained of the emotional blackmail practised on the public when referring to their life-saving exploits and the daily risk to their lives.

A meeting was organised at the House of Commons by Jim Fitzgerald MP, a former fireman, to discuss proposals for a national strike against attempts to modernise the service. All MPs were invited to attend. I was the only Conservative MP to attend and the only woman present. I could sense the hostility all around me.

When the meeting was thrown open to the floor, I spoke.

'I have always supported the firemen in my constituency until recently when they staged twenty-one lightning strikes in a year, putting my constituents at risk. If your union continues striking across the country your union will end up like the print unions and the dockers, out of a job,' I told them.

'We can do without the support of Conservatives like the member for Billericay and I could tell her what to do with her advice. We all know her views on the working classes. She wants to privatise everything,' Ken Cameron, the firemen's militant leader, shouted back.

After the meeting I saw, huddled together in the corridor with Ken Cameron, Jim Fitzgerald and Andrew Dismore, the union's legal adviser and Labour MP for Hendon. I knew Dismore well from my days on Westminster City Council. He had orchestrated the campaign in 1986 to discredit Shirley Porter and Conservative councillors. He was a master of running anti-sleaze campaigns.

Soon afterwards Elizabeth Filkin, the Parliamentary Commissioner for Standards, received a letter from a Mr. Thomas, a retired fireman in Derbyshire, complaining about my entry into the Register of Members' Interests relating to the sale of my business when I was first elected.

His knowledge of parliamentary procedure was quite remarkable and would have done credit to any MP who took a special interest in embarrassing Conservative MPs. The complaint was trivial, but the select committee's response was not. I was 'required' to offer an apology to the House, which I did through gritted teeth.

And so began a two-year campaign of character assassination with the co-operation of the left-leaning *Independent*, which culminated in my suspension from the House of Commons for one month. So what were the complaints all about? Well anybody who thinks they were purely about wrongdoing by me is taking a pretty naïve view of how Labour operate. As soon as I arrived in Parliament, I made a full declaration of what I owned and we started to dispose of both Jim and my interests. We were clearing the decks.

At one stage, Filkin demanded that my husband, Jim,

should attend an inquiry which she would conduct. Jim is pensioner of 76 with prostrate cancer and a failing memory. Our doctor advised that this was a demand that he couldn't possibly meet.

All this fuss was about assets acquired before I became an MP. There was no conceivable way I could benefit myself from those assets through being an MP.

This was in sharp contrast with the Labour Ministers who have been reported to the Committee.

There was Geoffrey Robinson, a Treasury Minister and a friend of Chancellor Gordon Brown, whose affairs are still a mystery, and who didn't declare the full extent of his business dealings with Robert Maxwell. Robinson has, since becoming an MP, acquired assets which others have valued at £50 million, which no doubt he has declared. Then there was Peter Mandelson, who acquired, whilst an MP, a £700,000 house with a £373,000 mortgage loan from Robinson which he failed to declare.

The 'Passports for the Hindujas' affair caused the second resignation of Peter Mandelson – for misleading his colleagues. It also led to the downfall of Foreign Office Minister, Keith Vaz. He and his wife have acquired some five homes and a company which traded with the Hindujas since he became an MP.

All those Labour Ministers were acquiring assets or had used their influence without declaring their interests. Yet the Committee brushed the complaints aside.

Even the Committee's own Labour Chairman, Robert Sheldon, saw his family business expand to £6 million a year turnover whilst an MP, but then failed to declare the full extent of his interests in it as he was required to do by the rules of the House of Commons.

And there you have it. The Ethics Commissioner and the overwhelmingly Labour Standards and Privileges Committee attacked me, a Conservative MP, who had disposed of her interests. Meanwhile Labour MPs have been acquiring interests from which they benefited and which they failed to declare either in the Register or when making speeches. Apart from a few criticisms, those failings by Labour MPs have not been the subject of similar censure by the Committee.

It is a basic principle of English justice that without proof, an accused person must be given the benefit of the doubt. The Commissioner's lack of legal training may account for her failure to demand hard evidence to support the allegations from those making complaints against me. It has been left to me to discover this evidence.

I consider the verdict to have been very unfair and damaging to my reputation and I cannot help but feel dissatisfaction with the committee.

Sadly, the Tories have shown no stomach for a fight to change the way such complaints are investigated. Labour runs rings around us. My only recourse is to the European Court of Human Rights, where my case awaits a decision.

The Father of the House, Tam Dalyell, Labour member for Linlithglow, has said that he is uncomfortable with the way in which the Commissioner Elizabeth Filkin operates, entertaining trivial and frivolous complaints. He said, 'For a

Member of the House, reputation is all important. Absolutely critical. If sullied, it is almost impossible to recover. Mud sticks.'

The Fire Brigade Union may believe that they had a victory, but they did not call their national strike. Little has changed within the union – and we have yet to see the outcome of my appeal to a higher court.

* * * * *

There is a world of difference between the sad stories of politicians' private lives and the real sleaze which exists at the heart of the Labour Party where political favours are given in exchange for financial support. The cash-strapped Labour party went in for this, wholesale, in their climb back to power.

With the help of his tennis partner, Mr Levy, now Lord Levy, Blair has distributed more peerages than Lloyd George. Media types, whose fortunes came from Thatcher's policies of denationalisation, dug deep into their pockets to put Labour, the party opposed to privatisation, back into power.

Lord Falconer, an barrister with no qualifications for politics other than an MOT certificate (Mate of Tony), received a peerage and was given the task of getting Peter Mandelson out of trouble, by taking the flak for the doomed Dome.

Power is slowly draining from Parliament. And the Conservative Party finds itself between a rock and a hard place. Will we stand by and watch our respect for Parliament and the law being undermined while we adopt an entirely political programme dictated by Europe, or will we lead the country back to independence?

One thing is certain: politics is no longer a game of cricket. It is a vicious and nasty game of sleaze and smears and the destruction of reputations. We can no longer afford to be the party of gentlemen. We must play the new game by the new rules.

Chapter Twenty-Four

FINALE

'Being an MP feeds your vanity
and starves your self respect.'
MATTHEW PARRIS

I made up my mind to leave Parliament in 1999, as I was walking home in the small hours of the morning from another late-night session in the Commons designed to irritate Labour by keeping them up all night. The streets around Parliament Square were deserted but for a line of taxis waiting to ferry home the Commons catering staff.

Enoch Powell once said that 'All political lives end in failure, because that is the nature of politics, and of human affairs'. As I walked away from the House that night, I found myself wondering whether my being an MP had been worthwhile. Would I leave any legacy worth mentioning, or was it just an exercise in vanity? I'd tried to live up to my mother's advice not to be a grain in a rice pudding. But her other advice to be independent did not go down too well with the party. I won some small things: the introduction of pooper-scoopers to keep the streets clean; the right of women to do their shopping on Sundays. But the big issue, together with my colleagues in Fresh Start, was the guarantee of a referendum on whether we sacrifice our pound for their Euro. For hundreds of my constituents, I battled bureaucrats, who it should be said, are only implementing regulations that politicians create. And I did my best to keep Billericay in the headlines. I raised some of the many problems faced by women in our unequal society. Seventy-five years have gone by since we achieved votes for women, but we still have to achieve more women to vote in the Commons. I dressed brightly in the Chamber, and spoke my mind. I did everything an aspiring politician should avoid if they want to be taken seriously. But Essex loved it. 'You talk our language,' they told me. A great compliment. But, 'You are not a team player,' said the Whips. Which team? Ours or Europe? All my rebellions were against further integration, which neither I, nor my fellow Conservatives, voted for.

My well-meant advice to William Hague was not heeded. William was regularly photographed with Seb Coe in the picture – as if he expected some of Seb's Olympic stardust to rub off on him — and it conveyed the wrong message for someone who wanted to be taken seriously as a future prime minister. Bearing this in mind, I wrote him a letter halfway through his term as leader:

Dear William,
I hope you will take a piece of advice from an old hand at the political game.
You are doing wonderfully well in the Commons, but it damages your image as Leader of our Party always to appear in the media with Seb Coe in tow, like a parrot on your shoulder.
Regards, Teresa

Unlike John Major, William ignored my advice. Sadly, he lost the leadership, and the parrot ended up in the Lords.

* * * * *

I was tempted to have one last stab at politics by putting my name forward for Mayor of London. Dick Whittington, the first Mayor of London, was a self-made man from humble origins. A clever lad, he came to London in 1363, aged thirteen, to seek his fortune. This was about the time when our house in Orsett was built. He learned the wool trade, and became a successful merchant. So far, so good.

Then he turned his mind to politics. Moving up the civic ladder from common councillor to Sheriff of London, he reached the pinnacle of his political career when he became Lord Mayor. His special interest was in building works, which included Bart's Hospital and rebuilding Newgate Gaol. And, of course, he had a trusty cat. My CV was not dissimilar to his; if he could wind up as Mayor of London, perhaps I could, too.

The Conservative Party had already chosen a candidate: Lord Jeffrey Archer, a cross between Walter Mitty and Billy Liar. His career has been well documented by Michael Crick in his book *Stranger than Fiction*. He was the apple of the Conservative Party's eye, endorsed by both Margaret Thatcher and William Hague. It therefore came as a real shock when Ted Francis, a former friend of his, exposed the novelist's fake alibi about his whereabouts on a certain night, which he used in a libel action against the *Daily Star*. Francis said that he could not stand by and see Jeffrey become London's mayor. When the story broke, Jeffrey was forced to withdraw his candidacy.

The party would be looking for a new candidate and I was well qualified for the job. London was my home town, I knew it like the back of my hand. I had served on Westminster City Council, which administers the heart of London and I was a member of the Select Committee on Transport, where I had spent many months studying reports on London's Underground and interviewing all the key players.

I made my bid to Central Office. But at 9 p.m. the same day, I received a telephone call to say that my application had been rejected. If my selection for the seat in Billericay was the fastest in the history of the Conservative Party, then this must have been the fastest rejection!

I later found out that that there had been a bitter row that evening at the Party's London Executive, where they had decided, at a private meeting, to reject my application. Some members said that I had done immense damage to the party over Europe and therefore should not be allowed anywhere near the mayoral contest. Others argued that, as one of only three nationally known members offering themselves for selection, I should be allowed to go through at least to the vetting stage, particularly after the party chairman, Michael Ancram, publicly welcomed my application.

The London mayoral contest was a shambles. The Tories' candidate chosen to succeed Archer, the relentlessly heterosexual Steve Norris, promptly had a sulky rift with the party over the unlikely issue of homophobia. But, of course, we were not the only party having problems with the selection of a candidate for the mayoral election. Labour's favoured candidate, Frank Dobson, was fed up at being bullied out of the Cabinet post he loved in order to fight a dirty campaign for a doomed job. The Labour Party also waged a vicious campaign to stop Ken Livingstone from standing, even though he was by far and away the most popular candidate with the public. I spent a year with Ken Livingstone hosting a Sunday morning phone-in on London's LBC radio in which he relentlessly plugged his application to revive his career by reminding the listeners of his record as leader of the GLC (Greater London Council) and particularly his 'fares fair' campaign. The whole thing smacked to me of political bribery. No wonder he was way out in the polls.

This was an office for which Londoners showed no enthusiasm. The turnout to vote in the referendum on whether we should have a mayor at all was derisory: less than twenty per cent of Londoners voted, and of those, only a tiny majority were in favour. The whole exercise was being inflicted on us by Labour because of the European policy of dividing Britain into twelve regional authorities, of which London was one. This was another example of the tail wagging the dog.

My main objective was to frustrate Labour, whose intentions were to gain power over the centre of the capital, the Cities of London and Westminster, which they have always failed to win by fair means. We did not need to end up with our capital run on the same disastrous lines as some of the Labour-dominated boroughs. That is what Ken Livingstone may well lead us to.

* * * * *

How can we lift the spirits of the Conservative Party to bring them back to their rightful place in government? By being the party of the nation. By halting the advance of the European train. By rekindling the faith in free markets which, under Margaret Thatcher, brought our economy back from the abyss. And applying that faith to the public sector which is languishing from over-regulation, trade union straightjackets, and hostility to new ideas. We need to revive a new spirit of enterprise, with opportunities in the public sector for individual creativity. This cannot happen unless state control over the delivery of education, health and welfare is removed. People must be offered the opportunity to make their own choices. This means lower taxes and more personal responsibility. Above all we need a leader who will trust people, not patronise them. A leader who will liberate us from control freakery which dominates our lives.

We pack our benches with young men, who lust after a political career when most of their contemporaries are lusting after women. They have plenty of theories, but no practical experience of the day-to-day problems outside our closeted world.

Only when we re-establish contact with the aspirations of our natural supporters, and restore pride in our country, will we be re-electable. Let us pray this happens before Blair and his cronies destroy forever our right to govern ourselves.

I was pleased Iain Duncan-Smith won on Thursday 14th September. He has many virtues. Not least, he is brave, as well as honest and amiable. Yet I wonder if we acted in a friendly way in placing him in such a difficult role. Fighting the incompetent socialist governments of the past was easy. Mr. Blair and Mr. Brown often seem to have stolen our free market credentials. This makes them difficult to wound.

It seems to me the only natural conclusion is that Iain Duncan-Smith must make us the Party committed to seceding from the European Union. It has to be as a party open to the world, and without any hint of protectionism. We can match Margaret Thatcher's successes by tackling the monopolists of the public sector and their unions.

I think Iain's shy smile is far more appealing than Tony Blair's false grin. It is not impossible that he can win the next election.

EPILOGUE

'Today is the last day of an era past.'
BORIS YELTSIN

I was taking my usual shortcut home through the Lords to avoid the tourists who crowd the pavement outside the Commons, when someone called out to me.

'Hello Teresa, I hear you are not standing again?'

It was Roger Freeman – now Lord Freeman – a former minister in Margaret Thatcher's government. He was in charge of selecting candidates. A very influential man.

'I think it is wiser to leave five minutes too soon than to continue for five years too long, in politics.'

'What will you do with yourself?'

'I don't know. You only live once. I might even fit in another career before I pop my clogs.'

He smiled. 'Have you thought of joining us in the Lords? We are very short of women to fill our quota. You'd be great.'

I was amazed and to be honest, a bit flattered. I valued his good opinion. 'What? With my reputation, I would be surprised if the party would want me causing mischief in another place. I've spent fourteen years on the green benches, not exactly hiding my light under a bushel. Why would I want to spend the next fourteen years in the Lords? I'm not ready to join the Klingons.'

Roger smiled again. 'We could do with your energy at this end. We do a lot of work. Very necessary.'

I shook my head.

'I know, and I'm flattered to be asked. But I'm not ready for the old folks' home yet.'

If anyone could have persuaded me, it would have been Roger. For his sake I would have liked to say 'Yes' but I just couldn't bring myself to abandon my principles. I believe that the Lords has had its day. It needs replacing.

Roger looked sad. Instinctively, I took hold of his hand and squeezed it.

I took a deep breath.

'Its nice of you to ask, Roger, really it is. But I can't do it – not even for you.'

INDEX

INDEX